D0484576

SHAKESPEARE'S WORLD

D. L. JOHANYAK

Professor of English
The University of Akron Wayne College

PEARSON

Prentice
Hall

Upper Saddle River, New Jersey 07458

Library of Congress Cataloging-in-Publication Data

JOHANYAK, D. L.
  Shakespeare's world/by D. L. Johanyak—1st ed.
    p. cm.
  Includes bibliographical references and index.
  ISBN 0-13-097101-4
    1. Shakespeare, William, 1564-1616—Outlines, syllabi, etc. 2. Dramatists,
English—Early modern, 1500-1700—Biography—Outlines, syllabi, etc. 3. History,
Modern—16th century—Outlines, syllabi, etc. 4. History, Modern—17th century—Outlines,
syllabi, etc.   I. Title.

  PR2895.J64 2004
  822.3'3—dc21
                                                        2002192986

Editor in Chief: Leah Jewell
Senior Acquisitions Editor: Carrie Brandon
Editorial Assistant: Jennifer Migueis
Production Editor: Maureen Benicasa
Production Assistant: Marlene Gassler
Copyeditor: Martha Williams
Prepress and Manufacturing Buyer: Brian Mackey
Senior Marketing Manager: Rachel Falk
Marketing Assistant: Adam Laitman
Director, Image Resource Center: Melinda Reo
Manager, Rights and Permissions: Zina Arabia
Interior Image Specialist: Beth Boyd-Brenzel
Cover Image Specialist: Karen Sanatar
Image Permissions Coordinator: Carolyn Gauntt
Image Permissions Researcher: Abby Reip
Cover Designer: Robert Farrar-Wagner
Cover Art: Willem Janzoon Blaeu, World Map 1635, with two polar insets in the body of the map
and border panels depicting the four elements, the seven known planets, the four seasons, and the
seven wonders of the world. The Granger Collection, New York. William Shakespeare, 1610, Artist
Unknown, oil on canvas. National Portrait Gallery, London/SuperStock, Inc.

This book was set in 10/12 Optima by Interactive Composition Corporation and was printed and
bound by Courier Companies, Inc. The covers were printed by Phoenix Color Corp.

For permission to use copyrighted material, grateful
acknowledgment is made to the copyright holders
on pages 272–273, which are considered an extension
of this copyright page.

© 2004 by Pearson Education, Inc.
Upper Saddle River, New Jersey 07458

All rights reserved. No part of this book may be
reproduced, in any form or by any means,
without permission in writing from the publisher.

Printed in the United States of America
10 9 8 7 6 5 4 3 2 1

ISBN-0-13-097101-4

Pearson Education LTD., London
Pearson Education Australia PTY, Limited, Sydney
Pearson Education Singapore, Pte. Ltd
Pearson Education North Asia Ltd, Hong Kong
Pearson Education Canada, Ltd., Toronto
Pearson Educación de Mexico, S.A. de C.V.
Pearson Education—Japan, Tokyo
Pearson Education Malaysia, Pte. Ltd
Pearson Education, Upper Saddle River, New Jersey

*This book is dedicated
to
readers of Shakespeare the world over*

What should I say? his deeds exceed all speech . . .
(*King Henry VI—Part One,* I.i.15)

CONTENTS

PREFACE

B ooks about William Shakespeare continue to proliferate. By 1999, the year commemorating the four hundredth anniversary of the Globe Theater's opening, studies about Shakespeare, Elizabethan England, the European Renaissance, and New World colonialism filled library shelves with facts and theories about this fascinating period.

This book combines perspectives from those realms to offer an integrated approach to the study of Shakespeare's world, a global society that nurtured and challenged the talented writer from the English midlands. While some view Shakespeare as a middle-class upstart who wrote from pastoral experience and a classic education, deeper layers of meaning await discovery between the lines of his sonnets and plays.

With a window on the world from his Bankside theater, Shakespeare observed everyday English life while keeping an ear attuned to global events. His plays reflect contemporary influences as well as information and speculation about distant regions and diverse peoples. Shakespeare enjoyed thwarting stereotypes. His drama stimulated interest in the commonplace and in little known or misunderstood aspects of "otherness."

I wrote *Shakespeare's World* to help students appreciate the depth and breadth of Shakespeare's global awareness. These chapters explore topics not commonly associated with Shakespeare study: England's trading ventures, the Reformation and Counter-Reformation, Renaissance arts and science, and New World discoveries. Enacted on the Globe Theater floorboards, allusions to key events, important figures, and exotic lands tell us that Shakespeare was not merely a merchant's son or a London playwright, but a man of the world who dramatized his perceptions to create a lasting legacy of his times.

TO THE READER

This text provides an overview of Shakespeare's world, an age of discovery and adventure set against the backdrop of the Renaissance and the Reformation. Topics included in this work provide a colorful picture of Shakespeare's society by giving readers a spectrum of views about sixteenth and seventeenth century life. Obviously, not everything can be included, and selections were based on a topic's scope or impact on Shakespeare's life or times.

Period documents sometimes are quoted verbatim from primary sources, which means that spelling and vocabulary may be inconsistent. In some cases the print uses "v" for "u" or a character resembling "f" for "s" which makes the text difficult to read. I have followed printing conventions, even when they differ from document to document. Some secondary sources use modern spelling.

Quotes from Shakespeare's plays are referenced from the second edition of the *Riverside Shakespeare* (G. Blakemore Evans and J. J. M. Tobin, eds. [Boston: Houghton Mifflin, 1997]). I chose this edition because it enjoys a reliable reputation, and it has been used by Shakespeare students for many years.

Questions at the end of each chapter provide opportunities for review and application of the material. Critical thinking and research activities allow students to explore key topics and related issues. Students may utilize these activities on their own or teachers may assign them for credit. A list of additional resources may guide readers to further study.

I hope readers will enjoy this material as much as I do, and that this work will enhance their study of Shakespeare's world.

Acknowledgments

Few books are published on individual merit. I completed this text with the help of those whose assistance or support made the project especially worthwhile.

Jeffrey T. Andelora, Mesa Community College
Arthur D. Barnes, Louisiana State University
Richard Burt, University of Massachusetts, Amherst
Andre Lamers, Bakersfield College

The Folger Shakespeare Library and the Shakespeare Birthplace Trust provided gracious assistance with information about and access to many helpful documents and source materials.

Carrie Brandon, Maureen Benicasa, and Martha Williams at Prentice Hall were instrumental in bringing this book to publication.

Michael Johanyak ushered my technological research skills into the twenty-first century.

Stephen and Bethany Johanyak displayed great patience and enthusiasm. Jason and Mathew Kamalie fanned my confidence while squelching my fears. My father John Holodnak (1924–1999), and my mother Lee Shock Holodnak (1924–1991), urged me to academic pursuits. Becky, John, and Scott offered unflagging support, while Annie's humor helped to smooth those rough days that accompany long-term projects.

Like Shakespeare's Falstaff and Prince Hal, everyone craves occasional respite, and the friendly folk at Borders Café, especially Donna C., Crystal L., Crystal W., and Janice B., provided specially made café mochas for much-needed breaks.

And humble gratitude to God,
without Whom everything else is meaningless.

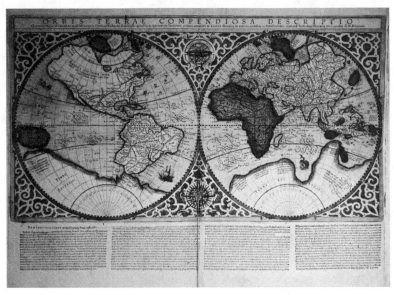

Blaeu World Map, c. 1635.

1

INTRODUCTION TO SHAKESPEARE'S
WORLD

Show minutes, times, and hours.
(*King Richard II*, V.v.58)

A s Shakespeare scholars enter a new millennium of study and debate, period studies on topics such as women, the economy, and colonialism dot the literary landscape like an Elizabethan map of the uncharted world. New research continues to investigate old myths and legends that survive England's greatest dramatist, and to pore over the hundred or so documents that bear his name or signature. Much of the Bard's life remains a mystery, though research continues to reveal key findings. Son of a farmer and subject of a queen, Shakespeare came of age in a world that pitched and tossed with the rebirth of classical learning and a cataclysmic split of the Christian church.

This book was written to guide students through the maze of facts and fictions comprising Shakespeare's cultural and dramatic worlds. *The Riverside Shakespeare's* opening lines describe the value of a global approach to literary figures and their eras:

> Now and again the observation is offered about a great writer that he has created a world of his own. Such artificial worlds are necessarily smaller than the one we live in; otherwise they would not help us much to understand it; like a map, they locate situations by reducing them to a comprehensible scale. Lifelike and large as these representations of truth may seem to us, they are limited nonetheless by the means and motives of their creation. . . . Indeed, if it were not for Shakespeare, we might well doubt whether any single creative genius could have encompassed so much of the variety, the profundity, and the abundance of life as it has been lived in the modern era of civilization. (Evans and Tobin 1997, 1)

Shakespeare's World explores William Shakespeare's life, works, culture, and global influences. Attuned to his unique time period, Shakespeare's writing includes numerous references to "world," punning the significance of the "globe." *Othello,* set in Venice and Cypress, contains 28 or more references to some form of "world" while *Hamlet* offers at least two dozen. Clearly, Shakespeare's vision extended beyond England's borders to far horizons of both Old and New Worlds.

All of the plays mention foreign lands, from neighboring countries like France and Scotland to distant Africa, Asia, the North Pole, and the South Sea. Peoples such as Poles, Russians, Turks, Negroes, and Jews are introduced as bit players or well-defined characters. (See the table at the end of Chapter 1.) Writing from the bank of the Thames River, William Shakespeare had the world at his fingertips, and he utilized that knowledge to enhance his writing. Chapter 1 provides an overview of the global entities that flowed through London society and Shakespeare's pen. Chapter 2 introduces Shakespeare's Stratford life and spotlights his London career. Chapters 3 and 4 highlight his poems and dramas, with synopses for convenient reference. Moving to the next sphere of influence, Chapters 5 through 8 examine Elizabethan and Jacobean England through the window of political, religious, and social events.

Chapter 9 looks across the English Channel to European influences that held special meaning for Shakespeare's audiences. Just as places like Hollywood, New York, and the Bahamas suggest certain connotations to today's readers, we will consider what Shakespeare may have intended when alluding to places like Jerusalem, Rome, and Tripoli. Chapter 10 explores the intellectual effects of the Renaissance with its emphasis on classical study and scientific inquiry. While today's postmodern society honors researchers like Jonas Salk and Linus Pauling, the Renaissance brought to light important theories by figures like Leonardo DaVinci and Johannes Kepler.

The final section of this text explores the furthest reaches of English rule: Russia, Africa, and the Orient of the Old World in Chapter 11, and the Americas, or West Indies, of the New World in Chapter 12. Here we find accounts of English and European adventurers who sailed the globe, returning with evidence of new discoveries and the enticement of new opportunities. These exciting movements are woven through the complex texture of Shakespeare's writing to reveal a detailed tapestry of his society.

THE BIRTH OF THE BARD

> *Where ever the bright sun of heaven shall shine,*
> *His honor and the greatness of his name*
> *Shall be.* (*King Henry VIII,* V.iv.50–52)

William Shakespeare was born in Stratford-upon-Avon, a mid-sized market town about a hundred miles northwest of London. His father John Shakespeare was a dealer in farm products—wool, timber, fleeces, and leather. John's wife came from a genteel family and the couple must have enjoyed a comfortable, middle-class lifestyle.

John Shakespeare's success in local politics undoubtedly inspired his son with the drive to achieve success on his own terms. John served on the town council and eventually earned a position equivalent to mayor. He would have been something of a local celebrity, a role that may have fed young Will's taste for the spotlight of public performance.

As a teenager Will Shakespeare married a farmer's daughter, Anne Hathaway. The couple soon had three children: daughter Susanna and twins Hamnet and Judith. A few years later, references to Shakespeare's writing began to surface in London. What led Shakespeare to leave Stratford? Theories abound, including one that comes packaged with a rendition of what may be Shakespeare's earliest verse. Allegedly Shakespeare was arrested and possibly whipped for poaching deer in Charlecote Park, owned by Sir Thomas Lucy, a neighborhood aristocrat. In revenge the mayor's son may have composed and circulated the following verses, as recalled in the early 1700s by Thomas Jones of Tardebigge, aged 90, with Jones's regional accent reflected in his recitation:

> A parliament member, a justice of the peace,
> At home a scarecrow, at London an ass,
> If lousy is Lucy, as some volk miscall it,
> Then Lucy is lousy whatever befall it.

He thinks himself great
Yet an ass in his state
We allow by his ears but with asses to mate.
If Lucy is lousy, as some volk miscall it,
Sing lousy Lucy, whatever befall it.

(Fido 1978, 15)

Whether Shakespeare wrote or even heard of the stanzas can be conjecture only. As "evidence" of Shakespeare's longstanding disdain for Sir Thomas, some critics point to the dozen white louses of Justice Shallow's insignia in *The Merry Wives of Windsor* (I-T.16).

No evidence has surfaced to suggest that Shakespeare received a university education. However, an interesting hint beckons from his play, *King Henry IV—Second Part,* probably written in the mid-1590s:

Shal. . . . I dare say my cousin William is become a good scholar.
  He is at
Oxford still, is he not?
Sil. Indeed, sir, to my cost.
Shal. 'A must then to the Inns a' Court shortly.

(III.ii.9–13)

The name "William" teasingly suggests the author, William Shakespeare, as is sometimes thought of the student named William giving a Latin recital in *The Merry Wives of Windsor* (IV.i). Shakespeare's extensive legal vocabulary has led some scholars to believe he received legal training, perhaps as a scribe. It is interesting to think William might have begun college until his father's fortunes declined or he married Anne, at which point he withdrew to find an apprenticeship. Alas, all we can do is speculate.

A London Career

Shakespeare's taste for pageantry, for excitement, and for the limelight took root in the rich soil of London's blossoming theater culture. Legends about young Will's start in drama emerged years after his death, so it remains unclear where, when, or how he entered the world of plays and players. In the late 1580s, London drama included popular works like Christopher Marlowe's *Doctor Faustus* and Thomas Kyd's *The Spanish Tragedy.* It is possible Shakespeare performed in these plays and others, and perhaps they fired a competitive spirit to write as well as, or better than, their authors.

In 1592 a London playwright by the name of Robert Greene published a pamphlet entitled *Greene's Groats-worth of Wit, Bought with a Million of Repentance. Describing the Folly of Youth, the Falsehood of Makeshift Flatterers, the Misery of the Negligent, and Mischiefs of Deceiving Courtesans.* The author states on the title page that it is "Written before his death and published at his dying request." Some of his scathing remarks criticizing drama-tists who lack a university degree appear to hint at Shakespeare:

> Yes, trust them not: for there is an upstart crow beautified with our feathers, that with his 'Tiger's hart wrapt in a player's hide,' supposes he is as well able to bombast out a blank verse as the best of you; and being an absolute Johannes Factotum, is in his own conceit the only Shake-scene in a country. (Fido 1978, 36)

Greene's invective against 28-year-old Shakespeare reveals envy. Following Greene's death, his publisher, stationer Henry Chettle, apologized for the refer-ence in an introductory "Epistle" to his 1593 *Kinde Heart's Dream:*

> . . . I am as sorry as if the original fault had been my fault, because my self have seen his [Shakespeare's] demeanour no less civil than he ex-cellent in the quality he professes. Besides, divers of worship have re-ported his uprightness of dealing, which argues his honesty, and his facetious grace in writing that approves his Art. (Fido 1978, 37)

Although Shakespeare generally is remembered as polite, not given to drinking or brawling, his legacy nevertheless includes stories to highlight a sense of mischief and humor. In 1602, John Manningham recorded this anec-dote with regard to Richard Burbage's role as Richard the Third and an arrange-ment to meet a female fan afterward:

> Shakespeare, overhearing their conclusion, went before, was enter-tained and at his game ere Burbage came. Then message being brought that Richard the Third was at the door, Shakespeare caused return to be made that William the Conqueror was before Richard the Third. (Halliday 1998, 92)

Joining the recently reorganized Lord Chamberlain's Men by 1594 or 1595, Shakespeare mingled with entrepreneurs like the Burbage family and aristo-crats like Henry Wriothesley, people who left their mark on the development of English drama. From acting in Ben Jonson's *Sejanus* to borrowing contempo-raries' themes, William Shakespeare received a solid apprenticeship in the drama profession and went on to become a master, drawing admiration not only in his own time but also in generations of theatergoers since.

Elizabethan actors built theaters, formed companies, and supported higher education, projecting the questionable occupation of drama into the respectable ranks of the middle class. The Lord Chamberlain's Men played before royalty, eventually taking the name of the King's Men when James I came to the throne in 1603 and brought the troupe under his protection. The palace of princes was a high pinnacle for a farmer's son from Stratford. Shakespeare competently man-aged his success, investing in a variety of income strategies and purchasing the second largest residence, New Place, in his hometown.

ELIZABETH'S ENGLAND

During the sixteenth and seventeenth centuries, Shakespeare's world was shifting almost beneath his feet in the wake of the northern Renaissance and the Christian reform movement. Queen Elizabeth's strong leadership maintained stability, yet, many cultural perceptions began to change, from views of the monarchy to middle-class norms and lower-class struggles.

In the tradition of her Tudor forebears, Elizabeth secured a solid European presence during her 45-year reign. She steered England through regional controversies like the Babington Plot and navigated European crises growing out of the Reformation. Not only did she win the war with Spain and plant colonies in distant provinces, but she managed it without the guiding influence of a husband despite many attempts to get her married to produce an heir. In the tumultuous wake of movements like the Counter-Reformation, Elizabeth kept her head literally and figuratively, though her mother and cousin were executed for treason, and the half-sister who preceded her had earned the epithet "Bloody Mary" for inciting civil strife to persecute Protestants.

Elizabeth's reign nurtured many positive developments. Social roles expanded as education increased and printed material proliferated. Women began to be valued as individuals, no longer mere extensions of fathers or husbands, as their accomplishments drew notice and appreciation. Though plague periodically swept away portions of the population and civil unrest broke out from time to time, the indomitable spirit of progress surged onward, evidenced by trends like new and restored buildings and improved sanitation. Elizabeth maintained a frugal, balanced budget that supported household and government staff. She entertained ambassadors from around the world who left samples of goods and manners. Elizabeth's councils started and prevented wars and loaned as well as borrowed funding. The last Tudor monarch relied on political savvy that dictated Mary Stuart's beheading and named Mary's son as successor. Addressing a hunger problem arising from crop failures, Elizabeth awarded concessions and relief for the poor while enacting vagrancy acts to evict or punish "masterless men." She patronized the arts and supported drama. She wrote poetry and songs, such as this one commemorating the defeat of the Spanish Armada:

A songe made by her Majestie and songe before her at her cominge from white hall to Powles through Fleete streete in Anno domini 1588

> songe in December after the scatteringe of the Spanishe Navy
>
> Lok and bowe downe thyne eare o Lorde
> from thy bryght spheare behould and see
> Thy hand maide and thy handy worke
> Amongest thy pristes offering to thee
> zeale for incense Reaching the skyes
> my self and septer sacryifise
> My sowle assende this holy place

Ascribe him strengthe and singe his prayse
For he Refraynethe peryures spyrite
And hathe done wonders in my Daies
he made the wynds and waters rise
To scatter all myne enemyes

This Josephes Lorde and Israells god
the fyry piller and dayes clowde
That saved his saincts from wicked men
And drenchet the honor of the prowde
And hathe preservud in tender love
The spirit of his Turtle Dove.

finis (Stevenson and Davidson 2001, 29–30)

Regulatory agencies like the guilds and artificers union helped to monitor medical practice and the quality of marketable merchandise. A primitive form of indoor plumbing emerged. The prevailing beverages were water or ale, and middle-class meals included several courses centered on meat dishes.

Life expectancy hovered around 40. People paid taxes and worshiped regularly. A child had a one-third chance of reaching adulthood. Many boys were educated; most girls were not. People generally married in their twenties, with many widowed before middle age. A majority of men held jobs, and the poor were prosecuted or driven from town. England expanded intellectually and philosophically to admit immigrants and export colonists. "Foreigners" were not always welcomed. Many viewed Moors as dangerous infidels linked to the Ottoman Empire that was devouring Eastern Europe. Jews had been banned centuries before, yet some lived in quiet communities largely unnoticed and usually unbothered. Gypsies were routed, sometimes tolerated, rarely extolled. Blacks—free and slave—were introduced to England and sold to the Americas while West Indies natives were brought to the Old World where some died. Confrontations with the concept of "otherness" forced England to study its cultural reflection and to make hierarchy distinctions between Negroes, Catholics, and Turks.

Shakespeare seemed to avoid much of the political intrigue that attracted other writers. But *The Merchant of Venice* with other anti-Semitic plays, like Christopher Marlowe's *The Jew of Malta,* were perhaps intended as a show of support for Elizabeth following the execution of her personal physician Roderigo Lopez. A converted Portuguese Jew, Lopez served Leicester and then Essex. When his correspondence with Don Antonio, pretender to the Portuguese throne, came to light, Essex accused the physician of treachery and claimed Lopez and Antonio planned to poison the Queen. Tried and executed in 1594, Lopez served as a representative image of the dangerous "outsider," though many believed him innocent.

Shakespeare's early patron Henry Wriothesley, earl of Southampton, later joined the Essex faction that rebelled against Queen Elizabeth at the turn of the seventeenth century. Reputedly the faction convinced Shakespeare's company to play *Richard the Second* to steer public sentiment in Essex's direction through the story of an overlooked loyalist who understandably seizes the kingdom. Records do not indicate the company was punished. Shakespeare found ways to humanize the worst social offenders, to force viewers of his plays to come to terms with the humanity of his characters, no matter how distasteful or heinous their conduct. *The Merchant of Venice* offers a humane understanding of Jews with Shylock's impassioned speech in Act III:59–73 that begins, "Hath not a Jew eyes? Hath not a Jew hands, organs, dimensions, senses, affections, passions?" And as Shylock leaves the courtroom a defeated man stripped of all public identity and status, our sympathy trails him. Even Aaron the Moor in *Titus Andronicus,* who may be Shakespeare's worst villain and whose lines mock decency ("If one good deed in all my life I did, / I do repent it from my very soul" [V.iii.189–190]), is softened by tenderness for his illegitimate son. Shakespeare prods the embers of our very souls, exposing our cultural prejudices and stereotypes.

RENAISSANCE EUROPE

As the Italian Renaissance washed over northern Europe, intellectual events left far-reaching impressions. From discovery and rediscovery, adventure and tradition, came debate about religion, politics, science, and philosophy. The classics awakened to renewed life through translations of ancient Greek and Latin manuscripts.

Reformers redefined personal and state faith as the Catholic Church struggled to regain footing on the slippery mount of spiritual authority. Facing an internal inquisition confirming doctrine and reorganizing worship, priests carried the message of salvation to distant colonies. Puritans sought religious freedom in the Old and New Worlds. Christianity secured a role as a leading global faith amid growing numbers of Islamic converts and the spread of other beliefs, as trade between East and West increased.

Scientific minds like those of Galileo and Kepler explored the universe and the "atomies," consolidating theories about the mysterious cosmos. Nicolaus Copernicus (1473–1543), chair of the Department of Mathematics at Rome, taught universal circular nature in 1507. Anatomical study of the human body and new treatments for old diseases advanced scientific findings through work like William Harvey's discovery of blood circulation.

EXPLORATION AND EXPANSION

As the medieval world ebbed before the Renaissance, explorers pursued tantalizing lures of wealth, fame, and power in the worlds that lay beyond vast territories and oceans. Vying for dominance, princes financed adventurers and merchants who explored faraway lands and conquered unsuspecting peoples.

Clergy and scholars recorded experiences in the newly discovered West Indies. A Dominican friar, Bartolomé de Las Casas, described the Spaniards' systematic destruction of native Indians. His work, entitled *Brevisima relacion de la Destruycion de las Indias occidentales* (1552), was translated into English in 1582 as "A briefe narration of the destruction of the Indies by the Spaniards." Used by the English to exemplify Spanish cruelty (and thus promote English superiority), his work illustrates some of the earliest relations between Europe and the New World:

> . . . God created all these innumerable multitudes in every sort, very simple, without subtletie, or craft, without malice, very obedient, and very faithfull to their naturall Liege Lords, and to the Spaniards whom they serve, very humble, very patient, very desirous of peace making, and peacefull, without brawles and strugglings, without quarrels, without strife, without rancour or hatred, by no meanes desirous of revengement. . . .
>
> Upon these Lambes so meeke, so qualified and endued of their Maker and Creator, as hath bin said, entred the Spanish incontinent as they knew them, as, Wolves, as Lions, and as Tigres most cruell of long time famished: and have not done in those quarters these fortie yeeres past, neither yet doe at this present, ought else save teare them in pieces, kill them, martyr them, afflict them, torment them, and destroy them by strange sorts of cruelties never neither seene, nor read, nor heard of the like . . . so far forth that of above three Millions of soules that were in the Ile of Hispaniola, and that we have seene, there are not now two hundred natives of the Countrey. The Ile of Cuba . . . is at this day as it were all waste. Saint Johns Ile, and that of Jamayca, both of them very great, very fertill, and very faire, are desolate. . . . (de Las Casas in Hadfield 2001, 251–252)

As Western civilization reached across the Atlantic to claim new territories, religious, social, and racial demarcations confirmed "differences" among peoples and societies. "Slaving" became the lucrative occupation of opportunists like John Hawkins. Shakespeare's plays use the word "slave" (or a variant) as a term of human baseness when not a literal social status reference, and the term is used often.

Rulers sent ships east and west in search of lands to claim and cultures to subdue. Delegates encountered other delegates at oriental courts, and adventurers pirated each other on the open seas. English explorers like Sir Francis Drake and Sir Walter Raleigh competed with the Spanish for Asian trade and American lands, eventually planting colonies like Jamestown and Plymouth.

Europeans eagerly mapped and territorialized untapped resources of the uncharted world. Explorers searched aboriginal regions of Africa, Australia, and the Americas, seeking rights to imaginary wealth they envisioned there. Strange and half-accurate reports filtered back to the Old World about "savages" who populated these lands and required taming—for their own "good," of course, but more importantly, to further the aims of conquering nations.

This was the world that Shakespeare surveyed, a world that engendered lively representations in his writing. As you explore *Shakespeare's World,* take time to become acquainted with the societies, the people, and the events that left their imprint on the fertile mind and pen-scratched pages of an English playwright named William Shakespeare.

SOURCES

Evans, G. Blakemore, and J. J. M. Tobin, eds. *The Riverside Shakespeare.* 2d ed. Boston: Houghton Mifflin, 1997.

Fido, Martin. *Shakespeare: An Illustrated Biography.* New York: Peter Bedrick, 1978.

Halliday, F. E. *Shakespeare.* New York: Thames and Hudson, Inc., 1956. Reprinted 1998.

Las Casas, Bartolome de. "A Briefe Narration of the Destruction of the Indies by the Spaniards." Trans. M.M.S. In *Amazons, Savages and Machiavels: Travel and Colonial Writing in English, 1550–1630, an Anthology,* ed. Andrew Hadfield. Oxford: Oxford University Press, 2001.

Stevenson, Jane, and Peter Davidson, eds. *Early Modern Women Poets: An Anthology.* Oxford: Oxford University Press, 2001.

Regions and Peoples Referenced in Shakespeare's Work
(Some cities or names affiliated with larger countries are indented.)

AFRIC, AFRICA AFRICAN	*Coriolanus, Cymbeline, King Henry IV—Part Two, The Tempest, Troilus and Cressida*
ALEXANDRIA	*Antony and Cleopatra*
ALPS	*Antony and Cleopatra, King Henry V, King John, King Richard II*
AMAZON, AMAZONIAN	*Coriolanus, King Henry VI—Part One, King Henry VI—Part Three, King John, A Midsummer Night's Dream, Timon of Athens*
AMERICA	*The Comedy of Errors* (see also **Indies** and **New World**)
ANTHROPOPHAGIAN	*The Merry Wives of Windsor*
ANTIOCH	*Pericles*
ARABIA, ARABIAN	*Antony and Cleopatra, Coriolanus, Cymbeline, Macbeth, The Merchant of Venice, Othello, Phoenix and the Turtle, The Tempest*
ARMENIA	*Antony and Cleopatra*
ASIA	*Antony and Cleopatra, The Comedy of Errors, King Henry IV—Part Two, Much Ado About Nothing*
ASSYRIAN	*King Henry IV—Part Two, King Henry V*
AUSTRIA	*All's Well That Ends Well, King John*
BARBARY	*As You Like It, Hamlet, King Henry IV—Part One, King Henry IV—Part Two, The Merchant of Venice, Othello, King Richard II*
BELGIA	*The Comedy of Errors*
BERMOOTHES	*The Tempest*

BLACKAMOOR/S	*Love's Labour's Lost, The Merchant of Venice, Troilus and Cressida*
BLACK	*Two Gentlemen of Verona* (see also **Moor** and **Negroes**)
BOHEMIA, BOHEMIAN	*The Merry Wives of Windsor, The Winter's Tale*
BRITAIN	*Cymbeline, King Lear*
BRITTANY	*King Richard II*
CANNIBALS, CANNIBALLY	*Coriolanus, King Henry IV—Part Two, King Henry VI—Part Three, Othello*
CARTHAGE	*The Taming of the Shrew, The Tempest, A Midsummer Night's Dream*
CONSTANTINE	*King Henry VI—Part One*
CONSTANTINOPLE	*King Henry V*
CORINTH	*Timon of Athens*
CYPRESS	*Antony and Cleopatra, Othello*
DALMATIANS	*Cymbeline*
DENMARK, DANE	*All's Well that Ends Well, Hamlet, Othello*
DESERT	*Macbeth*
DUTCH, DUTCHMAN	*All's Well that Ends Well, Cymbeline, Love's Labour's Lost, The Merry Wives of Windsor, Much Ado About Nothing, Twelfth Night*
HOLLANDER	*King Henry VI—Part Three, Othello*
LOW COUNTRIES	*King Henry IV—Part Two*
EAST, EAST TO OCCIDENT, EAST, EAST AND WEST (INDIES), EASTERN	*Antony and Cleopatra, Cymbeline, Macbeth, The Merry Wives of Windsor*
EGYPT, EGYPTIAN	*Antony and Cleopatra, As You Like It, King Henry VIII, Othello, Pericles, Twelfth Night*
ALEXANDRIA	*Antony and Cleopatra*
NILE	*Cymbeline, Antony and Cleopatra*
PYRAMIDS	*Sonnet 123*
EPHESUS	*The Comedy of Errors, Pericles*
ETHIOP(E)	*As You Like It, Love's Labour's Lost, The Merry Wives of Windsor, A Midsummer Night's Dream, Much Ado About Nothing, Pericles, Romeo and Juliet, Sonnets to Sundry Notes of Music, Two Gentlemen of Verona, The Winter's Tale*
EUROPE, EUROPA	*Cymbeline, King Henry IV—Part Two, King Henry V, King Henry VI—Part One, King Henry VI—Part Three, Much Ado About Nothing, The Tempest, The Winter's Tale*
FLEMISH	*The Merry Wives of Windsor*
FRANCE, FRENCH, FRENCHMAN	*All's Well that Ends Well, As You Like It, The Comedy of Errors, Cymbeline, Hamlet, King Henry IV—Parts One and Two, King Henry V, King Henry VI—Parts One, Two, and Three, King Henry VIII, King John, King Lear, King Richard II, King Richard III, Love's Labour's Lost, The Merchant of Venice, The Merry Wives of Windsor, Much Ado About Nothing, Pericles*
GALLIA	*Cymbeline, Henry V*

GERMAN, GERMANY	*All's Well that Ends Well, Cymbeline, King Henry IV—Part Two, King Henry V, King Henry VI—Part Three, King Henry VIII, King John, King Lear, Love's Labour's Lost, The Merchant of Venice, The Merry Wives of Windsor, Much Ado About Nothing, Othello*
WITTENBERG	*Hamlet*
GIPSY, GYPSY	*Antony and Cleopatra, As You Like It, Romeo and Juliet*
GOTHS	*As You Like It, Titus Andronicus*
GREECE, GREEKS	*As You Like It, The Comedy of Errors, Coriolanus, Cymbeline, King Henry IV—Part Two, King Henry VI—Part One, King Henry VI—Part Three, Julius Caesar, Pericles, The Rape of Lucrece, The Taming of the Shrew, Titus Andronicus, Troilus and Cressida*
ATHENS, ATHENIAN	*Antony and Cleopatra, King Lear, A Midsummer Night's Dream, Timon of Athens, Troilus and Cressida*
GUIANA	*The Merry Wives of Windsor*
HELLESPONT	*Othello, Two Gentlemen of Verona*
HOLY LAND	*King Henry IV—Part One, King Henry IV—Part Two, King Richard II*
JERUSALEM	*King Henry IV—Parts One and Two, King Henry VI—Part One, King Henry VI—Part Two, King Henry VI—Part Three, King John*
HUNGARY	*Measure for Measure, The Merry Wives of Windsor*
ICELAND	*King Henry V*
ILLIUM	*Troilus and Cressida*
ILLYRIA, ILYRIAN	*King Henry VI—Part Two, Twelfth Night*
INDE, INDIA, INDIAN, INDIES (EAST AND WEST), WESTERN INDIES (SEE ALSO AMERICA AND NEW WORLD)	*All's Well that Ends Well, As You Like It, The Comedy of Errors, King Henry IV—Part One, King Henry VI—Part Three, King Henry VIII, Love's Labour's Lost, A Midsummer Night's Dream, The Merchant of Venice, The Tempest, Troilus and Cressida, Twelfth Night*
INFIDELS	*King Richard III* (see also **pagans**)
IONIAN SEA	*Antony and Cleopatra*
IRELAND, IRISH	*As You Like It, The Comedy of Errors, King Henry IV—Part One, King Henry V, King Henry VI—Part Two, King Henry VIII, King John, King Richard II, King Richard III, Macbeth*
ISLAND/S	*The Rape of Lucrece, The Tempest, Two Gentlemen of Verona* (Western isles = *Macbeth*)
ITHACA	*Troilus and Cressida*
ITALY (SEE ALSO ROME OR ROMAN EMPIRE), ITALIAN	*All's Well that Ends Well, Antony and Cleopatra, Coriolanus, Cymbeline, King Richard II, Love's Labour's Lost, The Merchant of Venice, Much Ado About Nothing, The Rape of Lucrece, The Taming of the Shrew, The Tempest*
FLORENCE	*Othello*
MANTUA	*Hamlet, Romeo and Juliet*
MILAN	*King John, The Tempest, Two Gentlemen of Verona*
NAPLES, NEAPOLITAN	*King Henry VI—Part Two, King Henry VI—Part Three, Othello, The Tempest, Troilus and Cressida*

PADUA	*The Taming of the Shrew*
TUSCANY	*All's Well That Ends Well*
VENICE	*The Merchant of Venice, Othello*
VERONA	*Romeo and Juliet, Two Gentlemen of Verona*
JEW(S), JEWRY, HEBREW	*Antony and Cleopatra, King Henry IV—Part One, King Henry V, Love's Labour's Lost, Macbeth, A Midsummer Night's Dream, The Merchant of Venice, The Merry Wives of Windsor, Much Ado About Nothing, Two Gentlemen of Verona*
LAPLAND	*The Comedy of Errors*
LIBYA	*Troilus and Cressida, The Winter's Tale*
LYDIA	*Antony and Cleopatra*
MACEDON	*King Henry V*
MAHOMET	*King Henry VI—Part One*
MAURITANIA	*Othello*
MESOPOTAMIA	*Antony and Cleopatra*
MESSINA	*Much Ado About Nothing*
MEXICO	*The Merchant of Venice*
MOOR	*The Merchant of Venice, Othello, Titus Andronicus*
MOROCCO	*The Merchant of Venice*
NEGROES	*King John* (see also **Black men**)
NETHERLANDS	*The Comedy of Errors*
NEW WORLD	*The Merry Wives of Windsor, Twelfth Night* (see also **America** and **Indies**)
NORTH POLE	*Love's Labour's Lost*
NORWEYAN, NORWAY	*Hamlet, Macbeth*
ORIENT, ORIENTAL	*All's Well That Ends Well, Antony and Cleopatra, King Henry IV—Part Two, The Merchant of Venice, A Midsummer Night's Dream, The Passionate Pilgrim, King Richard III, Sonnet 7, Venus and Adonis*
OTTOMITES	*Othello*
PAGANS	*King Henry IV—Part One, Richard II* (see also **infidels**)
PALESTINE	*King John, Othello*
PERSIA, PERSIAN	*The Comedy of Errors, King Lear, The Merchant of Venice, Twelfth Night*
DARIUS	*King Henry VI—Part One*
MEDIA	*Antony and Cleopatra*
PARTHIA, PARTHIAN	*Antony and Cleopatra, Cymbeline*
PHILIPPI	*Julius Caesar*
PIGMY, PYGMIES	*King John, Much Ado About Nothing*
PO RIVER	*King John*
POLACKS, POLAND	*The Comedy of Errors, Hamlet, Measure for Measure*
PORTUGAL	*As You Like It*
LISBON	*The Merchant of Venice*
PRAGUE	*Twelfth Night*

RHODES	*Othello*
ROME, ROMAN EMPIRE, ROMISH, ROMANS	*Antony and Cleopatra, Coriolanus, Cymbeline, Hamlet, King Henry V, King Henry VI—Parts One and Two, King Henry VIII, King John, Julius Caesar, Measure for Measure, The Rape of Lucrece, Titus Andronicus*
RUSSIA, RUSSIAN	*King Henry V, Love's Labour's Lost, Macbeth, Measure for Measure, The Winter's Tale*
SARDINIA	*Antony and Cleopatra*
SARDIS	*Julius Caesar*
SCOT(S), SCOTCH, SCOTLAND	*The Comedy of Errors, King Henry IV—Part One, King Henry IV—Part Two, King Henry V, King Henry VI—Part One, King Henry VI—Part Three, King Richard III, Macbeth, The Merchant of Venice, Much Ado About Nothing*
SCYTHIA, SCYTHIAN	*King Henry VI—Part One, King Lear, Titus Andronicus*
SICILIA, SICILY, SICYON	*Antony and Cleopatra, King Henry VI—Part Two, King Henry VI—Part Three, The Winter's Tale*
SOUTH SEA	*As You Like It*
SPAIN, SPANIARD, SPANISH	*All's Well that Ends Well, The Comedy of Errors, Cymbeline, King Henry IV—Part One, King Henry IV—Part Two, King Henry V, King Henry VI—Part Three, King Henry VIII, Julius Caesar, King John, Love's Labour's Lost, Othello, Much Ado About Nothing, Pericles, Romeo and Juliet*
ARRAGON	*Much Ado About Nothing*
CASTILIAN	*The Merry Wives of Windsor*
NAVARRE	*Love's Labour's Lost*
TOLEDO	*King Henry VIII*
SPARTA	*Troilus and Cressida*
SYRACUSE	*The Comedy of Errors*
SYRIA	*Antony and Cleopatra, Pericles*
ALEPPO	*Macbeth, Othello*
TARTAR(S)	*All's Well that Ends Well, The Comedy of Errors, King Henry V, King Lear, Macbeth, The Merchant of Venice, The Merry Wives of Windsor, A Midsummer Night's Dream, Romeo and Juliet*
TRANSYLVANIAN	*Pericles*
TRIPOLI	*The Merchant of Venice, The Taming of the Shrew*
TROY, TROYAN	*King Henry IV—Part Two, Pericles, Troilus and Cressida, A Midsummer Night's Dream*
TUNIS	*The Tempest*
TURK/S, TURKISH, TURKEY	*All's Well that Ends Well, As You Like It, The Comedy of Errors, Hamlet, King Henry IV—Part Two, King Henry V, King Henry VI—Part One, King Lear, King Richard II, King Richard III, Macbeth, The Merchant of Venice, The Merry Wives of Windsor, Much Ado About Nothing, Othello, The Taming of the Shrew*
SULEYMAN	*The Merchant of Venice*
TYRE, TYRIAN	*Pericles, The Taming of the Shrew*
VIENNA	*Hamlet, Measure for Measure*
WEST	*King Henry IV—Part Two, King Henry VI—Part Two*

Portrait of William Shakespeare.

2

WILLIAM SHAKESPEARE'S LIFE

'A was a man, take him for all in all,
I shall not look upon his like again.
(*Hamlet*, I.ii.188)

The scene opens in April 1564 in the bustling market town of Stratford-upon-Avon. A clergyman records the birth of a lad named William born to John and Mary Shakespeare. As we watch his life unfold, we see William standing beside his father at town's center, avidly listening to a property debate between John Shakespeare and other civic leaders.

The scene changes and we observe an adolescent Will stack timber and bag barley to prepare for market day. Once more the scene opens, this time inside a small country church where 18-year-old William exchanges vows with Anne Hathaway, a farmer's daughter from nearby Shottery. At the conclusion of the first act, Will fathers three children in as many years. Then the curtain mysteriously falls over the next few years of his life.

The second act of this compelling drama opens in the early 1590s in London. William Shakespeare sits at a wooden desk in his rented room, quill pen scratching out line after line on the parchment before him, capturing events that leap from history texts and translated romances scattered about. He glances up, musing on recent encounters and conversations. Stretching to relieve writer's cramp, he recalls with a smile his days as a player before turning his attention to the scribbled words that will compose a host of comedic, romantic, and tragic plays to support Anne and the children back home.

Then the spotlight glows on William's final years, following retirement to Stratford. The last act opens on a balding fellow with a paunch and crow's feet, sitting in his lovely garden at New Place under a spreading tree to read the latest London news in a letter from a fellow player. Granddaughter Elizabeth plays among the flowerbeds and shrubs.

Finally it is 1616 and we view a weakened Shakespeare in bed, hearing his revised will read, leaving the bulk of his estate to daughter Susanna with bequests to Anne and Judith. His thoughts seem to wander to 11-year-old Hamnet, Judith's twin, who died 20 years before, leaving the anguished father bereft of son and heir. Perhaps his pale lips recite the lines of an early poem that recalls his beloved son's passing. Although many critics believe the sonnets were written in the early 1590s before Hamnet's death, it is possible some were penned later. *Sonnet 33* may allude to this poignant loss, if we keep in mind Shakespeare's penchant for homonyms and double meanings:

> Full many a glorious morning have I seen
> Flatter the mountain tops with sovereign eye,
> Kissing with golden face the meadows green,
> Gilding pale streams with heavenly alcumy;
> Anon permit the basest clouds to ride
> With ugly rack on his celestial face,
> And from the forlorn world his visage hide,
> Stealing unseen to west with this disgrace:
> Even so my sun one early morn did shine
> With all-triumphant splendor on my brow,
> But out, alack, he was but one hour mine,
> The region cloud hath mask'd him from me now.
> Yet him for this my love no whit disdaineth:
> Suns of the world may stain, when heaven's sun staineth.

In this study of Shakespeare's world, we embark on a journey of acquaintance with the greatest playwright in English history.

SHAKESPEARE'S ANCESTRY

. . . your father lost a father, That father lost, lost his, and the survivor bound
In filial obligation, for some term
To do obsequious sorrow. (*Hamlet*, I.ii.89–92)

William Shakespeare came from a long line of peasant farmers, or yeomen, and the Shakespeare name is recorded in places like Kent and Ireland. Documents show dozens of spellings for the name "Shakespeare." An early progenitor, William Saksper of Clopton in Gloucestershire, was hanged for robbery in 1248.

William's grandfather Richard Shakespeare was a tenant farmer who owned 60 acres in the district of Snitterfield, three miles north of Stratford, where he valued property of deceased neighbors. Records show that Richard was fined for keeping too many cattle on the common pasture in 1535 and for keeping a dunghill in town. Years later his son John also was fined for keeping a dunghill on the street where he lived rather than where it belonged. Shakespeare uses the dunghill as a comic or derogatory image in several plays, as seen in this example from *As You Like It*: ". . . I (his brother) gain nothing under him but growth, for the which his animals on his dunghills are as much bound to him as I" (I.i.14–15). Richard also was cited for not keeping his hedges trimmed and for not traveling six miles to attend the Warwick manor court. In 1543 Thomas Atwood bequeathed Richard a team of four oxen, a sizable gift. Richard and his two sons leased land from the Robert Arden family in Wilmcote where he raised barley, a crop that requires dung year-round, according to Eric Sams (1995), author of *The Real Shakespeare: Retrieving the Early Years, 1564–1594*. Robert's daughter Mary later married Richard's son John, and they became the parents of William Shakespeare. Richard died in 1561 before meeting grandson Will. Clearly Richard was a man who liked doing things his way and did not mind challenging the law.

Shakespeare's mother Mary Arden descended from landed gentry. Ardens had been High Sheriff in Warwickshire before the Norman Conquest (A.D. 1066) and as late as 1575. Mary's grandfather Thomas Arden held property with son Robert Arden who is buried at Aston Cantlow Church. Mary's father died in 1556, leaving her the estate of Asbies in Wilmcote plus a few pounds in money.

Henry Shakespeare, Edmund Lambert, and Alexander Webbe, Shakespeare's uncles, likewise farmed that part of England. Records show that Henry was fined for drawing blood during a fight and later was arrested for debt. Rumor suggests the family was Catholic though they publicly worshipped at the Church of England as required by law. Shakespeare's drama demonstrates knowledge of country matters and folklore. Family themes like twins, brothers, and stepparents provide material for his plays. It is interesting to ponder the effect of lineage on Will's writing.

Shakespeare's birthplace.

JOHN AND MARY SHAKESPEARE

My father—methinks I see my father. (*Hamlet,* I.ii.184)

John Shakespeare (1529–1601) was a farmer who also worked as a glover, wool dealer, and moneylender.

John had moved to Stratford by 1552, the year he was fined for keeping a dunghill in Henley Street. In 1557 he married Mary Arden (1540–1609). Eight children were born to the couple: Joan (1558), Margaret (1562–63), William (1564–1616), Gilbert (1566–1612), Richard (1574–1613), Joan (1569–1646), Anne (1571–79), and Edmund (1580–1607). Eldest son and third child, William was baptized in Holy Trinity Church on April 26, 1564; he had probably been born three days earlier on April 23, the day celebrated as the birth of St. George, England's patron saint.

Sixteen years younger than William, Edmund followed his brother to London and became an actor. He died at age 27 or 28 and was buried December 31, 1607, in St. Saviour's, Southwark, close to the Globe Theatre. His son had died just a few months earlier. Perhaps both were killed by the plague epidemic.

Shakespeare's father became increasingly involved with local government, as detailed by Dennis Kay in *William Shakespeare: His Life and Times* (1995). In 1556 John served as an ale taster, checking beer and bread for quality and price. In 1558 he became one of four constables elected to keep the peace and supervise firefighting preparations. In 1559 he became an affeeror for the Leet, or manor court, assessing fines not given by statute. In 1561 he was elected to serve as one of 14 burgesses and was then appointed as one of two chamberlains in charge of borough finances and property. On July 4, 1565, John was elected alderman, entitling him to wear a thumb ring and a black, fur-trimmed gown—no small honor, considering later dress limitations imposed by Elizabeth's sumptuary laws. When elected as bailiff in 1565—the chief elected officer of the borough—he would have been escorted to and from the Guild Hall and church by sergeants with maces. With his wife he would have taken front-row seats for Guild Hall presentations by touring drama companies. In 1571 he was elected chief alderman.

DECLINE OF FAMILY FORTUNES

> *No villainous bounty yet hath pass'd my heart;*
> *Unwisely, not ignobly, have I given.* (Timon of Athens, II.ii.174)

After 1575 the family fortunes declined, probably because of debt or Catholic loyalties. By 1601 half the town's population—about 700 Stratfordians—were poor. In 1578 John Shakespeare did not pay his poor tax and stopped attending Stratford Council meetings. He also mortgaged a piece of property and sold part of his wife's inheritance. In 1587 he was replaced as alderman because he failed to attend meetings, and in 1592 he was cited for failure to attend church, possibly fearing prosecution for debt.

There is some question about the family's religious beliefs. In April 1757 a six-leaved manuscript was found in the roof of the Henley Street house. The document was a Catholic confession listing 14 articles of faith; it was believed to belong to John Shakespeare, though it has since disappeared.

John Cottam, William Shakespeare's teacher, was a Catholic whose brother was executed as a Catholic priest in 1582. It is possible Cottam was the source of John Shakespeare's spiritual testament if the document actually existed. There is speculation as to whether William may have been an actor/musician tutor for the Alexander Houghton family, who also were Catholics, at Lea in 1581 as Alexander's will refers to a "William Shakeshafte." Shakespeare's early patron Henry Wriothesley (1573–1624) was Catholic too. Shakespeare evidenced knowledge of Puritan beliefs as indicated in references to John Foxe's (1516–87) *Book of Martyrs* (1563). The acquaintance may have been greater than reading; Foxe tutored Sir Thomas Lucy (1532–1600) in Stratford.

Shakespeare's family attended Holy Trinity Church, which reflects their compliance with the 1559 government mandate for Protestant worship. Services included Bible readings, prayer book litanies, and the homilies. Many of Shakespeare's plays include biblical allusions to most if not all books of the Bible.

In 1596 William successfully renewed his father's application with the Heralds' Office for a coat-of-arms, resulting in official gentleman status. The family insignia is a shield crossed by a spear on which a falcon perches. Just a few years later in 1601, John again held a position on the town council, though he died that same year, about the time his son produced *Hamlet*.

STRATFORD-UPON-AVON

> *Look, I am going. Commend me to my wife.* (Coriolanus, III.ii.134–5)

One of three business centers in the county of Warwickshire near England's center, Stratford was given a town charter in 1553 by King Edward VI.

Sketch of New Place, Shakespeare's Stratford residence.

Approximately 1,500 residents occupied 200 houses during Shakespeare's early years. The town's Parish Register indicates that "Gulielmus filius Johannes Shakspere" was baptized on April 26, 1564, the year that 200 residents died of the plague.

John and Mary Shakespeare lived in a dwelling made of two joined houses, one of which served as John's workplace.

Although Shakespeare spent most of his adult years in London, in 1597 he bought the second largest house in Stratford, called New Place, where he lived from 1612 until his death on April 23, 1616. He was buried in Holy Trinity Church, "full seventeen foot deep" according to the rector of Acton in Middlesex.

SHAKESPEARE'S EDUCATION

> *. . . you have learn'd . . . to sigh, like a schoolboy that had lost his A B C;* (Two
> Gentlemen of Verona, II.i.18–19, 22)

Children typically began "petty school" (the Elizabethan notion of kindergarten) by age five where they learned to read and write. By age eight the pupils moved on to grammar school, which in Shakespeare's case was located next door. There they studied classical writers, spending hours each day translating Latin into English, then back into Latin. Students were trained in rhetoric, logic, and history and they read a wide selection of Latin literature with some contemporary European writers and a little Greek. Shakespeare and his classmates attended daily chapel.

William probably received a quality education. Later in life, perhaps dazzled by the University Wits or dismayed by his lack of academic credentials, learning-related themes and language surface in his writing, evidenced in references like "schoolboys" and "schoolmaster" in several works. His narrative poem *The Rape of Lucrece* and tragic play *Coriolanus* include terms like "books," "school," and "pen," with an "ABC book" in *King John*. Kissing "by the book" and "schoolboys" appear in *Romeo and Juliet*, while Hamlet is depicted as a "scholar," and "scholars" is referenced in *Pericles*, *The Merchant of Venice*, and *Much Ado About Nothing*. Allusions to "school" and "education" appear in *As You Like It*, and *All's Well That Ends Well* mentions "college" and "schools." *The Taming of the Shrew* describes a learning plan:

> Let's be no Stoics nor no stocks, I pray,
> Or so devote to Aristotle's checks
> As Ovid be an outcast quite abjur'd.
> Balk logic with acquaintance that you have,
> And practice rhetoric in your common talk,
> Music and poesy use to quicken you,
> The mathematics, and the metaphysics,
> Fall to them as you find your stomach serves you.

> *(I.i.31–40)*

Clearly education lay close to William's heart.

In *The Merry Wives of Windsor* is a scene where a schoolmaster leads a student named William through a Latin grammar exercise, apparently following, William Lily's *Short Introduction of Grammar*. Shakespeare enlivens the teacher with a pronunciation difficulty and erudite manner. A student named William suggests this scene may be a humorous sketch drawn from Shakespeare's childhood:

SIR HUGH EVANS:	Come hither, William; hold up your head; come.
MRS. PAGE:	Come on sirrah; hold up your head, answer your master, be not afraid.
SIR HUGH EVANS:	William, how many numbers is in nouns?
WILLIAM:	Two.
. . .	
SIR HUGH EVANS:	What is "lapis," William?
WILLIAM:	A stone.
SIR HUGH EVANS:	And what is a stone, William?
WILLIAM:	A pebble.
SIR HUGH EVANS:	No; it is lapis. I pray you remember in your prain.[brain]
WILLIAM:	Lapis.
SIR HUGH EVANS:	That is a good William. What is he, William, that does lend articles?
WILLIAM:	Articles are borrow'd of the pronoun, and be thus declin'd, 'Singulariter, nominativo, hic, haec, hoc.
SIR HUGH EVANS:	Nominativo, hig, hag, hog:—pray you mark; genitivo, hujus. Well, what is your accusative case?

WILLIAM: Accusativo, hinc.

· · ·

SIR HUGH EVANS: Show me now, William, some declensions of your
                      pronouns.

WILLIAM: Forsooth, I have forgot.

· · ·

MRS. PAGE: He is a better scholar than I thought he was.

The Merry Wives from IV.i.17–81.

Roger Ascham's *The Schoolmaster* (1570) enjoyed popularity as a model of Elizabethan educational theory.

Shakespeare may have been a law clerk because his father, a local legal officer, was illiterate; legal training would have enabled son William to draft Latin documents. William's signature appears in a 1568 legal text entitled *Archaionomia*, and his drama displays familiarity with legal jargon and conventions. Scholar Eric Sams believes these and other hints support the possibility of Will's training as a scribe or legal assistant ("noverint").

LITERARY INFLUENCES

I, thus neglecting worldly ends, all dedicated
To closeness and the bettering of my mind. (*The Tempest*, I.ii.89–90)

Shakespeare's schoolmaster probably studied at Oxford. The school day was long, beginning at 6 A.M. Shakespeare's plays suggest familiarity with Ovid, Virgil, Juvenal, and other classic writers. Ben Jonson snidely refers to Shakespeare's "small Latin and less Greek," but Shakespeare's plays contain many Latin phrases. Arthur Golding's 1567 English version of Ovid's *Metamorphoses* and Sir Thomas North's 1579 translation of Plutarch's *Lives of the Noble Grecians and Romans* were widely read, and Shakespeare's writing suggests knowledge of both. Shakespeare also uses many French and Italian expressions, though we do not know if he ever left England or studied these languages.

William Painter's *Palace of Pleasure*, a popular collection of tales, includes themes that may have influenced Shakespeare's comedies. Holinshed's *Chronicles of the Kings of England* provided important information for Shakespeare's histories. Sir Philip Sidney's *Arcadia* and his sonnet sequence *Astrophil and Stella*, Spenser's *Faerie Queene*, Thomas Lodge's *Rosalynde*, and writers like Thomas Nashe influenced Shakespeare's themes and style, as did a host of other sources.

Oxford and Cambridge, founded to train clerics, were the only universities in England at this time, though London's Inns of Court provided higher learning in the law. Many commoners remained illiterate and could not write their names.

Shakespeare's drama and poetry hold their own against the writing of university scholars like Christopher Marlowe and Ben Jonson. In fact, it was

Shakespeare's lack of formal training that spawned the anti-Stratfordian movement, initiated by those who deny a commoner named Shakespeare could have produced the plays attributed to him.

EARLY DRAMATIC INFLUENCES

Before permanent theaters were established, drama troupes traveled about England and many stopped at Stratford. In 1569 the Queen's players were paid nine shillings for performing in Stratford while the Earl of Worcester's men received one shilling for their entertainment.

Between 1575 and 1587 actors' troupes performed dozens of engagements in Shakespeare's birthplace. In January of 1576 the Earl of Worcester's Men returned, followed by Leicester's Men in 1576–77 who played for 15 shillings. In 1587 at least five companies visited Stratford.

John Shakespeare's role as magistrate allowed him to approve players' entertainment and payment, and he probably enjoyed front-row seats. William Shakespeare may have had significant exposure to the exciting world of drama through the many troupes that visited Stratford during his youth. He might have witnessed business negotiations between his father and troupe managers.

Given the fall of family fortunes ("for that Mr. Shakespeare doth not come to the halls when they be warned nor hath not done of long time"), a teen marriage followed closely by fatherhood, and an uninhibited genius, it is perhaps no surprise that young William soon found a career on the London floorboards.

MARRIAGE AND CHILDREN

But do thy worst to steal thyself away,
For term of life thou art assured mine. (Sonnet 92)

Shakespeare's wife Anne Hathaway (1556–1623) was the daughter of Richard Hathaway, a prosperous farmer living in Shottery about a mile from Stratford. Her grandfather John Hathaway was listed as an "archer" in 1536 and a "constable" in 1548. Richard Hathaway's will, dated September 1, 1581, references his daughter's engagement. During this period marriages were legally recognized when bride and groom spoke vows with parental consent, usually before family and friends. Following a formal engagement, some couples set up housekeeping as though married even before the church ceremony. Due to ecclesiastical law marriages could not be performed during Advent and Lent, so in 1582 couples could not marry between December 2, 1582, and April 7, 1583, except by special license. On November 28, 1582, an appeal for special licensing was made to the Episcopal Church court at Worcester, the diocese of Bishop John Whitgift, later Archbishop of Canterbury (1583–1604). When approved, the license allowed William Shakespeare to marry "Anne Whatley of

Temple Grafton" without proclamation of the banns on three successive Sundays as was usually mandated. While some scholars question the "Whatley" name of Shakespeare's fiancée, the variant spelling of "Hathaway" is generally attributed to clerical error. It is possible Anne was living with her mother's relatives at Temple Grafton following her father's death; his will left ten marks to be paid on her wedding day.

Temple Grafton church where William Shakespeare may have married Anne Hathaway.

Anne was eight years older than her husband, 26 to Will's 18. His plays disparage marriage to an older woman, as evidenced in his adaptation of the Venus and Adonis myth representing an experienced Venus unsuccessfully pursuing a youthful lover. *Twelfth Night* includes the duke's recommendation that women not marry younger men:

> Let still the woman take
> An elder than herself, so wears she to him;
> So sways she level in her husband's heart.
> For, boy, however we do praise ourselves,
> Our fancies are more giddy and unfirm,
> More longing, wavering, sooner lost and worn,
> Than women's are.

> *(II.iv.29–34)*

The degree to which these words may be autobiographical is anybody's guess. Another passage in *King Henry VI—Part One* speaks against forced marriage:

> For what is wedlock forced, but a hell,
> An age of discord and continual strife?

Whereas the contrary bringeth bliss,
And is a pattern of celestial peace.

(V.v. 62–65)

Burial certificate for Shakespeare's son Hamnet.

Daughter Susanna (1583–1649) was born on May 26, 1583. Two years later twins arrived, a boy named Hamnet (1585–96) and a girl named Judith (1585–1662). They were probably named after Judith and Hamnet Sadler; the husband was a Stratford baker and Shakespeare's lifelong friend. William's son Hamnet died at 11, possibly of plague. Susanna was named executrix of her father's will, and with her husband inherited most of her father's estate. By law, however, her mother automatically received a one-third share. Susanna could sign her name, suggesting some level of education, and she married physician John Hall on June 5, 1607. Hall had practiced medicine in Stratford since 1600 and held B.A. and M.A. degrees from Cambridge University. The couple's only child, daughter Elizabeth, was born February 21, 1608.

Elizabeth married Thomas Nash in 1626; he died in 1647. In 1649 she married John Bernard and became Lady Bernard. Having inherited Shakespeare's home, New Place, Lady Bernard entertained Queen Henrietta Maria for two nights during the Civil War in 1642 as the queen traveled to Oxford to meet the King. Elizabeth died childless in 1670, ending William Shakespeare's direct bloodline.

Shakespeare's second daughter, Judith, signed documents with her mark rather than a signature, suggesting she was illiterate. Like her mother she wed a younger man, at 31 marrying 26-year-old Thomas Quiney. Her three sons—Shakespeare, Richard, and Thomas—died young. Husband Thomas was excommunicated from the church and fined for swearing and selling unwholesome wine. He moved to London in 1652, leaving his family behind.

Bust of William Shakespeare.

RETIREMENT AND DEATH

> *. . . and thence retire me to my Milan, where*
> *Every third thought shall be my grave.* (*The Tempest,* V.i.311–12)

New Place, Shakespeare's Stratford residence, was noted for an attractive appearance and had formerly been owned by Stratford's leading citizen. Shakespeare continued to produce plays and to maintain an interest in two playhouses, the Blackfriars and the Globe, until perhaps 1610 or 1611, when he retired to Stratford.

A major fire broke out in Stratford in 1614, though we do not know of any effects on Shakespeare's family. In January 1616 Shakespeare prepared his Last Will and Testament with the help of a solicitor, Francis Collins of Warwickshire.

His signature appears clear and firm. However, Judith married in February and Shakespeare changed the will in March, when his signature appears shaky. Perhaps his health failed naturally or maybe his daughter's choice of spouse proved unsettling. A late play, *The Tempest*, displays parental anxieties in protecting a daughter from a dishonorable suitor:

> . . . If thou dost break her virgin-knot before
> All sanctimonious ceremonies may
> With full and holy rite be minist'red,
> No sweet aspersion shall the heavens let fall
> To make this contract grow; but barren hate,
> Sour-ey'd disdain, and discord shall bestrew
> The union of your bed with weeds so loathly
> That you shall hate it both.
> Therefore take heed,
> As Hymen's lamps shall light you.
>
> *(IV.i.15–23)*

A few weeks after changing his will, Shakespeare died. No cause of death was recorded, but stories abound, including one that says he caught a cold following a drinking binge with cronies Ben Jonson and Francis Drayton.

While Susanna received most of his estate, Judith, who may have married against his wishes, received a "broad silver gilt bole" and a marriage portion (or dowry) to be paid within a year. Shakespeare's dramatic lines reveal disillusionment with "modern" unions: ". . .Reason and love keep little company together now-a-days" (*A Midsummer Night's Dream* III.i.143–4). Perhaps because wife Anne received a third of the estate by law, she was given only "the second best bed." For centuries scholars have pondered this bequest, wondering if Anne's affections were of secondary importance to the writer who lived most of his life in London, or whether the bequest connotes a private romantic meaning.

William Shakespeare was buried in the chancel of Stratford's Holy Trinity Church beneath the floor, an honor reserved for those of noble birth or distinctive achievements. Shakespeare may have written his epitaph if he followed his own advice from *Much Ado About Nothing* (V.ii.77–80): "If a man do not erect in this age his own tomb ere he dies, he shall live no longer in monument than the bell rings and the widow weeps." The following words appear over his place of interment in Trinity Church:

> Good frend for iesus' sake forbeare,
> To dig the dvst encloased heare.
> Blese be ey man ty spares thes stones,
> And cvrst be he ty moves my bones.

Later a painted bust was erected over the site. Every year thousands of visitors come to pay homage to the great playwright of humble origin.

LEGENDS ABOUT WILLIAM SHAKESPEARE

For he hath found to end one doubt by death
Revives two greater in the heirs of life. (*King Henry IV—Second Part*, IV.i.197–8)

Intriguing rumors survive Shakespeare's life. Thomas Fuller, who died in 1661, claims "many were the wit combats between him [Shakespeare] and Ben Jonson." He describes them as "encounters between a Spanish great galleon and an English man-of-war: Master Jonson, like the former, was built for higher in learning, solid but slow in his performances; Shakespeare, with the English man-of-war, lesser in bulk but lighter in sailing, could turn with all tides, tack about and take advantage of all winds by the quickness of his wit and invention."

In his *Brief Lives* John Aubrey claims that Shakespeare's father was a butcher, "that as a boy Shakespeare exercised his father's trade, but when he killed a calf he would do it in a high style, and make a speech." He also writes that the youthful Shakespeare had been a schoolmaster in the country. Aubrey collected information from William Beeston, son of an actor who had joined the Chamberlain's Men by 1598. His notes describe Shakespeare "the more to be admired" [because] "he was not a company keeper . . . wouldn't be debauched."

On journeys between London and Stratford Shakespeare allegedly stayed at John Davenant's Oxford tavern. John's son was the poet and playwright Sir William Davenant, who allowed himself to be thought Shakespeare's illegitimate son. In the late seventeenth or early eighteenth century a clergyman named Richard Davies recorded the story that Shakespeare used to poach deer and rabbits at Charlecote from Sir William Lucy "who had him often whipped and sometimes imprisoned, and at last made him fly his native country to his great advancement, and also that he died a papist [Catholic]" (Halliday 1998, 36).

Around 1657 Thomas Plume stated, "Will was a good honest fellow, but he durst have cracked a jest with him at any time." John Ward, Stratford vicar from 1662–81, recorded that "Shakespeare, Drayton, and Ben Jonson had a merry meeting, and it seems drank too hard, for Shakespeare died of a fever there contracted" (Halliday 1998, 112).

William Shakespeare left such a vibrant legacy that it is tempting to seize the unknown portions of his life and fabricate stories to fill the gaps. While most of these are based on little substance, it is amusing to consider the possibilities as we strive to complete a composite of this marvelous writer.

SUMMARY

Shakespeare's work leaves us with the desire to know more about the man who created fascinating characters like Hamlet and historical figures such as Henry the Fifth. While many documents support the existence of a man named William Shakespeare to discredit the anti-Stratfordian theory discussed in Chapter 4, few offer details of his day-to-day existence: Did he write all the works attributed to him? To what extent did young Hamnet's death affect his life and career? Were he and Anne happy in their marriage? Did Elizabethan audiences appreciate his plays as much as we do today?

Questions like these may never be answered. Although the man is gone, his work remains to entertain and inspire us. English literature owes a debt of gratitude to the middle-class writer from Stratford whose stories of sorrow and laughter continue to intrigue us today.

SOURCES

Bentley, Gerald. *Shakespeare: A Biographical Handbook*. New Haven, Conn.: Yale University Press, 1961.

Fido, Martin. *Shakespeare: An Illustrated Biography*. New York: Peter Bedrick, 1978.

Fox, Levi. *The Shakespeare Handbook*. Boston: G.K. Hall, 1987.

Frye, Roland Mushat. *Shakespeare's Life and Times*. Princeton, N.J.: Princeton University Press, 1967.

Halliday, F. E. *Shakespeare*. New York: Thames and Hudson, Inc., 1956. Reprinted 1998.

Hyland, Peter. *An Introduction to Shakespeare: The Dramatist in His Context*. New York: St. Martin's, 1996.

Kay, Dennis. *William Shakespeare: His Life and Times*. New York: Twayne, 1995.

Rowse, A. L. *William Shakespeare: A Biography*. New York: Harper, 1963.

Sams, Eric. *The Real Shakespeare: Retrieving the Early Years, 1564–1594*. New Haven, Conn.: Yale University Press, 1995.

Schoenbaum, S. *Shakespeare's Lives*. New ed. Oxford: Clarendon, 1991.

Wells, Stanley. *Shakespeare: A Life in Drama*. New York: W.W. Norton, 1995.

QUESTIONS

1. How might ancestral stories have influenced young Shakespeare?
2. Which plays reflect themes and traits found in Shakespeare's family tree?
3. Why might traveling actors have appealed to a boy like Shakespeare?
4. What types of market and commercial images appear in Shakespeare's writing?
5. What roles do farm images play in his work?
6. Why would a young man leave his family in Stratford and go to London to make a living?
7. Which rumors about Shakespeare's life seem most realistic? What do such stories suggest about Shakespeare's character and reputation?

CRITICAL THINKING AND RESEARCH PROJECTS

1. Explore possible links between dates of actors' visits to Stratford and events in Shakespeare's life.
2. Why do you suppose so little information exists about Anne Hathaway? Look up records about the sixteenth-century Hathaway family. Compare findings to what we know of Shakespeare's wife and marriage.

3. What role did children play in Shakespeare's writing? How might his marriage and family have influenced those images?

4. Why do readers continue to enjoy Shakespeare's writing today? Which of his themes are universal? Why are his works more popular than those by writers like Ben Jonson or Christopher Marlowe?

For Further Reading

Duncan-Jones, Katherine. *Ungentle Shakespeare: Scenes from His Life*. London: Arden Shakespeare, 2001.

Fraser, Russell. *Shakespeare: The Later Years*. New York: Columbia University Press, 1992.

Granville-Barker, Harley, and G. B. Harrison, eds. *A Companion to Shakespeare Studies*. New York: Doubleday, 1960.

Gurr, Andrew. *William Shakespeare: The Extraordinary Life of the Most Successful Writer of All Time*. New York: HarperPerennial, 1995.

Halliwell, James Orchard, Esq. F.R.S. *The Life of William Shakespeare*. London: John Russell Smith, from 1848.

The Rape of Lucrece by Titian, 1515.

3

SHAKESPEARE'S POEMS AND PLAYS

—my library was dukedom large enough.
(*The Tempest*, I.ii.109–110)

Tudor England was exciting and precarious to shrewd entrepreneurs like William Shakespeare, who learned to navigate the political upheavals and cultural evolutions of this era. Despite London officials' efforts at certain intervals to limit theater activity, Shakespeare's troupe enjoyed great popularity and made personal fortunes. When James I came to the throne in 1603, the Lord Chamberlain's Men officially became the King's Men, with the reputation of being England's greatest dramatists.

It is uncertain when or how William Shakespeare came to London, but scholars think it is possible he spent some time as a theatrical apprentice, perhaps even holding horses (an Elizabethan parking attendant!) for well-to-do patrons. He is listed as an actor in several plays, including those with roles that may have included the ghost in *Hamlet*.

Eric Sams believes Shakespeare's earliest work includes the first version of *Pericles* in 1588 and perhaps *Titus Andronicus* in 1589, as well as *Hamlet, The Taming of the Shrew,* and *The Troublesome Reign of King John*. In 1588 Thomas Nashe attacked unlearned writers, perhaps including young Shakespeare, in *The Anatomy of Absurdity*. But, the evidence is inconclusive.

Within a few years, however, Shakespeare established a reputation as a popular playwright, as indicated in Green's attack and Chettle's retraction. During the 1590s Shakespeare wrote histories and lighter comedies, like the Henry plays and *The Comedy of Errors, A Midsummer Night's Dream,* and *As You Like It*. Tragedy emerged in works like *Romeo and Juliet,* though the darker dramas came later.

Critics categorize Shakespeare's drama periods in varying ways. Some see the 1590s as a combination of histories, comedies, and a few tragedies, with his best work appearing from 1600 to 1609 in tragedies like *Othello* and *Macbeth*, and edgy romances. Neither decade is definitive with respect to genre. The histories appeared intermittently, as did plays with classical themes. Toward the end of his career Shakespeare collaborated with John Fletcher to produce *King Henry VIII, The Two Noble Kinsmen,* and *Cardenio* (now lost). It is possible he also worked with Thomas Middleton on *Timon of Athens*. After Shakespeare's death, theater colleagues organized his plays for publication in 1623, categorizing them into three main types in the First Folio: comedies, tragedies, and histories. Nowadays critics sort the works in more complex fashion, viewing the genres of some as mixed and in other cases, as perplexing.

What seems clearer than his genres is Shakespeare's adherence to poetical conventions of the time to produce narrative poems and sonnets that attracted critical acclaim. The chronology appearing at the beginning of this chapter offers potential rather than absolute publication dates. Above all, Shakespeare's writing evidences a keen mind and sensitive spirit housed in a body that hungered for love and fame.

Most of the poems probably appeared early in his career, perhaps during a period when plague closed the theaters. Two narrative poems dedicated to aristocrat Henry Wriothesley helped to establish Shakespeare's literary reputation.

THE NARRATIVE POEMS

He had the dialect and different skill,
Catching all passions in his craft of will. (*A Lover's Complaint*, ll.125–6)

Although Shakespeare is best known for writing 36 plays and 154 sonnets, his early career was advanced by two erotic narrative poems based on Elizabethan conventions. Both are dedicated to a youthful patron, Henry Wriothesley, and they display a metrical rhythm that enhances their seductive themes.

Venus and Adonis by Titian (Venetian, c. 1485–1576), "Venus and Adonis." National Gallery of Art, Washington, D.C.

Venus and Adonis

Over one arm the lusty courser's rein,
Under her other was the tender boy,
Who blush'd, and pouted in a dull disdain,
With leaden appetite, unapt to toy. (ll.31–32)

Shakespeare's *Venus and Adonis* (1592–93) is based on a story from Ovid's *Metamorphoses* that recounts the myth of a love-smitten Venus in pursuit of a handsome but indifferent youth. Pronouncing her love for his physical beauty and making sexual overtures to seduce the nonchalant boy, Venus reflects characteristics associated with the traditional male suitor and the historical dark lady. Adonis eludes her seductive wiles only to be gored by a wild boar, destroyed by a traditional male pastime sought in preference to Venus's love. Critics note the domineering nature of the aggressive woman and question whether Shakespeare wrote from experience. In this adaptation Venus reflects the dark lady of sensual lure and romantic appetite whose pursuit of an inexperienced male results in tragedy.

Lucrece

> *But she hath lost a dearer thing than life,*
> *And he hath won what he would lose again;*
> *This forced league doth force a further strife,*
> *This momentary joy breeds months of pain,*
> *This hot desire converts to cold disdain;*
> *Pure Chastity is rifled of her store,*
> *And Lust, the thief, far poorer than before.* (II.687–693)

In 1593–94 Shakespeare produced *Lucrece* with a plot derived from Livy's *History of Rome* elaborating on the theme of sexual aggression by depicting the beautiful fidelity of a wronged woman. The title was not changed to *The Rape of Lucrece* until 1616. In this poem victim and victor die following a villain's assault of his friend's wife. As the faithful wife Lucrece's victimization recalls Helen's rape in classical literature, and the family's downfall parallels the fall of Troy, a common image in Shakespeare's writing found in works like *Troilus and Cressida* and *Othello*. The violated wife calls her husband home, and after divulging the crime, stabs herself. Tarquin the rapist is forced into exile. A key theme of this work is that uncontrolled lust is destructive. Lucrece feels stained beyond redemption and takes her life to protect her husband from sharing her humiliation. Violated women usually die in Shakespeare's works, as evidenced in *Titus Andronicus*.

Sexual aggression leads to tragedy in both narrative poems. The seductive Venus fails to divert youthful Adonis from a fatal hunt; consequently, he (and not she) dies. In *Lucrece* the rapist's deed leads to shame, despair, and death. Dedicating these works to young Wriothesley allowed Shakespeare to steer a young aristocrat away from sexual temptation and toward marriage and family. The theme of needful procreation appears in the sonnets as well.

The Passionate Pilgrim

> *Did not the heavenly rhetoric of thine eye,*
> *'Gainst whom the world could not hold argument,*
> *Persuade my heart to this false perjury?*
> *Vows for thee broke deserve not punishment.* (III.1–4)

Five of Shakespeare's sonnets, along with poems by Richard Barnfield, Bartholomew Griffin, and Christopher Marlowe, and some by other Elizabethan poets, appear in a collection of twenty romantic verses entitled *The Passionate Pilgrim*. The earliest version of the work includes a title page that claims "W. Shakespeare" as author, with a 1599 publishing date. While it is clear that Shakespeare did not write all the poems, it is significant that the publisher attributes the collection to Shakespeare.

A Lover's Complaint

> *For lo his passion, but an art of craft,*
> *Even there resolv'd my reason into tears,*
> *There my white stole of chastity I daff'd,*
> *Shook off my sober guards and civil fears.* (ll. 295–8)

Publisher Thomas Thorpe included *A Lover's Complaint* in the 1609 collection of Shakespeare's sonnets. The key figure in the poem is a young woman who laments her abandonment by a seducer. The poem, in rhyme royal, takes a confessional tone as she pours out her heart to an aging shepherd who seems to represent a priestly figure. Yet her words lack a truly repentant tone for she admits she might again be seduced if her lover were to return, based on her attraction to his good looks and emotional appeal. While some critics do not believe Shakespeare wrote the poem, it strikes an interesting balance between regret and lingering temptation.

The Phoenix and the Turtle

> *Beauty, Truth, and Rarity,*
> *Grace in all simplicity,*
> *Here enclos'd, in cinders lie.* (ll.53–55)

The Phoenix and the Turtle (1601) became part of Robert Chester's *Love's Martyr, or Rosalin's Complaint*. Shakespeare's poem parallels the doomed union of the title creatures to the hopelessness of mismatched humans, yet balances sorrow with a tribute. The phoenix may represent Queen Elizabeth, based on the allegorical potential of her famed Phoenix portrait, while the turtledove may refer to one of her favorites, or to her monarchy or realm. As the northern Renaissance moved into England by the late sixteenth century, Shakespeare and other writers drew on poetic conventions like the funereal threnody or dirge to praise lofty values that symbolically, at least, had become lost or overshadowed with shifting cultural norms. As we often do today, perhaps in this poem Shakespeare bemoans the loss of the "good old days."

THE SONNETS

> *Will you then write me a sonnet in praise of my beauty?* (*Much Ado About Nothing*,
> V.ii.4–5)

Sonnet writing originated in France and Italy during the Renaissance and grew in popularity in Elizabethan England, peaking in the 1590s. Sir Philip Sidney's

1591 sonnet sequence *Astrophil and Stella* inspired poets like Barnabe Barnes, Giles Fletcher, and Michael Drayton to create their own sonnet collections. Playwrights turned to poetry when plague closed the theaters. Single sonnets frequently appeared in print and became available to the general public, but the most popular was the cycle or series of sonnets addressed to a beloved woman or man, usually telling a story or following the development of a personal relationship.

Some of Shakespeare's sonnets appear in plays like *Love's Labour's Lost* and *Romeo and Juliet*. But most appeared in the 1609 collection that included *A Lover's Complaint* issued by publisher Thomas Thorpe and printer George Eld under the title, *Shakespeare's Sonnets*. Many scholars believe these were mainly written in the 1590s. Francis Meres alludes in his 1598 *Palladis Tamia* to Shakespeare's "sugared sonnets among his private friends," regarding him as "mellifluous and honey-tongued," worthy of comparison to Ovid.

The 154 sonnets sometimes are divided into three groups. The first 17 urge a young man to marry. The next 109 vary, though the majority seems to address a man. Most of the last 28 concern at least one woman. It is unclear whether any of the people or events in the sonnets are real, although the speaker's emotions seem genuine. Candidates for the dark lady, or temptress, include Mary Fitton, one of the Queen's ladies-in-waiting who bore a number of children to a variety of men. Another possibility is Lucy Morgan, also called Lucy Parker, Lucy Negro, or Black Luce. Lucy actually was a white woman who ran a well-known London brothel in the 1590s.

The speaker's affection for the young man appears to reflect a strong friendship or aesthetic attraction rather than sexual magnetism, though scholars interpret the poems in varying ways. The sonnets exhibit an "ababcdcdefefgg" rhyme scheme and in the first 12 lines pose a dilemma that is resolved in the final couplet. One of the major themes emphasizes the lasting beauty of an individual's love or fame.

Because Shakespeare dedicated his two long narrative poems to a patron, many believe his sonnets, written about the same time, also may be dedicated to the earl of Southampton and that Henry Wriothesley may be the attractive young man of the verses. The sonnets sometimes are studied as a single unit of material and as smaller combinations of poems. Mostly they are viewed individually, though readers often look for connecting themes or patterns.

THE PLAYS

Speak the speech, I pray you, as I pronounc'd it to you. (Hamlet, III.ii.1–2)

Shakespeare found themes for his plays in historical sources like Holinshed's *Chronicles of England, Scotland, and Ireland,* English mythology that included folklore and superstition, the Bible, and classical legends drawn from Ovid's *Metamorphoses* and Plutarch's *Lives of the Noble Grecians and Romans.* Morality plays and "interludes" introduced the use of stock characters named for representative qualities, like "Cruelty" or "Shame." *King Henry IV—Part Two* opens with a prologue by a character named "Rumour." In the comedies, such characters are modified as less obvious reflections of personality traits evidenced, for example, in the character of Dull (a constable) in *Love's Labour's Lost*, and Froth, a "foolish Gentleman" in *Measure for Measure*.

Shakespeare's writing suggests the influence of earlier English works such as Nicolas Udall's *Ralph Roister Doister* (1540), Thomas Norton's *Gorboduc* (1561), and Thomas Preston's *Cambyses, King of Persia* (c. 1569). Contemporary drama also proved inspirational, including Thomas Kyd's *The Spanish Tragedy,* Christopher Marlowe's *Tamburlaine,* and a host of European sources such as Italy's Ariosto who themselves tapped classical and medieval conventions.

It can be difficult to distinguish Shakespeare's characters and plots from each other, so a brief synopsis of each play appears below.

The Comedies and Romances

If this were play'd upon the stage now,
I could condemn it as an improbable fiction. (Twelfth Night, III.iv.127–8)

Comic drama satisfied audiences by bringing a complex plot to a happy ending. Shakespeare's comedies typically include two lines of action. The primary plot centers on main characters and a series of events that advance the story line. A second, lesser plot focuses on clownish figures that enact their own drama and sometimes interface with the main characters. Realistic figures drawn from everyday life and language can be crude, but by the final act, the unbalanced world returns to normal.

The theory of comedy can be traced back to classical views in Plato's *Republic* and Horace's *Ars Poetica*. It was considered important not to laugh at base behavior, as though to diminish or encourage its harmful effect. A distinction was made between comic action, or what we call "slapstick" humor today, and wit, or wordplay. Adapted from agrarian festivals, comedy relies on a fictional plot, social protocol, and everyday figures. Plautus' comedies (205–184 B.C.) emphasize verbal joking and identity confusion, while the work of Terence (c. 160 B.C.) highlights the complexities of interpersonal relationships.

Comedy continued to evolve during the Renaissance. Italy's Ariosto and Dolce, for example, produced "commedia erudita" utilizing verbal wit. By the mid-1500s, "commedia dell'arte," deriving from street pageantry and physical jests, enjoyed popularity. Shakespeare seems to have been familiar with works like Ariosto's *Orlando Furioso,* Tasso's *Aminta,* and Matteo Bandello's *Novelle,* published by the late 1500s in works like John Harington's 1591 English translation (Clubb 2002, 34).

Shakespeare's comedy of the 1590s follows the traditions of John Lyly (1554?–1606) and Christopher Marlowe, along with Italian plots and themes. Later comedies reveal an edge, however, with love overshadowed by violence and personal ambition.

The Comedy of Errors (1592–93)

> *By men of Epidamium he and I,*
> *And the twin Dromio, all were taken up;*
> *But by and by rude fishermen of Corinth*
> *By force took Dromio and my son from them,*
> *And me they left with those of Epidamium.* (V.i.350–54)

This play provides an early indication of Shakespeare's awareness of and interest in the New World, evidenced in sideline banter about a woman's symbolic physical features: "Where America, the Indies?" (III.ii.133). Opening to a conflict between the regions of Ephesus and Syracuse, Aegeon, a Syracuse merchant, when arrested, relays his family history to Solinus, duke of Ephesus. Aegeon reveals his twin sons (both named Antipholus) were tended by twin servant boys (both named Dromio). During a stormy voyage his wife Aemilia and one of the sons with his servant were presumed lost at sea. The remaining son set out on his eighteenth birthday with his servant to find the missing family members. Five years later, Aegeon has come to Ephesus to look for all of them. The duke allows Aegeon until nightfall to pay his fine or face execution. Meanwhile, Antipholus of Syracuse and servant Dromio arrive in Ephesus, and a series of mix-ups confuse everyone—twins included—beginning with the mistaken identity of one Antipholus for another by the wife of the brother from Ephesus. When Angelo the merchant gives a commissioned gold chain to the Syracuse brother, the Ephesus Antipholus refuses to pay and is arrested. Thinking her husband mad, Adriana and her sister Luciana seek medical treatment for him. The real husband with his servant, Dromio, flees the well-meaning efforts of his wife by hiding in an abbey. The other twins tie up the doctor and escape, arriving at the duke's palace as Aegeon prepares for execution. While they recount their story, the other twins arrive with the abbess Aemilia, Aegeon's long-lost wife. Revelation and restoration usher in a happy ending, capped by the engagement of Antipholus of Syracuse to Luciana.

The Taming of the Shrew (1593–94)

> *I swear I'll cuff you, if you strike again.* (II.i.220)

With references to Aristotle and Ovid, this play conveys a scholarly air as the backdrop of a crude and lusty suit between strong-minded lovers. The lovely Bianca, daughter of rich Baptista of Padua, entertains a variety of suitors, but her father will not allow her to wed before her older sister marries. Bad-tempered Katharina lacks courtiers until a determined young man arrives to woo her. Attracted to Katharina's dowry and challenged by her contentious reputation, Petruchio of Verona courts his bride with an enormous dose of her own medicine. Marrying Katharina or "Kate" against her wishes, Petruchio pretends she is simply coy and rushes her to his home where he finds fault with her every wish, denying food, rest, and new clothing by claiming nothing is good enough. Wearied, Kate submits to her husband's will, supporting all statements and actions, no matter how illogical or contradictory to her own wishes. They return to her father's home for Bianca's wedding, and Katharina's example and scolding of the other wives win Petruchio a handsome bet.

The Two Gentlemen of Verona (1594)

> *I'll to the ale-house with you presently.* (II.v.8–9)

Two fast friends of Verona share all pastimes but romance. Proteus loves Julia, but Valentine goes to Milan to seek his fortune. There he falls in love with Silvia, daughter of the duke of Milan. The duke encourages his daughter to a suit with Thurio, a well-placed suitor whom Silvia disdains. Meanwhile, Proteus's father sends him to Milan to improve his prospects. Proteus and Julia reluctantly part with vows of fidelity. In Milan Proteus likewise falls for Silvia, and to get his friend Valentine out of the way, reports the couple's planned elopement to her father. The duke banishes Valentine to Mantua; he is caught by a troop of robbers who threaten to kill him unless he becomes their leader. He agrees on condition of sparing women and the poor. Proteus pursues Silvia, but she remains constant to Valentine. Julia and servant Lucetta arrive from Verona disguised as men. Julia becomes "Sebastian" to serve as Proteus's replacement servant. He sends her to Silvia with the ring Julia had given him in Verona, but Silvia continues to reject his suit. Silvia departs for Mantua to find Valentine but is caught by a robber who plans to take her to his captain. Proteus arrives and rescues Silvia, witnessed by Julia in the guise of Sebastian. Valentine comes to inquire about the female reported by his thieves, and reconciliation is effected for all parties: Valentine offers Proteus the hand of Silvia, which he refuses when his love for Julia is restored upon finding she has followed him to Milan, and Valentine wins the duke's approval.

Love's Labour's Lost (1594–95)

> *Our late edict shall strongly stand in force:*
> *Navarre shall be the wonder of the world;*
> *Our court shall be a little academe,*
> *Still and contemplative in living art.* (I.i.11–14)

In another play with an academic backdrop, Ferdinand, king of Navarre, proposes a three-year term of study with no women allowed within a mile of court. Courtiers Berowne, Longaville, and Dumaine agree. The clown Costard is sentenced to punishment for wooing a country girl, Jacquenetta. Ferdinand has forgotten the French princess is due to arrive, but he must keep his vow. She and her ladies are disturbed by this treatment and return to their camp to plot revenge. When King Ferdinand finds his men are smitten with the ladies-in-waiting of the

French princess to whom he is attracted, he breaks his vow and the men visit the ladies in disguise where they are rebuffed. Costard mixes letters of Berowne for Rosaline and Armado for Jacquenetta. The ladies assail the men with their own words of banishment, followed by resolution of the conflict. News of the death of the princess's father forces her departure. She promises to return and marry the king in a year, and her ladies promise the courtiers the same if the men remain cloistered during the mourning period.

A Midsummer Night's Dream (1596)

> *Fair lovers, you are fortunately met;*
> *Of this discourse we more will hear anon.* (IV.i.177–78)

Love interests are switched in this mythological farce. Hermia and Lysander are in love, as are Helena and Demetrius. But Demetrius begins to love Hermia, encouraged by her father. Both pairs of lovers escape to the woods. Oberon and Titania, king and queen of the fairies, argue over Titania's adopted Indian boy. Oberon orders his servant Puck to place a potion in Titania's eyes so that she will love whatever she first looks upon when she awakens. Likewise, Demetrius is to receive drops so he will love Helena. Thanks to Puck's mischief, Titania awakens to fall in love with Bottom, a weaver-turned-actor with a donkey's head in lieu of his own. Puck accidentally places drops in Lysander's eyes, causing him to fall for Helena who believes both suitors are mocking her. Oberon puts the four to sleep and reconciles them when they awaken. Bottom's human head is restored as is Titania's good sense, and Bottom's acting company plays *Pyramus and Thisbe* at the wedding of three couples.

The Merchant of Venice (1596–97)

> *The quality of mercy is not strain'd,*
> *It droppeth as the gentle rain from heaven.* (IV.i.184–85)

Melancholy merchant Antonio offers to finance his friend Bassanio's courtship of Portia, an heiress. Portia favors Bassanio's suit, but before dying her father concocted a plan whereby each suitor must choose correctly from a gold, silver, or lead chest to reveal his worthiness for Portia's hand. So far none has chosen the correct casket. Antonio applies to the Jewish moneylender Shylock for a loan of three thousand ducats on Bassanio's behalf, promising to repay the money when his ships arrive within three months. Shylock lends the money, taking as surety the promise of a pound of flesh should Antonio renege. Bassanio chooses the lead casket, allowing him to marry Portia. His friend Gratiano claims Nerissa, Portia's handmaid. Shylock's daughter Jessica elopes with her Christian suitor Lorenzo, robbing Shylock of a daughter, a prized ring, and some gold. Shylock's comic servant Launcelot also flees. Antonio learns his

THE EXCELLENT

History of the Merchant of Venice.

With the extreme cruelty of *Shylocke*
the Iew towards the saide Merchant, in cut-
ting a iust pound of his flesh. And the obtaining
of *Portia*, by the choyse of
three Caskets.

Written by W. SHAKESPEARE.

Printed by *J. Roberts*, 1600.

Merchant of Venice title page, 1600.

ships have been lost at sea and Shylock demands his pound of flesh. At court Portia and Nerissa dress as judge and clerk to hear the case. When Shylock insists on the flesh, Portia mandates he must take one pound of flesh only, without a drop of blood. Shylock surrenders to enforced conversion and to sharing his fortune with Jessica and Lorenzo. Antonio learns his ships are safe. Portia and Nerissa take their husbands to task for giving away their betrothal rings, though the women themselves had demanded them while in disguise. The couples happily reconcile.

Much Ado About Nothing (1598–99)

> *Mess. I see, lady, the gentleman is not in your books.*
> *Beat. No, and he were, I would burn my study.* (I.i.79–80)

The play opens with the announcement that Don Pedro's military force is about to visit Leonato, governor of Messina. One of the soldiers, Claudio, is lauded for courage. Leonato's niece Beatrice inquires after Benedick, a long-time acquaintance and object of her criticism. When the expedition arrives Claudio falls in love with Leonato's daughter Hero. Beatrice and Benedick banter. Don Pedro offers to intercede for Claudio with Hero at the evening festivities. Don John, bastard brother of Don Pedro for whom he is filled with envy and hate, attempts to deceive Leonato into believing Don Pedro truly loves Hero. The plot fails and reconciliation follows. Don John hatches a second plot with the help of Borachio to make it appear that Hero is seeing another man at night. This plot causes Claudio to renounce Hero in church. She faints and her death is announced falsely to gain sympathy and time for the evil plot to be revealed. Benedick and Beatrice are led to believe that each cares for the other, and they fall in love. Reluctant to believe the allegations against Hero, they make efforts to uncover the plot. Constable Dogberry and sidekick Verges announce the perpetrator's arrest due to suspicious behavior and the treachery is revealed. Hero and Claudio are reunited and Benedick and Beatrice officially woo.

As You Like It (1599)

> *Ros. It is not the fashion to see the lady the*
> *epilogue; but it is no more unhandsome than to*
> *see the lord the prologue.* (Epilogue 1–3)

Duke Ferdinand replaces his older brother as ruler. The elder duke stays in the Forest of Arden while daughter Rosalind remains at court. Two brothers, Oliver and Orlando de Boys, arrive at court in conflict. Orlando wins a wrestling match and Rosalind's affection, but flees to the forest from his brother's wrath. Rosalind, dressed as the boy Ganymede, departs for the forest accompanied by the usurper duke's daughter Celia, her friend and confidante. There she meets

Orlando and encourages him to practice his romantic hopes for Rosalind on Ganymede. Meanwhile Phebe falls for Ganymede who evades her passion. Orlando saves Oliver from a lion and the brothers are reconciled as Oliver falls for Celia. The authentic duke promises to marry them when he is restored to his rightful place. Phebe marries Silvius and Touchstone the clown marries Audrey. The rightful duke learns the false duke has repented and surrendered his role as duke to live a holy life, allowing the rightful duke to reclaim his rule.

Twelfth Night (1600)

You are betroth'd both to a maid and man. (V.i.263)

A shipwreck separates twins Viola and Sebastian. Viola dresses like a boy and becomes a page, Cesario, to the duke of Orsino with whom she secretly falls in love. In carrying messages to his intended Olivia, Viola finds that Olivia has developed an attraction to Cesario. Olivia's uncle Sir Toby Belch convinces fop Sir Andrew Aguecheek to pursue Olivia fruitlessly. Olivia's servants persuade her steward Malvolio that Olivia loves him, and he is later confined for madness as he foolishly responds to the jokesters' pranks. Meanwhile Antonio saves Sebastian from the shipwreck. Olivia mistakes Sebastian for Cesario and proposes marriage, to which he agrees, while Antonio confuses Viola for Sebastian. The play climaxes when all appear before the duke for their causes. Sebastian and Viola discover each other, Olivia learns she has actually wed Sebastian, and Orsino and Viola confess mutual love. When the prank on Malvolio is revealed, Belch marries Maria.

The Merry Wives of Windsor (1597)

I have suffer'd more for their sakes—more than the villainous inconstancy of man's disposition is able to bear. (IV.v.107–109)

In an alleged response to Queen Elizabeth's request for a play about Falstaff in love, Shakespeare depicts Falstaff making advances to two married women. The two wives plot to falsely encourage him and arrange separate trysts to get revenge. Two former victims of Falstaff's conniving report his plans to Page and Ford, the women's husbands. Ford pretends to seek Falstaff's help in wooing Mistress Ford. When Falstaff is nearly caught, he hides in a basket of dirty laundry that gets thrown in the river. When the setup is repeated, Falstaff dresses as an old woman and is beaten. A third plot arranges for the two wives to meet him in the woods, but Page's daughter Anne leads a contingent of children disguised as fairies who assault Falstaff. Anne eludes her parents' choice of husband to marry Fenton whom she loves, and this revelation is well received by her parents who bestow pardon and acceptance.

All's Well That Ends Well (1602–03)

So there's my riddle: one that's dead is quick— (V.iii.303–304)

Bertram becomes count of Rossillion when his father dies. Helena, an orphaned physician's daughter, lives in his household and loves Bertram whose mother approves. Bertram goes to Paris to attend the seriously ill king of France, followed by Helena who brings a cure. The grateful king offers Helena marriage to any of the court bachelors. Helena chooses Bertram who rejects her unimpressive birth and status. Though the king forces their union, Bertram refuses to consummate the marriage until she gets his ring and bears his child, seemingly impossible conditions. Bertram leaves for Italy with his friend Parolles and there woos Diana. Helena follows and lodges with Diana and her widowed mother where she discovers Bertram's deception. Diana agrees to get Bertram's ring and let Helena take her place in bed. After the plan is carried out, Bertram hears a rumor that Helena is dead and returns to France. The king catches him in lies and then Diana arrives with her mother to bring charges. Helena returns with this ring and with child to reveal all. Bertram repents and vows his love for her.

Measure for Measure (1604)

The tempter, or the tempted, who sins most, ha? (II.ii.163)

The duke of Vienna, Vincentio, appoints Angelo to rule while he takes a break. Feeling he has been lax, Vincentio believes Angelo will be stricter (and disliked), and he disguises himself as a friar to observe. Zealous Angelo condemns Claudio to death for impregnating Juliet before marriage. Claudio's sister Isabella pleads for her brother's life, but Angelo will pardon Claudio only in exchange for Isabella's virtue. Vincentio persuades Isabella to pretend to agree and then to switch places with Angelo's former love Marina. Afterward, Angelo refuses to release Claudio. Vincentio substitutes a condemned prisoner for Claudio and tells Isabella to seek justice when the real duke returns. Vincentio resumes his identity as the duke, Marina, and Isabella confront Angelo who confesses and receives a pardon when he agrees to marry Marina. The duke marries Isabella and Claudio weds Juliet.

Richard II (left), Henry V (right)

King Richard III portrait.

THE HISTORY PLAYS

Beauty and honor in her are so mingled
That they have caught the King; and who knows yet
But from this lady may proceed a gem
To lighten all this isle? (*King Henry VIII*, II.iii.76–79)

Shakespeare dramatically revealed the conflicting natures of England's former kings. Contrasts between strong and weak rulers like Richard II and Richard III or change within an individual, such as Henry V in youth and maturity, provided material for historic plots. Themes include nationalism, expansion, and the divine right of kings. Shakespeare revised history to recast characters into molds he found suitable for the stage. He portrayed Joan of Arc, for example, in unfavorable terms. Dates and events are maneuvered to accommodate plot development and staging techniques. Sources for these plays derive from Raphael Holinshed's *Chronicles of the Kings and Queens of England,* published in 1577. Other sources include Robert Fabyan's *New Chronicles of England and of France* and Edward Halle's *Chronicles.*

King Henry VI — Part One (1589–90)

> *Good Lord, what madness rules in brainsick men,*
> *When for so slight and frivolous a cause*
> *Such factious emulations shall arise!* (IV.i.111–113)

The play opens with the funeral of Henry V, just seven years after his defeat of the French at Agincourt. English nobles accuse clergy of controlling the heir Henry VI, and the French rebel under King Charles. The English army is weak. At Orleans the Dauphin meets Joan Pucelle, a prophetess serving the French cause whom we have come to know as Joan of Arc. The Dauphin lets her fight the English and he later marries her. The English Talbot faces Pucelle and loses. The countess of Auvergne calls Talbot a "silly dwarf" and tries to imprison him. In England, Richard Plantagenet reflects on his legacy because Henry V had executed Richard's father as a traitor, leading to the War of the Roses. Before dying Edmund Mortimer names Richard Plantagenet his heir. Henry VI goes to France to be crowned king. At Rouen the Dauphin and Joan fight the English but are forced to retreat. Falstaff is banished as a coward. Henry VI makes peace with France and promises to marry Margaret of Armagnac, a French noble's daughter. York sentences Joan to burn at the stake. Henry VI changes his mind and marries Margaret of Anjou. Suffolk plans to seduce Margaret to control Henry and the kingdom.

King Henry VI — Part Two (1590–91)

> *Henry my lord is cold in great affairs.* (III.i.224)

Margaret of Anjou comes to Henry minus a dowry; Anjou and Maine are returned to France. Gloucester fears all France will be lost. English nobles Buckingham, Somerset, and Cardinal plan to dispose of Gloucester. York plots to claim the kingship through the House of York in opposing Henry VI's claim through the House of Lancaster. Gloucester's wife Eleanor plots for the crown with magic and is arrested; her husband casts her off. Richard Plantagenet schemes for the English crown. France appears to be lost and Gloucester, arrested for treason, predicts Henry VI's downfall. York leaves to suppress Irish rebels and Gloucester is murdered. Henry banishes Suffolk who is murdered by pirates. Irishman John Cade plans to become the king of England and kills all the nobles he finds in London, burning the Tower of London and London Bridge. Alexander Iden kills Cade. York, supported by sons Edward IV and Richard III, tells Henry VI he wants the crown for himself. Henry VI, flanked by Somerset, Clifford, and Buckingham, faces York at the Battle of St. Albans where hunchback Richard III defeats Somerset.

King Henry VI — Part Three (1590–91)

> *Hadst thou been kill'd when first thou didst presume,*
> *Thou hadst not liv'd to kill a son of mine.* (V.vi.34–36)

York and Warwick storm the London castle so York can take the throne. Henry VI returns and promises to yield the throne when he dies. Furious, Queen Margaret divorces Henry and takes son Prince Edward to join Henry's supporters— Northumberland, Clifford, and Westmoreland. York faces Margaret with 20,000 men at the Battle of Wakefield and is killed. Margaret and the prince flee to France. Edward IV marries Lady Jane Grey. Henry VI names Warwick and the duke of Clarence as England's Protectors and orders Henry VII to Brittany for protection. Edward IV captures King Henry, Queen Margaret, Oxford, Somerset, and the prince at Tewksbury and kills Prince Edward. Richard III murders Henry VI in the Tower of London. Edward IV blesses Edward V and banishes Margaret to France.

King Richard III (1592–93)

> *I must be married to my brother's daughter,*
> *Or else my kingdom stands on brittle glass.*
> *Murther her brothers and then marry her.* (IV.ii.60–62)

Richard III, hunchback from birth, muses on his discontent despite the end of the civil wars. He kills his wife and several relatives to secure his claim to the throne. He plans to kill brother Clarence and marry Lady Anne whose husband he has already killed. Clarence is kept in the Tower. King Edward IV dies of apparent illness. Edward IV's son is supposed to be crowned, but fearing Richard, the queen flees with her other son, brother of the Prince of Wales. The two boys are sent to the tower, allegedly to await the coronation of the Prince of Wales. Richard executes Hastings and spreads rumors that the deceased king's sons are illegitimate. Richard then appears in public as a reluctant ruler. He arranges for Tyrell to murder the princes and is crowned king. Former supporter Buckingham is captured and executed. Ghosts trouble Richard on the battle-field. He pursues Richmond, and following hand-to-hand combat, Richard dies. Richmond is offered the crown and plans to marry Queen Elizabeth's daughter to unite the houses of York and Lancaster and end civil strife.

King Richard II (1595–96)

> *I wasted time, and now doth time waste me.* (V.v.49)

Richard II and his uncle John of Gaunt address a dispute between Gaunt's son Henry Bolingbroke and the duke of Norfolk who fight over the death of Richard's brother, the duke of Gloucester. Richard banishes the duke perma-nently and Bolingbroke for five years. Gaunt dies and Richard II claims his lands and money, acts which anger many nobles. Assisted by the earl of

Northumberland (Henry Percy) and his son Hotspur, Bolingbroke executes Bushy, Green, and the earl of Wiltshire as King Richard tries to maintain the crown. Richard's troops disperse when his death is rumored and the commoners rebel. Richard repeals Bolingbroke's banishment. Bolingbroke insists on being titled King Henry IV. Richard II is sent to northern England and the queen is exiled to her native France. Sir Pierce murders Richard II in prison and Henry IV executes the earl of Salisbury, Lord Spencer, the earl of Kent, and Sir Thomas Blunt, among others, for treason.

King John (1594–96)

France, hast thou yet more blood to cast away? (II.i.334)

Backing Arthur, the English king's nephew, the French demand that King John surrender the throne. John's troops meet the French at Angiers inconclusively. John arranges for the Dauphin to marry his niece Blanch and hands over limited English lands. The pope excommunicates John over the appointment of the archbishop of Canterbury and orders the French to continue fighting. English troops capture Arthur but he falls to his death before King John can execute him. Ironically, John's nobles believe he has killed Arthur and they desert to the French. The Pope's emissary Pandulph receives the crown from John, then returns it to him as a church vassal. French troops ignore orders to stop fighting. English deserters, fearful of reprisal under the French king, return to support John. Pandulph negotiates peace between the French and English, but John is poisoned by a monk at Swinstead Abbey and his son is crowned Henry III.

King Henry IV—Part One (1596–97)

My blood hath been too cold and temperate,
Unapt to stir at these indignities. (I.iii.1–2)

Former supporters of King Henry IV contest his claim for Wales, Scotland, and northern England. Henry IV matures from Falstaff's idle companion to ruler and warrior set on defending his kingdom. Preparing to face Hotspur, a contestant for the throne, Henry offers peace, but Worcester and Vernon fail to inform Hotspur, who is killed by Prince Henry. Coming upon Hotspur's corpse, Falstaff stabs it and allows others to believe he conquered the foe. King Henry plans to go after the Welsh who follow Owen Glendower while Prince John and Westmoreland attack the archbishop of York and Northumberland.

King Henry IV—Part Two (1597–98)

He hath eaten me out of house and home. (II.i.74)

Henry IV directs Westmoreland and Lancaster to rout the rebels. Falstaff remains at the Boar's Head Inn with Mistress Quickly until Prince Hal visits and they are called to war. Falstaff recruits fighting men but allows them to buy their way out of service. King Henry sends Prince John of Lancaster to negotiate with the rebels if they will disperse their army. They do, and Prince John's army captures and executes the leaders. While dying, King Henry reconciles with Prince Hal, realizing his potential greatness. Hal becomes King Henry V. When Falstaff sets out for London to meet his old friend, the King prohibits him from approaching within ten miles on penalty of death.

King Henry V (1598–99)

This story shall the good man teach his son. (IV.iii.56)

Henry V demonstrates new-found maturity in surrendering youthful behavior and companions, Falstaff included, who dies without a visit from the king. Henry claims the French throne, defeats treachery at home, and wins strategic battles in France before wooing Princess Katharine of France. Their marriage heals the conflict and joins their countries of France and England.

King Henry VIII (1612–13)

never, before
This happy child, did I get any thing. (V.iv.64–65)

Wolsey arrests and executes Buckingham for treason despite the queen's protests. At Wolsey's party King Henry falls for Anne Bullen (Boleyn), one of the queen's ladies-in-waiting. Henry, wishing to marry Anne, seeks Wolsey's advice about divorcing the queen who (Henry argues) was his brother's lawful wife, which may constitute incest and discredit their marriage. Wolsey advocates waiting for Rome's papal authority, but Henry becomes increasingly distrustful of Wolsey. Taking the matter into his own hands, Henry divorces the queen and marries Anne secretly. Wolsey and Queen Catherine die soon after. The new Archbishop Cranmer, accused of treason, is supported by Henry. Cranmer christens Anne Boleyn's daughter as Princess Elizabeth and predicts her glorious rule of England.

LATE ROMANCES

You speak a language that I understand not. (*The Winter's Tale*, III.ii.80)

Four later plays defy classification: *Cymbeline*, *Pericles*, *The Tempest*, and *The Winter's Tale*. While they may be defined as comedies in the strict sense that no major characters die and reunions occur in the conclusions, the dark side of human nature surfaces in each plot. Some critics use the term "tragicomedy" for drama of this nature. Self-interest, murder, and exile guide these plots. *The Tempest* includes elements of earlier comedies but likewise adds disturbing features like the demonic Caliban.

Cymbeline (1609–10)

> *Let a Roman and a British ensign wave*
> *Friendly together.* (V.v.479–480)

The widowed British ruler Cymbeline marries an evil queen. His daughter Imogen loves Posthumus, but the queen expects her to marry stepbrother Cloten. Imogen marries Posthumus whom the king then banishes. Before leaving, Posthumus gives Imogen a ring and bracelet. In Rome Posthumus bets Iachimo can't seduce Imogen. Traveling to Britain, Iachimo attempts this feat but is rebuffed. At night he hides in her room, steals the bracelet, and notes a mole on a hidden part of her body. Back in Rome Iachimo convinces Posthumus the deed is done, and the angry husband sends a letter telling servant Pisanio to kill Imogen. Pisanio only warns her and Imogen leaves court disguised as a page. Pisanio also gives her a sleeping potion that he believes is medicine. Rome declares war on Britain over unpaid tribute. Imogen gets lost and meets Belarius with Cymbeline's two sons whom he kidnapped 20 years before. Cloten arrives in Posthmus's clothes and is killed by Guiderius following an insult. Feeling ill, Imogen takes the sleeping potion and when the others believe she has died, they place her beside the beheaded corpse of Cloten. When she awakens, she sees the corpse in Posthumus's clothes and mourns her husband; she then enters the service of Lucius as a page. Britons defeat Rome and Imogen (as Fidele the page), Iachimo, and Lucius are brought to court. The dying queen confesses and all repent and are forgiven. Cymbeline makes peace with Rome and frees his prisoners.

Pericles (1607–08)

> *. . . make swift the pangs*
> *Of my queen's travails!* (III.i.13–14)

King Antiochus of Antioch discovers that Pericles knows of the incest with his daughter. To escape Antiochus' wrath, Pericles flees to Tyre, appoints Helicanus as regent, then is shipwrecked en route to Pentapolis. Surviving the wreck, Pericles wins Thaisa's hand in marriage in a tournament. He learns that Antiochus has died. The couple's daughter Marina is born aboard ship on a return voyage to Tyre. Believing Thaisa has died in childbirth, Pericles seals her body in a watertight coffin and sets it adrift. Washing onto the Ephesian shore, Thaisa revives, and believing her family lost, devotes herself to service in Diana's temple. Mournful Pericles leaves Marina at Tarsus with Cleon and Dionyza for 16 years. Dionyza, jealous of Marina's beauty, plots to kill her but pirates capture Marina and sell her to a Mitylene brothel where the governor finds and rescues her. Believing the girl dead, Cleon raises a monument to Marina's memory. After viewing Cleon's monument, Pericles goes to Mitylene and unknowingly engages Marina in conversation, soon learning she is his long-lost daughter. Lysismachus, the governor, receives permission to marry

Marina. Obeying a dream, Pericles visits Ephesus where he finds Thaisa in Diana's temple, and the family is united.

Two Noble Kinsmen (1613)

> *Hark how yon spurs to spirit do incite*
> *The princes to their proof!* (V.iii.56–57)

This play is based on Chaucer's *Knight's Tale*. Two kinsmen, Palomon and Arcite, fighting against Athens for Thebes, are captured and imprisoned. Both are attracted to Emilia, sister of Hippolyta, the wife of Theseus. Arcite is exiled while Palomon remains in prison. Later he escapes with the help of the jailer's daughter who eventually goes mad from unrequited love. The kinsmen meet in the forest and fight over Emilia. Theseus sentences both to death. Emilia and Hippolyta persuade him to banish the two instead, but they refuse. Theseus tells Emilia to choose one; the other will die. She cannot choose so a date is fixed for the following month. When the month is up, Arcite wins but is wounded in a riding accident. Dying, he gives the hand of Emilia to Palomon.

The Winter's Tale (1610–11)

> *Our Perdita is found.* (V.iii.121)

Sicilian ruler Leontes jails his wife Hermione, believing she has been unfaithful with his friend Polixenes. In prison Hermione gives birth to a daughter Perdita whom Leontes disowns, and he orders Antigonus to abandon the child in the desert. Leontes' son Mamilius dies of sorrow and serving-woman Paulina reports that Hermione also has died. A shepherd finds and raises the infant Perdita. Sixteen years later she falls in love with Florizel, son of Polixenes, who is unhappy with his son's peasant love, and the couple escapes to Sicilia from Bohemia aided by Leontes' advisor Camillo. Polixenes follows them to Leontes' court where Perdita's history unravels, leading to reconciliation with her father. Leontes and Polixenes bless their children's union. Paulina leads them to a lifelike statue of Hermione that is revealed as the real woman. The family is reconciled and Paulina and Camillo wed.

The Tempest (1611)

> *O brave new world,*
> *That hath such people in't!* (V.i.181–182)

Prospero rules an island of spirits where he and daughter Miranda were shipwrecked years before. They are served by spritelike Ariel and deformed Caliban, son of Sycorax the witch who is now dead. Another wreck brings several newcomers to the island, among them Alonso, king of Naples; Sebastian, his brother; Antonio, Prospero's brother who has usurped his role as duke of Milan; and Ferdinand, son of Alonso. In addition, Stephano, a drunken butler, and Trinculo, a jester, assume authority over Caliban. Miranda and Ferdinand fall in love and plan to marry. Prospero forgives Antonio and will reclaim his title upon return to civilization. Ariel is freed while Caliban remains in servitude. Fairy folk celebrate the marriage.

THE TRAGEDIES

> *Tut, I can counterfeit the deep tragedian,*
> *Speak and look back, and pry on every side,*
> *Tremble and start at wagging of a straw;*
> *Intending deep suspicion, ghastly looks*
> *Are at my service, like enforced smiles.* (*King Richard III*, III.v.5–9)

Shakespeare's tragedies are still performed with great pathos on today's stages and, in fact, constitute a hallmark pursued by actors and theater companies. To perform tragic Shakespeare is to perform the elite in stage drama.

Tragedies depict human limitations and relational contradictions, the danger of misplaced trust, and consequences of unbalanced reason or emotion. Features include high-born nobles, elevated rhetoric, and a deadly moral flaw that contributes to the fall of the protagonist. Most of Shakespeare's major tragedies were written in the first decade of the 1600s.

Classical sources include Aristotle's *Poetics* and Horace's *Technique of Poetry*. Additional influences include Plutarch's *History of the Noble Greeks and Romans* for stories like *Julius Caesar* and *Antony and Cleopatra*.

Titus Andronicus (1593–94)

> *What means my niece Lavinia by these signs?* (IV.i.8)

Roman general Titus defeats the Goths and returns to Rome with captives Queen Tamora and her sons. Titus's sons kill one of them, Alarbus. Tamora seduces the emperor while plotting revenge with Aaron, her Moor lover. Tamora's sons Demetrius and Chiron kill Bassianus, the emperor's brother and husband of Lavinia, Titus's daughter. They rape Lavinia and amputate her hands and tongue. Lucius is banned for a failed rescue while Quintus and Martius are blamed for Brassianus's death. Titus sends his amputated hand to the emperor to spare his sons' lives, but the hand is returned with their heads. Lucius and an army march on Rome. Titus kills Chiron and Demetrius, makes a pie of their remains, and serves it to Tamora when she asks Titus to intercede with Lucius. Titus kills Lavinia in mercy before killing Tamora in revenge. Saturnius slays Titus and Lucius kills Saturnius. Lucius is crowned emperor, Aaron is buried to his chest to die of starvation while his child by Tamora is saved, and Tamora's remains are exposed for scavengers.

THE
MOST EX=
cellent and lamentable
Tragedie, of Romeo
and *Iuliet*.

Newly corrected, augmented, and
amended :

As it hath bene fundry times publiquely acted, by the
right Honourable the Lord Chamberlaine
his Seruants.

LONDON
Printed by Thomas Creede, for Cuthbert Burby, and are to
be fold at his fhop neare the Exchange.
1599.

The title page from *Romeo and Juliet,* 1599.

Romeo and Juliet (1595–96)

For never was a story of more woe
Than this of Juliet and her Romeo. (V.iii.309–310)

Two noble families of Verona, the Montagues and the Capulets, chronically feud. The prince issues a death sentence to end their brawling. Young Romeo Montague, infatuated with Capulet's niece Rosaline, sneaks into a masked ball to see her. There he glimpses Juliet who steals his heart, and their mutual love is pledged on her balcony. Friar Laurence secretly weds the couple the following day. Tybalt challenges Romeo who refuses to fight so Mercutio accepts the challenge and is slain. Romeo stabs Tybalt and is banished, spending one night with his wife before leaving at daybreak. Juliet's parents arrange her marriage to Count Paris and to prevent it, Juliet conspires with the friar to take a sleeping potion to make her comatose for 42 hours until Romeo can come for her. Her rumored death reaches Romeo before the friar's explanation, and he comes to die in her tomb. Romeo kills Paris outside the tomb, then takes poison as he gazes on Juliet. She awakens to find his body, seizes his dagger, and kills herself. Friar Laurence explains what happened to the prince, and the families make peace.

Troilus and Cressida (1601–02)

They say all lovers swear more performance
than they are able. (III.ii.84–85)

As the Trojan War enters its seventh year, King Priam's youngest son Troilus romances the daughter of Calchas, a priest of Troy, encouraged by her uncle Pandarus. Meanwhile Achilles' apathy troubles the Greeks. Troilus's brother Hector challenges the Greeks and Ulysses arranges for Ajax's name to be drawn for hand-to-hand combat. Calchas deserts to the Greeks, promising information and his daughter for the release of a Trojan warrior. Agamemnon agrees, and Cressida takes Troilus's sleeve as a love token before parting. Cressida, enjoying Greek attention, is wooed by Diomedes to whom she gives Troilus's sleeve as he watches from a distance. Hector duels with Ajax before calling a truce. Achilles, enraged when Hector kills Patroclus, orders his men to slay Hector as he rests unarmed. Troy is defeated and Troilus curses Achilles and Pandarus.

Hamlet (1600–01)

The potent poison quite o'er-crows my spirit. (V.ii.353)

Hamlet returns to Denmark from Wittenberg for his father's funeral and witnesses his mother's marriage to his uncle Claudius within a month. A meeting with his father's ghost confirms Hamlet's suspicions that Claudius murdered the elder Hamlet. Young Hamlet pretends madness to plan revenge. Statesman Polonius believes the madness stems from Hamlet's love for his daughter Ophelia and he orders her to meet with Hamlet so the parents can secretly observe. Hamlet arranges a special play dramatizing his father's death, eliciting Claudius's guilty response, which confirms the ghost's story. Claudius sends Hamlet to England with Rosencrantz and Guildenstern who bear a secret order for Hamlet's death; Hamlet reverses it so they die instead. Returning to Denmark he finds Ophelia dead from her madness-induced suicide; he and her brother Laertes quarrel at her grave. Laertes and the king plot to kill Hamlet by arranging a fencing match to be augmented by poisoned wine and a poisoned sword. At the match the queen unwittingly drinks the wine and collapses, warning Hamlet before dying. Wounded by the sword, Hamlet receives Laertes' confession and is alerted to the king's duplicity. Hamlet stabs the king and forces him to drink poison. Hamlet dies and Fortinbras of Norway comes to rule.

Julius Caesar (1599–1600)

This was the most unkindest cut of all. (III.ii.183)

Julius Caesar's victories over the Gauls and Pompey are lauded by Rome. Mark Antony tries to have Caesar crowned, but Cassius expresses concern about Caesar's ambition and seeks the support of Brutus, an honorable and respected leader. Musing while a storm wracks Rome, Brutus finally agrees that Caesar must be stopped. Ignoring a seer's prophecy and his wife's concern, Caesar is stabbed at the Senate by Brutus and Cassius. Mark Antony asks to speak at Caesar's funeral and skillfully rouses the crowd against the conspirators. Antony joins forces with Caesar's nephew Octavius and Lepidus to control Rome. A battle follows and Cassius kills himself. Defeated, Brutus also kills himself. Antony eulogizes Brutus as a noble Roman.

Othello (1604)

I took by th' throat the circumcised dog,
And smote him—thus. (V.ii.355–356)

The Moorish general Othello secretly weds Desdemona, daughter of Venetian senator Brabantio. Othello promotes Cassio as his lieutenant instead of Iago, who becomes jealous and resentful. The couple with Iago and Cassio travel to Cyprus where a battle rages against the Turks. Iago incites Othello's jealousy by luring Cassio into conflict with Roderick, costing Cassio his position. Iago urges Cassio to seek Desdemona's intervention and then alerts Othello to his wife's alleged guile. Iago's wife Emilia finds Desdemona's prized handkerchief given her by Othello, and Iago plants it on Cassio who passes it to his girlfriend. Iago arranges for Othello to overhear

Cassio talking about the handkerchief with Bianca whom Othello believes is Desdemona. Othello strangles his wife and orders Iago to kill Cassio. Iago convinces Roderigo to attempt Cassio's murder, but he only wounds Cassio so Iago kills Roderigo. Iago also kills Emilia to keep her quiet. Letters found on Roderick exonerate Cassio and convict Iago. Othello stabs himself and dies beside Desdemona.

King Lear (1605)

Pray you now forget, and forgive; I am old and foolish. (IV.vii.83)

Britain's ruler divides his kingdom among three daughters, Goneril, Regan, and Cordelia. The first two lavish him with praise, but Cordelia simply claims to love her father as she should. Lear disowns her. He soon learns he has misjudged his daughters as Goneril and Regan revile him. Maddened with grief, Lear wanders the wilderness during a storm, accompanied by follower Kent and a fool. When Gloucester's illegitimate son Edmund betrays him, the duke of Cornwall blinds him. Both Goneril and Regan desire Edmund, and Goneril poisons her sister. The English defeat the French army. Captured by Edmund, Lear and Cordelia are sentenced to hang. Gloucester's legitimate son Edgar from whom he has been estranged fights with Edmund who repents while dying. Goneril kills herself upon hearing of Edmund's defeat. Edmund repeals the death sentence too late to save Cordelia who dies, followed shortly by her father. Gloucester reconciles with Edgar before dying, leaving Albany to rule Britain.

Antony and Cleopatra (1606–07)

I am fire and air; my other elements
I give to baser life. (V.ii.289–290)

Mark Antony's affair with Egyptian ruler Cleopatra lures him from duty. His wife's death and impending war with Pompey force his return to Rome where he argues with Octavius. Antony marries his commander's sister, Octavia, to pacify him. Octavia tries to reconcile Antony and Caesar, but Antony returns to Cleopatra who persuades him to engage the furious Caesar at sea rather than by land. During the battle Cleopatra's ship leaves the scene and Antony's follows, leaving Rome the victor. Caesar refuses Antony's peace offer, and he tries to bribe Cleopatra with clear title to Egypt if she will kill Antony, which she refuses to do. Troops clash and Antony wins. When Egypt pulls out again, Antony threatens Cleopatra and she circulates the rumor of her death. Antony falls on his sword in grief. Servants carry him to Cleopatra and they exchange pledges of love before his death. Caesar promises mercy to Cleopatra but knowing he will humiliate her in defeat, she arranges for an asp to bite her. She and Antony are buried together.

Coriolanus (1607)

> *Bid them wash their faces,*
> *And keep their teeth clean.* (II.iii.60–61)

Romans distrust the Senate. Marcius disdains the common people, but when Volscians attack, he captures their capital city of Coriolo, earning the name of Coriolanus. The Volscian general plots revenge. When the Senate offers Coriolanus a consulship, two tribunes, Brutus and Sicinius, turn the commoners against him. Coriolanus upbraids the two and is exiled to Antium. There Aufidius offers him half the Volscian army, and the two leaders march to Rome where Coriolanus's mother tries to persuade him to peace. Coriolanus reports to the Volscians that Rome can't be taken; they condemn him as a traitor and he is stabbed.

Macbeth (1606)

> *I have supp'd full with horrors.* (V.v.13)

The Scottish Macbeth, thane of Glamis, is a military hero. Returning from battle with the thane of Cawdor, he and Banquo meet three witches who prophesy that Macbeth will be thane of Cawdor and then king, and Banquo will father future kings. The men ignore these prophesies. At home Macbeth learns he will become thane of Cawdor as reward for military exploits. Lady Macbeth pushes her husband to become king immediately. The couple plots against King Duncan by stabbing the king, placing the dagger with drunken servants, and then killing them in alleged outrage. The king's sons Malcolm and Donalbain flee, which some interpret as guilt, and Macbeth is crowned king. Fearing suspicion, Macbeth pays killers to vanquish Banquo, but Banquo's son Fleance escapes. Banquo's bloody ghost appears to Macbeth at his coronation feast and Macduff leaves for England. Macbeth kills everyone in Macduff's household. Macduff and Malcolm raise an army against Macbeth and return to Scotland. Macbeth is emboldened by prophecies that he will not die until Birnam Wood comes to Dunsinane, and he will not be killed by man born of woman. When a messenger reports soldiers covered with branches and Macbeth learns his mad wife has died, he knows he has lost but continues fighting. Facing Macduff on the field, Macbeth triumphantly asserts that no man born of woman can best him, to which Macduff replies he was born prematurely by surgical rather than natural means. Macduff beheads Macbeth and takes the throne.

Timon of Athens (1607–08)

> *Ah, when the means are gone that buy this praise,*
> *The breath is gone whereof this praise is made.* (II.ii.169–170)

Generous Timon gives to everyone, depleting his wealth. When creditors come, he sends them to friends who claim they can't help. Timon invites former friends to another banquet, serving warm water, where he renounces them and all other humans. He goes to live in a cave and finds hidden gold. Captain Alcibiades, banished for pleading mercy for one of his men, marches on the city, accepting Timon's gold for sacking Athens. Robbers also visit Timon and though he offers them gold to loot the city, they reform. Athens seeks Timon's help, but he refuses. The senators give Alcibiades his enemies and those who refused to help Timon. Peace follows, with the report Timon has died.

SUMMARY

Shakespeare's plays take many forms, some of which are difficult to categorize. From high-spirited romance to dread-locked tragedy, his drama runs the gamut of human emotions, playing upon the lives of his characters in ways that render striking and harmonious themes transcending time and place. It is interesting to ponder how a teenage father escaped the pressures of middle-class life to pursue fame in the heart of London's entertainment district by exploring human nature in his writing.

Perhaps more striking is his success. From where did Shakespeare glean insight into the heart of an adolescent girl like Juliet? How could he probe the pain of an aging ruler in the story of Lear? No other playwright has been able to capture with such vividness and realism the hearts and souls of characters struggling with their humanity. Shakespeare's stories enhanced by ornate costuming and special effects illustrate his times and enlighten ours.

SOURCES

Bentley, Gerald Eades. *Shakespeare: A Biographical Handbook*. New Haven, Conn.: Yale University Press, 1961.

Bradbrook, M.D. *Shakespeare in His Context: The Constellated Globe*. The Collected Papers of Muriel Bradbrook, Vol. IV. London: Harvester Wheatsheaf, 1989.

Clubb, Louise George. "Italian Stories on the Stage." In *The Cambridge Companion to Shakespearean Comedy,* ed. Alexander Leggatt. Cambridge: Cambridge University Press, 2002.

Crewe, Jonathan, ed. *William Shakespeare: The Narrative Poems*. New York: Penguin, 1999.

Evans, G. Blakemore, and J.J.M. Tobin. *The Riverside Shakespeare*. 2d ed. Boston: Houghton Mifflin, 1997.

Fox, Levi. *The Shakespeare Handbook*. Boston: G. K. Hall, 1987.

Frye, Roland Mushat. *Shakespeare's Life and Times*. Princeton, N.J.: Princeton University Press, 1967.

Honan, Park. *Shakespeare: A Life*. Oxford: Oxford University Press, 1998.

Hyland, Peter. *An Introduction to Shakespeare: The Dramatist in His Context*. New York: St. Martin's, 1996.

Rouse, W. H. D., Litt.D. *Being Arthur Golding's Translation of the Metamorphoses.* London: De La More, 1904.

Rowse, A. L. *The Elizabethan Renaissance.* London: Macmillan, 1971.

Sams, Eric. *Retrieving the Early Years, 1564–1594.* New Haven, Conn.: Yale University Press, 1995.

Schoenbaum, S. *Shakespeare's Lives.* New Ed. Oxford: Clarendon, 1991.

Sorelius, Gunnar. *Shakespeare's Early Comedies: Myth, Metamorphisis, Mannerism.* Uppsala, Sweden: Acta University, Stockholm: Almquist and Wiksell, 1993.

Wells, Stanley. *Shakespeare: A Life in Drama.* New York: Norton, 1995.

Whalen, Richard F. *Shakespeare—Who Was He?* Westport, Conn.: Praeger, 1994.

Williams, David R. *Shakespeare Thy Name Is Marlowe.* New York: Philosophical Library, 1966.

QUESTIONS

1. Find references to biblical stories in Shakespearean plays your class is studying.
2. Why might Shakespeare use scriptural references more than his contemporaries?
3. Given Henry Chettle's apology, what effect might Greene's criticism have had on Shakespeare's career?
4. Why would a creative genius like Shakespeare plagiarize other sources?
5. Give an example or two of today's reworked popular songs or themes.
6. Why would a successful playwright such as Greene bother to criticize a relative newcomer like Shakespeare whom Greene considered inferior?
7. How would someone like Philip Henslowe actually help bankroll an aspiring acting troupe? Why would Henslowe want to do this?

CRITICAL THINKING AND RESEARCH PROJECTS

1. Explore the development of one of Shakespeare's narrative poems. Consider sources, influences, and popular themes to suggest a theory as to how or why Shakespeare might have written it.
2. Compare a Shakespeare play with a similar one by a contemporary, for example, Shakespeare's *The Merchant of Venice* with Christopher Marlowe's *The Jew of Malta*. Discuss ways in which the works are similar and different, and examine reasons why.

FOR FURTHER READING

Blayney, Peter W. M. *The First Folio of Shakespeare.* Washington, D.C.: Folger, 1991.

Bloom, Harold. *Shakespeare: The Invention of the Human.* New York: Riverhead Books, 1998.

———, ed. *William Shakespeare: The Tragedies,* with intro. New York: Chelsea House, 1985.

Callaghan, Dympna, ed. *A Feminist Companion to Shakespeare*. Malden, Mass.: Blackwell, 2001.

Chedgzoy, Kate, ed. *Shakespeare, Feminism, and Gender*. New York: Palgrave, 2001.

Danson, Lawrence. *Shakespeare's Dramatic Genres*. Oxford: Oxford University Press, 2000.

Dubrow, Heather. *Captive Victors: Shakespeare's Narrative Poems and Sonnets*. Ithaca, N.Y.: Cornell University Press, 1987.

Muir, Kenneth. *The Sources of Shakespeare's Plays*. New Haven, Conn.: Yale University Press, 1978.

Neill, Michael. *Issues of Death: Mortality and Identity in English Renaissance Tragedy*. Oxford: Clarendon, 1997.

Patterson, Annabel. *Reading Holinshed's Chronicles*. Chicago: University Press of Chicago, 1994.

Shaheen, Naseeb. *Biblical References in Shakespeare's Comedies*. Newark: University of Delaware Press, 1993.

Spiekerman, Tim. *Shakespeare's Political Realism: The English History Plays*. Albany: State University of New York Press, 2001.

Thompson, Bard. *Humanists and Reformers: A History of the Renaissance and Reformation*. Grand Rapids, Mich.: William B. Eerdmans, 1996.

Vendler, Helen. *The Art of Shakespeare's Sonnets*. Cambridge, Mass.: Harvard University Press, 1997.

Wells, Stanley, Gary Taylor, John Jowatt, William Montgomery. *William Shakespeare: A Textual Companion*. Oxford: Clarendon Press, 1987.

West, Anthony James. *The Shakespeare First Folio: The History of the Book*. Oxford: Oxford University Press, 2001.

South Bank and London Bridge by Loggan.

4

PERFORMANCE AND CRITICISM

O, it offends me to the soul to
hear a robustious periwig-pated fellow tear a passion to totters.
(*Hamlet*, III.ii.8–10)

For centuries scholars have pored over the plays and poems of William Shakespeare, searching for clues to help us understand the man and his writing. Research has uncovered important facts about Shakespeare, including where he was born and buried, where he lived, and who his ancestors were. We also know something of his property dealings and his work in London theater.

But there are those who believe the writings attributed to William Shakespeare were produced by another person or persons, perhaps even Queen Elizabeth or a playwright of the day such as Christopher Marlowe. Supporters of this theory are called anti-Stratfordians.

Most scholars think William Shakespeare wrote most of the works attributed to him. The beauty, consistency, and universality of the plays point to their authorship as someone with the character and background associated with William Shakespeare from Stratford.

ANTI-STRATFORDIAN THEORIES

Most mighty Duke, behold a man much wrong'd. (*The Comedy of Errors*, V.i.331–332)

More than a hundred documents help us trace the activities of a man named William Shakespeare. The years 1585 to 1592 are sometimes called "the lost years" because little evidence survives about Shakespeare's life during that period. The Stratfordian's will leaves bequests to Heminges, Burbage, and Condell, London actors with the King's Men. Some critics believe that plays attributed to Shakespeare were written by others but published under Shakespeare's name; thus, they argue, a dramatist by the name of William Shakespeare never lived.

Two perceptions support the anti-Stratfordian movement: (1) The plays written under Shakespeare's name show learning common in a university education, which it appears William Shakespeare did not have. The response to this argument is that Stratford's grammar school offered a very strong education which would have prepared Shakespeare to write the plays attributed to him. (2) Many find it hard to accept Shakespeare's work as written by someone of common parents from a small country town. Authors such as the earl of Essex, the earl of Derby, or Sir Walter Raleigh have been proposed as writers of Shakespeare's work. But the plays abound with simple pastoral scenes and homely images.

Recent literary criticism favors Edward de Vere, the earl of Oxford (1550–1604). De Vere earned a Master of Arts degree at Oxford and Cambridge universities before pursuing legal training at Gray's Inn. In 1571 he married Anne Cecil, daughter of Queen Elizabeth's secretary of state. De Vere traveled abroad for several months and later fathered an illegitimate child by Anne Vavasour, which sent him to the Tower of London for a time. De Vere eventually wrote poetry, including *The Paradise of Dainty Devices* (1576), *The Phoenix Nest* (1593), and *England's Parnassus* (1600), and he was ranked by some as one of England's greatest Elizabethan poets. Francis Meres praised de Vere's comedy. The earl of Oxford died in London, possibly of plague, and was buried in Westminster Abbey.

However, the writing of other people does not resemble Shakespeare's. Other literary figures such as John Webster, Thomas Middleton, Thomas Dekker, and Thomas Heywood have been credited with Shakespeare's plays, though it remains unclear why these men, if the true writers, failed to reveal themselves. Several died while plays continued to be published under Shakespeare's name. It is unlikely that anyone but Shakespeare produced the work attributed to him.

SHAKESPEARE AND THE BIBLE

> *The Hebrew will turn Christian.* (The Merchant of Venice, I.iii.178)

Shakespeare's writing contains more references to the Bible than other drama of this period. His work also alludes to the apocrypha. Shakespeare references most if not all of the books of the Bible, either directly or through paraphrase, in passages like these:

> Not that Adam that kept the Paradise,
> but that Adam that keeps the prison; he that goes in
> the calve's-skin that was kill'd for the Prodigal.
>
> *(The Comedy of Errors, IV.iii.17–19)*

> I am as poor as Job, my lord, but not so
> patient.
>
> *(King Henry IV–Second Part, I.ii.126–127)*

> Though some of you, with Pilate, wash your hands,
> Showing an outward pity, yet you Pilates
> Have here deliver'd me to my sour cross,
> And water cannot wash away your sin.
>
> *(King Richard II, IV.i.239–242)*

With an ear for language, a mind for detail, and a heart for people, Shakespeare must have eagerly absorbed the Bible readings of church worship and school chapel.

Attuned to supernatural influences as were many in his age, Shakespeare uses angel references in many plays, including such diverse works as *Cymbeline, Pericles, Hamlet, Julius Caesar, Antony and Cleopatra, The Comedy of Errors*, and some of the history plays. In Shakespeare's lexicon, an "angel" may refer to a coin or represent a celestial being. He likewise makes use of "devil," "fiend," or "Lucifer" in plays like *Troilus and Cressida, The Tempest, Measure for Measure, Love's Labours Lost*, and history plays. Shakespeare's monarchs often defend their rule through the divine right of kings as orchestrated by God to form part of the great chain of being.

The civic code of justice upheld biblical standards, condemning behavior such as sexual misconduct (fornication, adultery, homosexuality) and fraud (bribery, embezzlement, inaccurate measures). Shakespeare explores the relationship of mercy and justice in *The Merchant of Venice*.

Old Testament figures like Adam, Abel and Cain, Noah, Samson, Jepthah, Deborah, Jezebel, Esther, and Job are cited in Shakespeare's drama, along with New Testament allusions to Herod, Mary, Pilate, Stephen, and Philip. Biblical allusions include the fall of humanity, the Flood, the Prodigal, Golgotha, Ascension Day, Pentecost, and the last judgment. Shakespeare knew his Bible well.

Bible Versions

John Wycliffe translated the Bible from the Latin Vulgate in the fourteenth century. William Tyndale (c. 1494–1536) first translated the Bible into English from Hebrew and Greek. His English New Testament was printed at Worms in 1526, followed by the Pentateuch in 1530. Further translations followed in the Matthews Bible as compiled by associate John Rogers. Persecuted for this work, Tyndale was strangled and then burned at the stake on October 6, 1536. The Matthews Bible was the first licensed by Henry VIII after his break from the Church of Rome, followed in 1539 by the Great Bible intended for use by Church of England clergy. Both drew heavily on Tyndale's work.

Translators working in Geneva revised Tyndale's 1534 New Testament in English into a new edition by 1557 with the help of John Calvin's brother-in-law, William Whittingham. The Geneva Bible followed in 1560 with extensive marginal notes, and was revised by Calvinist editors. Preferred by laypersons, it was dedicated to Queen Elizabeth and was widely read. Shakespeare would have been most familiar with this version.

The Bishops' Bible, prepared by a group of learned bishops in 1568, was used more in churches. Later, King James organized 47 men at Westminster, Oxford, and Cambridge to prepare the "Authorized, or King James, Version" (KJV) of the Bible that was published in 1611. It is still widely used today. Here is an excerpt from the KJV preface:

> And to the same effect say we, that we are so far off from condemning any of their labors that travailed before us in this kind, either in this land or beyond sea, either in King Henry' time or King Edward's (if there were any translation or correction of a translation in his time), or Queen Elizabeth's of ever renowned memory, that we acknowledge them to have been raised up of God, for the building and furnishing of his church, and that they deserve to be had of us and of posterity in everlasting remembrance. . . .

The Elizabethan Settlement

When Elizabeth I followed her half–sister "Bloody Mary" to the throne, she enacted the Elizabethan Settlement to heal the breach between Catholics and Protestants, giving freedom with restrictions to both denominations. She also authorized the adoption of a more equitable version of the Book of Common Prayer in 1559, replacing earlier, dogmatic editions. Here is an excerpt:

When they come at the grave, whiles the corpse is made ready to be laid into the earth, the priest shall say, or the priest and clerks shall sing. Man that is born of a woman hath but a short time to live, and is full of misery. He cometh up and is cut down like a flower; he flieth as it were a shadow, and never continueth in one stay. [Job 14.] In the midst of life we be in death: of whom may we seek for succor but of thee, O Lord, which for our sins justly art displeased.

Compare Shakespeare's handling of Ophelia's rites when she is suspected of suicide:

PRIEST: No more be done: We should profane the service of the dead
            To sing a requiem, and such rest to her as to peace-parted souls.

LAERTES: Lay her i' the earth, And from her fair and unpolluted flesh
            May violets spring! I tell thee, churlish priest,
            A minist'ring angel shall my sister be
            When thou liest howling. . . .

QUEEN: [scattering flowers.] Sweets to the sweet, farewell!

(V.i.235 242)

Because Shakespeare's parents may have been secret Catholics, it is possible that he was familiar with Catholic liturgy. Many religious rites appear in his plays. For example, the ghost in *Hamlet* describes torment in purgatory, and the character of Hamlet rejects suicide as forbidden by the Almighty. While the role of Catholicism in the Shakespeare household is unclear, William's writing demonstrates persistent interest in Christian themes and beliefs. Later works like *King Lear* and *The Tempest* suggest familiarity with pagan rites, perhaps reflecting the popular influence of classical themes.

SHAKESPEARE'S CONTEMPORARIES

But to say I know more harm in him than in myself,
were to say more than I know. (King Henry IV—First Part, II.iv.466–467)

Shakespeare's work brought him into contact with other London writers. It is believed, for example, that Shakespeare acted in Ben Jonson's *Sejanus*. It is clear that Shakespeare and his peers influenced each other.

Christopher Marlowe

Christopher Marlowe (1564–93), son of a shoemaker, was born in Canterbury. He received a scholarship to Corpus Christi College of Cambridge University where he earned Bachelor of Arts and Master of Arts degrees. Marlowe was one of the first so-called "University Wits" because of his education and literary interests.

Marlowe achieved fame in drama between 1587 and 1598 with plays like *Tamburlaine the Great I* and *II* which feature the effects of heredity, education, and death; *The Jew of Malta*, which illustrates the pursuit of power through money; and *The Tragical History of Dr. Faustus*, which explores the conflict between secular and spiritual power.

His experiments with blank verse led to its popularity. Sensuous use of heroic couplets produced *Hero and Leander*. Marlowe's style suggests Machiavellian influence. Thomas Walsingham, cousin of Sir Francis Walsingham, Queen Elizabeth's secretary of state, was Marlowe's patron.

Associated with atheism and known as a free thinker, Marlowe also was reputed to be a homosexual and an undercover government spy. Stabbed during a tavern dispute, some believe his death was faked to allow him to escape the consequences of religious heresy.

Marlowe roomed with Thomas Kyd, another atheist. Kyd (1558–94) is best known for writing *The Spanish Tragedy* sometime between 1585 and 1589, which enjoyed great popularity. Many credit Kyd with creating the revenge tragedy as a literary form; he blamed Marlowe when atheistic pamphlets were found in their belongings.

Sir Francis Bacon

Francis Bacon was born in 1561 to wealthy Londoner Nicholas Bacon, Queen Elizabeth's Lord Keeper of the Great Seal. Francis studied law and statecraft at Cambridge University's Trinity College where he received a master's degree. He then studied law at Gray's Inn.

Bacon explored the method of inquiry, using experiments to challenge or confirm truth. He rejected common viewpoints in a practical style that utilized maxims. His writings include *The Essays* in 1597, with *The New Atlantis* and *The Advancement of Learning* in 1605. Yet he lacked the popular appeal of William Shakespeare or Ben Jonson.

Bacon's aristocratic lineage, upbringing, education, and familiarity with court circles have led some to believe Bacon wrote Shakespeare's works. He died in 1626 with the titles Baron Verulam and Viscount St. Albans.

John Donne

John Donne (1572–1631) is celebrated for philosophical and scientific views. He was born into a Catholic family at a time when Catholics were persecuted. Donne's mother was related to Sir Thomas More and an uncle led the Jesuit mission in England. Donne's father died early and his mother married another Catholic. In 1593, his brother died during a prison term for harboring a priest.

Donne attended Oxford and Cambridge, but his religious beliefs prevented his receiving a degree when he refused to take the Oath of Supremacy required at graduation. At this point he may have begun to renounce Catholicism, and religious skepticism dominated many of his writings.

His first book of poems was called *Satires*, followed by *Songs and Sonnets*. An inheritance was spent on theater and women. His search for an aristocratic patron led to acquaintances with Sir Walter Raleigh and the earl of Essex. Eventually he became secretary to Sir Thomas Egerton, Lord Keeper of the Great Seal.

In 1601 he married Ann More, followed by a brief imprisonment and 14 years of poverty. His wife died after the birth of their twelfth child in 1617.

Under James I, Donne was encouraged to pursue advancement through church service rather than literary effort. Reluctantly he was ordained in 1615, and he wrote the *Holy Sonnets* in 1618; he served the last ten years of his life as dean of St. Paul's. Shortly before dying, he wrote *Death's Duel*.

Donne earned a reputation as the greatest of England's metaphysical poets; his early work contains ironic and erotic love images. Later religious poems illustrate a pursuit of God as he struggles with doubt. His oldest daughter Constance married Edward Alleyn (then aged 58) in 1623.

Ben Jonson

Born in 1572, educated, intellectual, and arrogant, the "gaunt, muscular" Ben Jonson was Shakespeare's friend and rival, and a favorite dramatist of both Queen Elizabeth and James I. Awarded an honorary degree by Oxford University, he was one of the most learned men of his time.

Shunning his father's bricklaying profession, he served military duty in the Lowlands and then returned to London and married. Early in his career he killed Gabriel Spencer, a former inmate at Marshalsea prison, where Jonson also served time due to government anger over Jonson and Nashe's *The Isle of Dogs*. For Spencer's death, Jonson pleaded benefit of clergy by citing Psalm 51 and was branded with a hot iron on the base of his left thumb.

Working first as an actor and then as a playwright, Jonson's genius manifested flair in works like *Every Man in His Humour* in 1598 and *The Alchemist* in 1610.

Jonson believed writers should be moral educators, and his religious faith vacillated between Catholicism and Protestantism. His classic themes were developed after Marlowe's type of virtú, leading to the tragic *Sejanus His Fall* in 1603. A lofty style and sense of beauty contributed to the writing of masques for King James's court. While Jonson's style was more elegant, Shakespeare's was quick-witted. Jonson once claimed of Shakespeare, "I loved the man this side idolatry" (Fido 1978, 81).

Jonson met the Native American princess Pocahontas during her visit to London in 1616. It is said he spoke with her a few moments, then gazed upon her in wonder for three-quarters of an hour. He died in 1637.

Sir Philip Sidney

Sir Philip Sidney (1554–86) was the nephew of Robert Dudley, earl of Leicester and named for his grandfather, Philip II of Spain. He attended Oxford but did not earn a degree. Later he traveled to Paris, Frankfort, Venice, and Vienna, and in 1577 was appointed English ambassador to the court of the German emperor.

Sidney's works include 108 sonnets and 11 songs. Among his most famous writings are *Arcadia*, *The Defense of Poesy*, and *Astrophil and Stella.*

Sidney fought the Spanish in 1586 at Zutphen where he was wounded in the thigh. He died three weeks later and was given the funeral of an honored courtier, drawing public crowds for a man beloved of the English people.

Edmund Spenser

Edmund Spenser (1552–99) received a bachelor's degree from Cambridge University in 1573 and a master's degree in 1576. In 1579 he entered the earl of Leicester's employment where he was befriended by literary figures like Philip Sidney, Edward Dyer, and Fulke Greville. Spenser referred to their group as "Aeropagus," and Leicester sought their support in religious and political matters.

In 1581 Spenser was appointed Clerk in the Chancery for Facilities. Later he served with Lord Grey of Wilton, Lord Deputy of Ireland, and he married Elizabeth Boyle. His writings about Ireland provide anecdotal information of the times.

Spenser highlighted the power of musical verse with narration. His themes celebrate love, chivalry, and Christian morality. As opposed to writers like Marlowe who embraced Machiavellian "virtú," Spenser celebrated the notion of "volupta."

His writings include *The Shepheardes Calender* and *The Amoretti*. When he died in 1599, he was buried in Westminster Abbey.

Francis Beaumont and John Fletcher

The collaborative team of Francis Beaumont (1584–1616) and John Fletcher (1579–1625) began as Elizabethan drama drew to a close. Beaumont, who was educated at Oxford and had studied law, displayed a philosophical orientation that was missing in Fletcher, who studied at Cambridge.

The duo specialized in the tragicomedy form with love and honor as principal themes in the mode of writers like Corneille and Racine. They used conventions such as disguise, brazen soldiers, and weak rulers.

Their plays include *Philaster* (1609) and *The Faithful Shepherdess* (1608), the latter of which was produced by Fletcher. His later works show the influence of Spanish authors.

John Webster

John Webster (c. 1580 to 1625) wrote comic drama from Italian Renaissance themes. His characters exhibit virtú. Plots include revenge, the macabre, and the human heart, celebrated with blank verse. Works such as *The White Devil* (1612) and *The Duchess of Malfi* (1616) show the influence of Sidney, Shakespeare, and Bandello.

Thomas Middleton

Born in 1570, Middleton wrote several masques and pageants between 1613 and 1626, with romantic comedies and tragedies between the years 1600 and 1614. His best-known work is *The Changeling* (1621), an Italian tragedy. He helped to popularize the comedy of manners in the style of Ben Jonson.

Thomas Heywood

Heywood is perhaps best known for *Arden of Feversham* (1592). After attending Cambridge University he wrote *A Woman Killed with Kindness* in 1603. The tragic plot leads to a nonviolent solution with the punishment of a wife's infidelity, in the form of a domestic tragedy.

SHAKESPEARE'S CRITICS

> *What can you vouch against him, Signior Lucio?*
> *(Measure for Measure,* V.i.322–323*)*

Scholars believe Shakespeare was acting roles and writing plays by the early 1590s, largely due to allusions made to Shakespeare in a pamphlet written by Robert Greene.

One of the so-called "University Wits," Greene received a Bachelor of Arts degree at Cambridge University and made a reputation as playwright and pamphleteer. His best work was probably *James IV* or *Friar Bacon and Friar Bungay*. Greene lived a debauched life, and his invective against the youthful Shakespeare was composed at a time when Greene suffered illness and loneliness shortly before his death.

The "tiger's hart" refers to *King Henry VI—Part 3* (I.iv.137). Obviously Greene resented the popular success of rival William Shakespeare, who lacked a university education. After Greene's death, Shakespeare (and possibly others like Christopher Marlowe who were maligned by the pamphlet) protested the untruths, and Henry Chettle apologized for the attack:

> To the Gentlemen Readers.
>
> Sorry, as if the original fault had been my fault, because myself has seen his demeanor no less civil than he excellent in the quality he professes. Besides, divers of worship have reported, his uprightness of dealing, which argues his honesty . . . "and his facetious grace in writing, that approves his Art." (Halliday, 1998, 51; modern print and spelling added)

Others who wrote of Shakespeare's wit and style included Francis Beaumont who authored *The Knight of the Burning Pestle:*

> . . . here I would let slip
> (If I had any in me) scholarship,

as Shakespeare's best are, which our heirs shall hear
Preachers apt to their auditors to show
How far sometimes a mortal man may go
By the dim light of Nature.

Shakespeare's share of enemies and supporters suggested that he enjoyed a substantial level of success in London theater.

HENRY WRIOTHESLEY, THIRD EARL OF SOUTHAMPTON

To the Right Honourable Henry Wriothesley,
Earl of Southampton, and Baron of Titchfield (Dedication to *The Sonnets*)

Writers commonly dedicated a particular work to a patron, one who supported the project financially or socially. William Shakespeare dedicated his first two narrative poems in 1593 and 1594 to Henry Wriothesley. The dedication to *Venus and Adonis* illustrates an earnest protégé hopeful of pleasing his literary patron:

> To the Right Honourable Henrie Wriothesley, Earle of Southampton, and Baron of Titchfield.
>
> I know not how I shall offend in dedicating my unpolisht lines to your Lordship, nor how the worlde will censure mee for choosing so strong a proppe to support so weake a burthen, onelye if your Honour seeme but pleased, I account my selfe highly praised, and vowe to take advantage of all idle houres, till I have honoured you with some graver labour. But if the first heire of my invention prove deformed, I shall be sorie it had so noble a god-father: and never after eare so barren a land, for feare it yeeld me still so bad a harvest, I leave it to your Honourable survey, and your Honour to your hearts content, which I wish may alwaies answere your owne wish, and the worlds hopefull expectation.
> Your Honour's in all dutie, William Shakespeare. (Evans and Tobin, 1997, 1799)

Shakespeare's dedication of *The Rape of Lucrece* displays a similar tone.

By age 16 Wriothesley had received a Cambridge University degree. In 1589 he enrolled as a law clerk at Gray's Inn. Inheriting his estate at age eight, he became a ward of Queen Elizabeth who designated Lord Burghley his guardian. Burghley probably arranged a match with his granddaughter, Elizabeth Vere, daughter of the earl of Oxford, but in 1594 young Wriothesley paid a forfeit of £5,000 to be released from the engagement. In 1595 he began an affair with Elizabeth Vernon, cousin of the earl of Essex and maid of honor to Queen Elizabeth. They secretly married in 1598 just three months before their daughter's birth, and when discovered, they were imprisoned for contempt of the Queen.

In 1601 Wriothesley was sentenced to death for his part in the Essex rebellion, but King James commuted the sentence in 1603. In 1624 he died in Holland.

THE UNIVERSITY WITS VERSUS THE GRAMMARIANS

*Novi [hominem] tanquam te. His humor is lofty, his discourse peremptory,
his tongue filed, his eye ambitious, his gait majestical, and his general
behavior vain, ridiculous, and thrasonical. He is too picked, too spruce, too
affected, too odd as it were, too peregrinate, as I may call it.* (Love's Labour's
Lost, V.i.9–14)

In Tudor England a university education was reserved mostly for those born to
wealth or high social class. As drama evolved into a commercial enterprise, occupational writing emerged as a saleable source of revenue. Despite drama's
middle-class leanings, the aristocrats claimed it as their own and criticized the
"untutored" writers who were making a fortune in the theater.

University-educated aristocrats who gave themselves airs included those
with established literary reputations:

- John Lyly, c. 1554–1606
- George Peele, c. 1557–1596
- Robert Greene, 1558–1592
- Christopher Marlowe, 1564–1593
- Thomas Nashe, 1567–1601

While many women were well educated, they did not receive university
educations. The "Wits" wrote "real plays" from moral/didactic stories and histories. Robert Greene (1558–92) produced drama between 1587 and 1592. He
was a snob who criticized those he envied.

The Grammarians—so called because they held only a grammar school
diploma—included William Shakespeare and Thomas Kyd. They were accused
of borrowing from sources like Ovid, Seneca, and Holinshed, and it seems
likely Shakespeare was influenced by Marlowe. In Tudor times there were no
copyright laws to protect an individual's writing.

SHAKESPEARE'S THEATERS

*All the world's a stage,
And all the men and women merely players.*
(As You Like It, II.vii.139–140)

Dissatisfied with merely playing roles, Shakespeare went on to become a playwright and businessman. His writing success provided the means to secure an
interest in two playhouses, the Globe and the Blackfriars.

There is more hint than fact to suggest that Shakespeare got his start in the
acting profession in London's first playhouse, called the Theater. As the first
permanent structure of its type, built in 1576 in Shoreditch, it was managed by
James Burbage. When the Theater's lease was not renewed late in the century,
Burbage and his cronies pulled it down and rebuilt the structure on the south
side of the Thames River in Bankside, the "entertainment district," calling the

The Globe Theater from map of London.

new theater the Globe. Records show that William Shakespeare, with several other company members, held principal interests or shares in this enterprise.

The government of London found fault with early theaters, which were usually large residences or inn yards. In 1574 public outcry was made against "great Inns, having chambers and secret places adjoining to their open stages and galleries, inveigling and alluring of maids . . . specially orphans" (Fido 1978, 21). The government reacted swiftly to the outcry, closing some theaters for days or months at a time. Over the ensuing decades, however, the public became more tolerant of stage entertainment. Since many theaters like the Globe were built south of London on Bankside, there was little the city could do to districts that lay beyond its jurisdiction.

The Globe Theater

Built in 1599, the Globe had perhaps 20 sides and a stage that projected into the auditorium. Since neither blueprints nor building remains today, we have little factual detail, though the Globe probably was similar to other theaters like the Rose.

Structure   The Globe's polygonal frame would have been made of wood. The stage was raised about 5 feet from the floor with a probable depth of about 43 feet by 27.5 feet, while the lower space was concealed by a wooden barrier or curtains. Most playhouses had a roof supported by two wood columns; beneath, it was decorated with a sun, moon, and stars to emulate the "heavens."

Three tiers of seating on three sides of the stage held spectators. The lowest may have been about 12 feet high; the middle, 11 feet high; and the upper gallery, perhaps 9 feet high. The two uppermost galleries overhung by 10 inches the one below it. On another gallery above the stage at the rear, which was probably used by musicians, one might sit to be seen as well as to see. Over all was a thatched or tiled roof.

Performances

The building could hold no more than 3,000 patrons, and it was not always full. The groundlings (those who stood near the stage in the lowest area) paid a penny for admission; higher-level seating was more costly. Thomas Platter, a traveler from Basel, describes his theater observations in 1599:

> Thus daily at two o'clock in the afternoon, London has two, sometimes three plays running in different places, competing with each other, and those which play best obtain most spectators. The playhouses are so constructed that they play on a raised platform, so that everyone has a good view. There are different galleries and places, however, where the seating is better and more comfortable and therefore more expensive. For whoever cares to stand below only pays one English penny, but if he wishes to sit he enters by another door and pays another penny, while if he desires to sit in the most comfortable seats, which are cushioned, where he not only sees everything well, but can also be seen, then he pays yet another English penny at another door. And during the performance food and drink are carried round the audience, so that for what one cares to pay one may also have refreshment. The actors are most expensively and elaborately costumed; for it is the English usage for eminent lords or knights at their decease to bequeath and leave almost the best of their clothes to their serving men, which it is unseemly for the latter to wear, so that they offer them for sale for a small sum to the actors. (www.wwnorton.com/nael/NTO/16thC/wider/tplater.htm)

Beneath the gallery at the rear of the stage was the "tiring house" or dressing room, providing space for backstage functions—changing costumes, storage, concealing actors, and so on.

Built in a matter of weeks and covered partially with a thatched roof, the Globe was not indestructible. On June 29, 1613, the Globe caught fire during a performance of *Henry VIII* and within two hours burned to the ground. Fortunately, no one was hurt. The following year it was rebuilt at a cost of about £1,400.

The Blackfriars Theater

An open-air theater, the Globe, could not be used in winter. On August 9, 1608, seven sharers (including William Shakespeare and Richard Burbage) leased the Blackfriars enclosed playhouse about a hundred feet from the north bank of the Thames River. Smaller than the Globe, the playhouse could seat about six hundred. Both theaters offered about 150 performances per year.

Several additional theaters were operating in London by the end of the sixteenth century:

- The Theater (1576–97) was London's first permanent playhouse. When its lease ran out, the timbers were used to build the Globe in Southwark.
- The Curtain was close to the Theater but not as popular.
- Newington Butts was possibly a converted inn yard.
- The Rose, like the Globe, was located on the south bank of the Thames River, with a thatched roof and timber frame on a brick foundation. Excavations continue at the site today.
- The Swan was considered by a visitor to be the largest of London's theaters. A surviving drawing shows three galleries, stage doors, and a canopy supported by pillars.
- The Fortune in Shoreditch was a larger version of the Globe, both having been built by Peter Street.

Acting Troupes

Good my lord, will you see the players well bestow'd? Do you hear, let them be well us'd, for they are the abstract and brief chronicles of the time. After your death you were better have a bad epitaph than their ill report while you live. (Hamlet, II.ii.522–526)

By the 1580s drama was recognized as a rising if questionable entertainment, and witty new authors were needed to provide fresh material. The University Wits filled the void with their love of blank verse, eloquent rhetoric, and romance. Many consider Lyly's *Euphues* a good example of early English drama.

Several repertory companies went bankrupt due to the precarious nature of drama performance. A few companies had existed even before the first permanent theater was built. While the status of drama troupes was relatively insecure in English society, important developments helped to solidify this occupation.

Leicester's Men

In 1572 Elizabeth's government passed a vagrancy act that required "masterless men" to be punished and returned to their parishes unless they could produce evidence of employment by peers of the realm, or show licensing by two justices of the peace. Early on, James Burbage sought the patronage of the earl of Leicester:

> . . . vouchsafe to retain us at this present as your household servants . . . not that we mean to crave any further stipend or benefits at your Lordship's hands but our own liveries as we have had, and also your honour's License to certify that we are your household servants when we shall have occasion to travel amongst our friends as we do usually once a year. (Fido 1978, 20)

The earl of Leicester's Men had existed since about 1559, receiving a patent in 1574. Their group included James Burbage, a key player in the development of modern theater. Other acting companies included those employed by the earl of Sussex, the earl of Oxford, the earl of Derby, and the earl of Pembroke. Some troupes lasted as long as 20 years, but Shakespeare's company, the original Lord Chamberlain's Men, continued nearly half a century. After 1603 the company changed its name to the King's Company or King's Men under the patronage of James I.

English Dramatists Abroad

Occasionally English actors journeyed with European troupes. A company called Die Truppe Kemp appeared in various European locales in 1579, and the Brownesche Truppe was recorded in 1590. Reportedly, English actors were at the Danish court from 1579 to 1586 when Thomas Bull killed a countryman over a girl, a murder for which he was beheaded. William Kemp was at Elsinore in 1586 as a member of the earl of Leicester's players. Kemp enjoyed international fame as a clown and swordsman; he also wrote comedies.

The Lord Chamberlain's Men

Theater companies were cooperatives managed by their members. In June 1594 a gathering of players from other companies organized under the patronage of Queen Elizabeth's cousin and Lord Chamberlain, Henry Carey, first Baron Hunsdon, whose mother was the sister of Anne Boleyn. On October 8, 1594, "the time being such as, thanks be to God, there is now no danger of the sickness," Hunsdon asked the Lord Mayor of London to let his company perform during the coming winter at the Cross Keys Inn.

The Lord Chamberlain's troupe became the most successful in England, and they eventually performed before royalty more than any other group. On

March 15, 1595, Shakespeare was named in the treasurer's accounts of the Queen's Chamber as joint payee, with William Kemp and Richard Burbage, for two performances at Greenwich during the previous Christmas season. By age 30 Shakespeare was established as a leading member of the company. On February 21, 1599, the group's playwright was named among the syndicate of men responsible for building and running the Globe Theater.

Like its competitors, the Lord Chamberlain's troupe comprised three groups of men and boys. (Women were not permitted on the stage until the 1660s.) Senior actors, sometimes called "sharers" or "fellows," invested in the company, played principal roles, and managed business. Shakespeare's company had as few as five and as many as 12 sharers at any given time. Well-known figures included Richard Burbage who was an actor and a painter, and may have played roles like Prince Hal. John Davies of Hereford claimed that Shakespeare "played some kingly parts" (Fido 1978, 70). Thomas Pope was a heavyset clown who probably portrayed Falstaff and other military figures. John Hemmings, with 12 to 15 children, may have played a family man.

A second group included hired men who played minor roles or served as musicians, stage managers, wardrobe keepers, and prompters; they were paid weekly. Augustine Phillips, for example, was possibly a musician.

The third group was composed of boys who took roles of women and children until their voices changed.

The King's Men

In 1603 when James I came to the throne, the group was renamed the King's Men. They attained special status and a new patent. William Shakespeare's name headed the list of company actors in a document granting each player four-and-one-half yards of scarlet cloth nominally intended for livery to be worn in the coronation procession, though the actors may not have participated. The livery represented King James's patronage and protection; city officials could not harass the King's Men without due process.

The troupe continued until 1642 when civil strife condemned drama performances and closed the playhouses. The Globe was pulled down shortly thereafter.

Richard Burbage   Born in 1567, Richard Burbage became one of the most experienced dramatists of the period, with roles like Richard III, Hamlet, Lear, and Othello. His powerful voice and modulated manner earned him popular renown from the 1590s on.

Richard's father, James Burbage, was a key investor in London theater. In 1567 he attempted to build and operate the Red Lion in Stepney as an inn yard theater, but that enterprise failed. Later, however, he helped to manage the Globe and Blackfriars theaters.

Burbage and Shakespeare were colleagues. A well-known amateur artist, Burbage may have painted the Shakespeare portrait from which the Droeshout

Original portrait of Richard Burbage from Dulwich College.

engraving for the first folio was copied. In his will Shakespeare left money for Burbage and a few other actors to purchase memorial rings, a funeral custom.

Philip Henslowe   Philip Henslowe kept an account book, called his diary, which recorded business affairs near the turn of the century until 1604. From these we have valuable information about Shakespeare's acting troupe and the business of drama generally. Henslowe lent money to people like Mrs. Birde to get her husband out of jail and to Thomas Heywood to purchase silver garters. Property purchases and medical recipes also were recorded, but many entries detail theater-related transactions, such as lending money to pay a tailor or to purchase a play for production.

Like Shakespeare and Burbage, Henslowe was a man of business. Without such managers, the entertainment industry might well have foundered.

William Kempe   An original shareholder in the Lord Chamberlain's Men, Will Kempe is best known for comic roles in the mode of Richard Tarlton, a beloved public and royal favorite who died in 1588. Tarleton set the fashion for Elizabethan comedy, so successors like Kempe imitated his style.

Kempe was famous for clowning and dancing before joining the Lord Chamberlain's Men. Verbal confusion and physical antics rather than wit were his trademarks, evidenced in roles like Falstaff in the history plays, Bottom in *A Midsummer Night's Dream*, Dogberry in *Much Ado About Nothing*, and Peter in *Romeo and Juliet*.

William Kempe toured with the Earl of Leicester's troupe before joining Shakespeare's company in 1594, but he left the troupe in 1599, possibly not wanting to move to Southwark or limit himself to acting roles. Or perhaps it was due to the Lord Chamberlain's shift toward tragic drama about this time.

Kempe's nine-day morris dance from London to Norwich suggests a preference for individual fame. Allegedly he danced across the Alps as well as wrote comedies. He was replaced in the Chamberlain's Men by Robert Armin.

Robert Armin   Armin, a less roisterous clown figure, demonstrated an ability to play parts as the "outsider" who questioned and mocked the status quo. *As You Like It*'s Touchstone and *Twelfth Night*'s Feste were two roles suited to his style. He later played roles emphasizing alienation, including Thersites, Autolycus, and Lear's fool.

Other London Actors

Edward Alleyn was a melodramatic performer. Evidence suggests Alleyn was a large, physical type who often played villain or hero roles. Contemporaries praise Alleyn for a lifelike manner and a powerful voice. Records suggest a fiery temper and flamboyance.

The son of a Bishopsgate inn holder, he was orphaned early and wandered as a youth. He played with Worcester's Men in 1583 at age 16 and also performed with the Admiral's Men, another leading troupe. Later he joined Lord Strange's Men before moving on to join the Lord Chamberlain's Men at the Theater, where fellow players included John Heminges, Augustine Phillips, William Kemp, Thomas Page, and George Bryant, as well as Shakespeare. Alleyn played leading roles in *The Spanish Tragedy* and *Doctor Faustus*. His personal fortune was sizable.

While Philip Henslowe financed many actors, Alleyn developed managerial expertise. Together they patronized players and playwrights. In 1592 Alleyn married Philip Henslowe's daughter. Upon retiring from the theater, he bought the manor of Dulwich in 1605 and endowed a school called the College of God's Gift, providing money and theatrical records. In 1623 after his wife died, Alleyn married the daughter of John Donne, the dean of St. Paul's and a renowned poet.

Ben Jonson played a number of roles with Lord Pembroke's Men and he wrote several plays. Among his best writings are *Sejanus His Fall* and *The Masque of Blackness*. It is believed Shakespeare acted in Jonson's plays and the two reportedly were friends despite occasional exchanges of criticism, as Shakespeare stood godfather to one of Jonson's children.

Children's Theater Companies

Child actors were much in demand in the late sixteenth century, since women were not permitted on the stage. Most companies employed six or fewer young boys to play women's roles. Eventually children's companies provided serious competition to adult troupes like the Lord Chamberlain's Men. Children's groups reached the height of their popularity during the first decade of the seventeenth century. In troupes like the Children of the Chapel Royal and Children of St. Paul's, the children played instruments or sang.

SOURCES FOR SHAKESPEARE'S WRITING

> *Grandsire, 'tis Ovid's* Metamorphosis,
> *My mother gave it me.* (*Titus Andronicus*, IV.i.42–43)

William Shakespeare obviously studied the ancient Greek and Roman writers. With increased attention given to the classics during the Renaissance, English translations of these works abounded, though Shakespeare studied Latin and sometimes Greek in school.

Classical Influences

Publius Ovidius Naso (commonly known as Ovid), a Roman poet, lived from approximately 43 B.C. to A.D. 17. Ovid's best-known work is *The Metamorphoses*, a collection of legends and myths. Shakespeare relied on Arthur Golding's 1567 translation for his source material, such as themes used in *A Midsummer Night's Dream*. Translator Arthur Golding was born in 1536. He was connected by marriage to John de Vere, earl of Oxford, and a friend of Sir Philip Sidney. Golding translated many classical works as well as John Calvin's writings. Here is an excerpt from Golding's preface to *The Metamorphoses:*

> I would not wish the simple sort offended for too bee,
> When in this booke the heathen names of feyned Godds they see.
> The trewe and everliving God the paynims did not know:
> Which caused them the name of Godds on creatures too bestowe.
> For nature being once corrupt and knowledge blynded quyght
> By Adams fall, those little seedes and sparkes of heavenly light
> That did as yit remayne in man, endevering foorth to burst . . .
> (www.oldarcadia.com/golding.html#preface)

An ancient Greek biographer and philosopher named Plutarch (46? B.C.– A.D. 120?) is best known for his *Lives of the Noble Grecians and Romans*. Shakespeare demonstrates familiarity with Sir Thomas North's 1579 translation in plays like *Julius Caesar*.

English Sources

Shakespeare used works like Rafael Holinshed's *Chronicles of English History to 1575* for the history plays. Another source was William Harrison, chaplain to Lord Cobham and rector of Radwinter as well as assistant to navigator Richard Hakluyt. Harrison wrote descriptions of Britain and England using books, letters, maps, and personal observations. Topics among his writings included "Of Cities and Towns in England," "Of Gardens and Orchards," "Of the Navy of England," and "Of Universities," and many other facets of English life.

An interesting feature of Shakespeare's writing is his multiple references to dogs, not only a common pet and economic necessity for those who garnered food by hunting, but also a term indicating contempt, similar to today's profanity.

Shakespeare's work suggests familiarity with Richard Hakluyt's popular *Divers Voyages Touching the Discovery of America.* Thomas Hariot's *A Briefe and True Report of the New Found Land in Virginia* was based on Raleigh's 1585 Roanoke colony off the coast of North Carolina, a significant news event of its day. Shakespeare may have used sources like these for *The Tempest.*

The second edition of Holinshed's *Chronicles,* which appeared in 1587, provided a rich source of English history.

European Influences

European conventions, plots, characters, and themes inspired Elizabethan writers of the mid- to late-sixteenth century. Popular influences included Petrarch (Francesco Petrarca, 1304–74), Giovanni Boccaccio (1313–75), and Matteo Bandello (1485–1561), who wrote of scandals surrounding sensational figures like the Borgias. Pastoral romances in the manner of Ludovico Ariosto (1474–1533), author of *Orlando Furioso,* and poet Torquato Tasso (1544–99), also were in vogue.

Many English citizens traveled to Italy. Impressed with the Renaissance flowering throughout southern European regions, they returned to England laden with fresh ideas and translations of the classical writings.

Thomas Hoby translated Castiglione's *Book of the Courtier.* His companions Henry Killigrew and Peter Whithorne had served under Charles V and translated Machiavelli's *Art of War.* In 1549 William Thomas published *The History of Italy.* Thomas, who later became a clerk in the Privy Council, lived in Italy for four years and loved its opulent style, yet he denigrated the sexual laxity and class exploitation he witnessed there. In 1550 Thomas published *The Principal Rules of the Italian Grammar with a Dictionary for the Better Understanding of Boccaccio, Petrarch and Dante.* His writings, among others, stirred interest in the Renaissance and led to heightened taste for Italian culture. A number of Shakespeare's plays features Italian settings.

CHARACTERS AND THEMES

> *I would have such a fellow whipt for o'erdoing Termagant, it*
> *out-Herods Herod, pray you avoid it.* (*Hamlet,* III.ii.12–14)

Hamlet's emotional uncertainty, Macbeth's thirsty ambition, Cressida's pragmatic sexuality, and Lear's maddened despair echo events in today's news headlines and popular literature. Romances that survive shipwreck, tragedies that unite families, and histories that illuminate the past underscore common bonds among generations and global settings. Shakespeare's characters help us relate in meaningful ways to his culture and to ours.

The Dark Lady

. . . I have sworn thee fair, and thought thee bright,
Who art as black as hell, as dark as night. (Sonnet 147 11.13–14)

The historical dark lady left her imprint on William Shakespeare's work. She emerges as a seductress famed for erotic beauty and as a divisive character in the sonnets and in characters like Cleopatra and Tamora. Candidates for Shakespeare's inspiration include Mary Fitton, Jane Davenant at the Crown Tavern in Oxford (whose son hinted that Shakespeare was his father), and Lucy Negro, the abbess de Clerkenwell, head of the Black Nuns of Clerkenwall. Each of these women was noted for sexual transgressions, as illustrated by the life of Mary Fitton.

Mary Fitton came to serve the Queen at age 17 in 1595. Sir William Knollys promised her father to look after the girl but instead fell in love with her himself. He was married to an older woman, Lady Chandos, who lived to 1605. William, then 61, married 19-year-old Lady Elizabeth Howard when Mary Fitton spurned him.

Mary's affair with the earl of Pembroke resulted in a son who died. Pembroke refused to wed Mary and was imprisoned at the Fleet Prison. Upon his release he traveled abroad and after Queen Elizabeth's death, he married the earl of Shrewsbury's rich daughter, an unhappy union which produced no children. Fitton intrigued with several naval officers, bearing at least one more child before marrying.

Sensual allure, illicit offspring, ill-fated marriages, masculine behavior, and damaged reputations overshadowed the lives of Elizabethan dark ladies. Shakespeare's versions include Viola in *Twelfth Night*, who assumes a male identity to achieve her goals; Shylock's daughter Jessica, who abandons her father and Jewish identity while stealing part of his fortune; and Cleopatra, the proud, sultry queen who kills herself rather than submit to Caesar's authority. Roles like these add color, complexity, and tragedy to many of Shakespeare's plots.

The Fair Young Friend

The better angel is a man right fair. (Sonnet 144 1.3)

In some Shakespearean sonnets the dark lady is juxtaposed with a "fair friend," an attractive male who forms part of the romantic triangle shared by the author and the dark woman. While the lady seduces both men, the writer fears her control and tries to warn his young friend of her deadly influence, as exemplified in *Sonnet 134*:

So now I have confess'd that he is thine,
And I myself am mortgag'd to thy will,
Myself I'll forfeit, so that other mine
Thou wilt restore to be my comfort still:
But thou wilt not, nor he will not be free,

> For thou art covetous, and he is kind;
> He learn'd but, surety-like to write for me,
> Under that bond that him as fast doth bind.
> The statute of thy beauty thou wilt take,
> Thou usurer, that put'st forth all to use,
> And sue a friend, came debtor for my sake,
> So him I lose through my unkind abuse.
> Him have I lost, thou hast both him and me,
> He pays the whole, and yet am I not free.
>
> *(Evans and Tobin, 1997, 1867–68)*

Sonnets with this theme indicate that the writer, who may or may not be the author (Shakespeare), competes for the attention of a femme fatale who uses both men for selfish purposes. The fair friend is alleged to be any of several court favorites, from Sir Philip Sidney to Henry Wriothesley, Shakespeare's early patron. The triangle manifested in many sonnets may indicate romantic intrigues experienced by Shakespeare or a contemporary, or they may represent creative fictions.

Protagonists embodying the fair young friend in Shakespeare's drama include Claudio, who is deceived about the true nature of his love Hero in *Much Ado About Nothing,* and Adonis, who is unsuccessfully wooed by Venus in Shakespeare's *Venus and Adonis.*

The Braggart Soldier

Falstaff is the best known of Shakespeare's comic soldiers. A stock character in the Henry plays, Falstaff's weaknesses create an effective backdrop for the heroic valor of Prince Hal, later King Henry. Originating in classical writing like figures found in Plautus, the bluffing coward evolved into a roguish, clown-like buffoon.

Viewers of Shakespeare's plays relate to Falstaff, reflecting as he does the frailties to which we all succumb. His bravado, cowardice, laziness, and lust lead him into scrapes at which audiences can laugh and scorn simultaneously. Yet we feel for his fallibility in pitiable moments. In *Henry V* we smile with compassion as well as humor when the Hostess relates Falstaff's death:

> Nay, sure, he's not in hell; he's in Arthur's bosom, if ever man went to Arthur's bosom. 'A made a finer end, and went away and it had been any christom child. 'A parted ev'n just between twelve and one, ev'n at the turning o' th' tide; for after I saw him fumble with the sheets, and play with flowers, and smile upon his finger's end, I knew there was but one way; for his nose was as sharp as a pen, and 'a babbl'd of green fields. (II.iii.9–16)

Falstaff reduced from swaggering soldier to mindless victim plays hard on the audience's emotions, as undoubtedly Shakespeare intended.

Noble and Ignoble Rulers

Shakespeare tapped English history to resurrect fallen leaders. Plantagenets and Tudors spring into action from the pages of his scripts, bringing with them the glories and horrors of their reigns. Rafael Holinshed's *Chronicles* provided factual information about England's past. Shakespeare likewise was familiar with political treatises such as Machiavelli's *The Prince*, which supports the notion of absolute rule, helping to define the bloodthirsty characteristics of despots like Richard III, here quoting his misdeeds:

> The son of Clarence have I pent up close,
> His daughter meanly have I match'd in marriage,
> The sons of Edward sleep in Abraham's bosom,
> And Anne my wife hath bid this world good-night.
>
> *(King Richard III, IV.iii.36–39)*

Henry V is depicted as a conscientious ruler who matures from Falstaff's companion in vice to become a noble king

Gender Disguises and Mistaken Identity

A popular convention adopted from Italian drama is mistaken identity. Characters with similar names or features are mistaken for each other, as with the two sets of twin brothers in *The Comedy of Errors*. In *Twelfth Night* and *The Merchant of Venice,* women dress as men to protect themselves in unfamiliar territory (in the former), or to dispense justice (in the latter).

Sometimes identity shifts occur due to supernatural influences, as in *A Midsummer Night's Dream,* where Bottom the Weaver receives a donkey's head in place of his own, and the four lovers' affections are rerouted by a spell. In the tragedies, Hamlet stabs Polonius, believing him to be Claudius behind his mother's tapestry.

Cross-dressing was functional in part, due to the fact that women did not perform on the stage until 1660. Since boys played female roles, it was helpful for female characters to pretend to be boys. Confused identity contributed to comic or tragic tension, as when Balthasar erroneously reports to Romeo that Juliet has died after seeing her placed in the tomb, when in fact she is merely comatose and awaiting Romeo's rescue.

Relational Conflicts

Conflicts complicate circumstances in Elizabethan plot structure, following Aristotle's premise that conflict is necessary to tragedy. In many of Shakespeare's plays, tensions between family members or lovers highlight humor or underscore tragedy.

Plays such as *The Taming of the Shrew, Romeo and Juliet, Troilus and Cressida,* and *Othello* focus on relationships of key couples. Three of these couples marry, while one pair is separated. Two marriages end in death, one by suicide and the other by murder/suicide. In *The Taming of the Shrew,* Kate not only conforms to the desirable spousal pattern sought by her husband, she also reminds the other wives of their marital duties. The deaths of Romeo and Juliet reconcile their long-feuding families and bring peace to their conflict-torn city. Cressida becomes a spoil of war, which severs her romance with Troilus, but she helps to smooth difficulties between warring factions. *Othello, The Merchant of Venice,* and *Titus Andronicus* represent problems associated with "otherness" in European societies.

Other relationships that raise questions include a stepfamily in *Hamlet,* abandoned parents in *King Lear* and *The Merchant of Venice,* and illegitimate siblings in *Much Ado About Nothing.* In each case the breakdown of normal family ties may reflect larger conflicts that have a bearing on mainstream society.

Classical Sources

Influenced by contemporary translations of ancient writers, Shakespeare borrowed plots from their works to fashion his own. Both narrative poems dedicated to Henry Wriothesley, *The Rape of Lucrece* and *Venus and Adonis,* were adapted from classical sources. Several plays allude to Tarquin, the Roman rapist of antiquity.

Classical plots weave stories like *Julius Caesar, Troilus and Cressida,* and *Antony and Cleopatra.* Other plays like *Titus Andronicus, Timon of Athens,* and *Coriolanus* are set in cities of antiquity. Clearly the ancients drew Shakespeare's interest.

Other topics found in Shakespeare's drama include aging, astrology and dreams, the four bodily humors or personality "types," art as nature, history, and romance.

CRITICAL THEORY: APPROACHES TO READING SHAKESPEARE

Cultural Materialist

The materialist view relates a work to its culture and compares conflicting ideologies, with special focus on political, economic, ethnic, gender, and class underpinnings. *Othello* introduces racial questions while *The Merchant of Venice* dramatizes religious conflict. Derived from Marxism and social scientists like Jonathan Dollimore, a materialist study examines the power struggles that form a backdrop to the action or influence the characters directly.

Deconstruction

Deconstruction originated in France in the 1960's, based largely on the work of Jacques Derrida. This method examines a work apart from relying on words to convey complete meaning. Instead, critics view words and their meaning as complex and contradictory, indicative of an author's intended meaning, but incapable of transmitting actual meaning, thus necessitating a deconstructionist approach—examining the parts of a whole rather than their sum to extract meaning beyond the surface level.

Feminist and Gender Studies

Gender studies evaluate the sex roles of a work. Shakespeare's sonnets and plays provide examples of men and women drawn in a variety of shadings. Feminist study helps us understand an author's attitude toward women as well as society's responses to the writer's female characters. Germaine Greer and Lisa Jardine are among late twentieth-century scholars to examine feminist issues in the works of Shakespeare. Queer theory considers a writing's homosexual implications.

Formalist

A formalist approach explores the dramatic structure of a work to determine the overall "theatrical effect" with an emphasis of ideas over character. Closely related new criticism examines a work's textual detail.

New Historicist

This method places the work in historical context and shows how cultures use ideology and symbol systems. Jacques Lacan and Michel Foucault took the approach that history can be read—or misread—as a text. Drama based on past events, such as Shakespeare's history plays, renders fascinating insights with this mode of study.

Performance Criticism

Critics focus away from text and more on production aspects of drama, such as costume, makeup, movement and gesture, music, choreography, and so on.

Psychological

Using a largely twentieth-century approach, scholars draw theories from psychological pioneers like Sigmund Freud, Carl Jung, Jacques Lacan, and Michel Foucault to examine expressions of the ego and id or language in a work. The study of dreams, goals, and behavior play a part in helping researchers dissect the psychology of the author or characters.

Structuralist

Structuralism argues for accepting a work on its own merit rather than basing its assessment on the writer's standing. Theories continue to evolve, including reader response and reception theory, which emphasize the reader's interaction with the text.

SUMMARY

Performance theory and criticism existed long before Shakespeare's time—as far back as the classical writers of ancient Greece and Rome, evidenced in Aristotle's *Poetics*. The rise of staged drama in Elizabethan England led to a renewed interest in critical theory and in the way plays were written and performed. By and large, Shakespeare's work attracted positive reviews in his own time, though a few negative comments have surfaced as well, possibly from professional jealousy. Shakespeare's work has stood the test of time and remains a valuable canon of study in the twenty-first century.

SOURCES

Astington, John. "Playhouses, Players, and Playgoers in Shakespeare's Time." In Margreta DeGrazia and Stanley Wells, eds., *The Cambridge Companion to Shakespeare*, 99–113. Cambridge: Cambridge University Press, 2001.

Bentley, Gerald Eades. *Shakespeare: A Biographical Handbook*. New Haven, Conn.: Yale University Press, 1961.

Bradbrook, M.D. *Shakespeare in His Context: The Constellated Globe*. The Collected Papers of Muriel Bradbrook, Vol. IV. London: Harvester Wheatsheaf, 1989.

DeGrazia, Margreta, and Stanley Wells. *Shakespearean Criticism in the Twentieth Century*. Cambridge: Cambridge University Press, 2001.

Evans, G. Blakemore, and J. J. M. Tobin, eds. *The Riverside Shakespeare*. 2d ed. Boston: Houghton Mifflin, 1997.

Fido, Martin. *Shakespeare: An Illustrated Biography*. New York: Peter Bedrick, 1978.

Foakes, R. A., and R. T. Rickert. *Henslowe's Diary*. Ed. with supplementary material, introduction, and notes. Cambridge: Cambridge University Press, 1961.

Fox, Levi. *The Shakespeare Handbook*. Boston: G. K. Hall, 1987.

Frye, Roland Mushat. *Shakespeare's Life and Times*. Princeton, N. J.: Princeton University Press, 1967.

Honan, Park. *Shakespeare: A Life*. Oxford: Oxford University Press, 1998.

Halliday, F. E. *Shakespeare*. New York: Thames and Hudson, 1956. Reprinted 1998.

Hyland, Peter. *An Introduction to Shakespeare: The Dramatist in His Context*. New York: St. Martin's, 1996.

Knowlton, Edgar C. *An Outline of World Literature from Homer to the Present Day*. New York: Ronald Press, 1937.

Rouse, W. H. D., Litt. D. *Being Arthur Golding's Translation of the Metamorphoses*. London: De La More, 1904.

Rowse, A. L. *The Elizabethan Renaissance*. London: Macmillan, 1971.

Sams, Eric. *Retrieving the Early Years, 1564–1594*. New Haven, Conn.: Yale University Press, 1995.

Schoenbaum, S. *Shakespeare's Lives*. new ed. Oxford: Clarendon, 1991.

Wells, Stanley. *Shakespeare: A Life in Drama*. New York: Norton, 1995.

Whalen, Richard F. *Shakespeare—Who Was He?* Westport, Conn.: Praeger, 1994.

Williams, David R. *Shakespeare Thy Name Is Marlowe*. New York: Philosophical Library, 1966.

QUESTIONS

1. Why did Shakespeare use scriptural references in his work?
2. Evaluate one of the many contemporary works that might have influenced Shakespeare's writing.
3. How could Shakespeare have learned so much about human nature?
4. Give an example of how Shakespeare has influenced today's culture.
5. What would draw Henry Wriothesley and William Shakespeare to each other?

CRITICAL THINKING AND RESEARCH PROJECTS

1. Explore the development of a main theme in several of Shakespeare's works: mothers, teachers, aging, and so forth. Evaluate Shakespeare's treatment of the theme over the time period in which references appear in his works.
2. Study ways in which Shakespeare's genres evolve from early to later works. Consider events from his life and his society that may have contributed to the changes.

FOR FURTHER READING

Astington, John H. *English Court Theater 1558–1642*. Cambridge: Cambridge University Press, 1999.

Barroll, Leeds. *Politics, Plague, and Shakespeare's Theater*. Ithaca, N.Y.: Cornell University Press, 1991.

Beckerman, Bernard. *Shakespeare at the Globe, 1599–1609*. New York: Macmillan, 1962.

Bermel, Albert. *Shakespeare at the Moment: Playing the Comedies*. Portsmouth, N.H.: Heinemann, 2000.

Brown, John Russell. *Shakespeare: The Tragedies*. New York: Palgrave, 2001.

Cox, John D., and David Scott Kastan. *A New History of Early English Drama*. New York: Columbia University Press, 1997.

DeSousa, Gerald U. *Shakespeare's Cross-Cultural Encounters*. New York: St. Martin's, 1999.

Grady, Hugh. *The Modernist Shakespeare*. Oxford: Clarendon, 1991.

Gurr, Andrew. *Playgoing in Shakespeare's London*. 2d ed. Cambridge: Cambridge University Press, 1996.

Leggatt, Alexander, ed. *The Cambridge Companion to Shakespearean Comedy*. Cambridge: Cambridge University Press, 2002.

Levine, Nina S. *Women's Matters: Politics, Gender, and Nation in Shakespeare's Early History Plays*. Newark: University of Delaware Press, 1998.

McDonald, Russ. *Shakespeare and the Arts of Language*. Oxford: Oxford University Press, 2001.

Mulryne, J. R., and Margaret Shewring, eds. *Shakespeare's Globe Rebuilt*. Cambridge: Cambridge University Press, 1997.

Shaheen, Naseeb. *Biblical References in Shakespeare's Plays*. Newark: University of Delaware Press, 1999.

Taylor, Gary. *Reinventing Shakespeare: A Cultural History from the Restoration to the Present*. London: Hogarth, 1989.

Thomson, Peter. *Shakespeare's Professional Career*. Cambridge: Cambridge University Press, 1992.

Wells, Stanley, ed. *Shakespeare: A Bibliographical Guide*. Oxford: Clarendon, 1990.

WEBSITES

Arden Net: The Critical Resource for Shakespeare Studies
http://www.ardenshakespeare.com/main/ardennet/

Folger Shakespeare Library
http://www.folger.edu/

Renaissance.dm.net/sites.html
www.ch.org.uk/history/

World Shakespeare Online
http://www-english.tamu.edu/wsb/

Spanish Armada advancing through the English channel, c. 1590 (CORBIS/Bettmann).

 5

ELIZABETH'S ENGLAND

O England!
model to thy inward greatness,
Like little body with a mighty heart,
What mightst thou do, that honour would thee do,
Were all thy children kind and natural!
(*King Henry V*, Chorus 16–19)

As medieval feudalism crumbled under the growth of national identity, territorial lords united in support of the monarchy despite occasional treacheries or regional uprisings. London, England's capital and Europe's leading city, grew to a population of 200,000 by 1600. A rising merchant class provided economic stability and growth.

This chapter looks at Elizabeth's England, examining issues that impacted daily living and provided source material for writers and dramatists. Living in London for more than two decades, William Shakespeare witnessed the monarchy's struggles and successes. His history plays, deftly written to skirt the censors and appeal to the masses, reflect expertise in manipulating political subtleties for mass appeal while soothing royal anxieties. His reworking of English history provides strokes of insight and character shadings creating a tasteful blend of raw and varnished fact.

Shakespeare took great interest in English history, especially Tudor rule. His treatment of Henry VIII, Elizabeth's father, appeared a decade after her death, manifesting political prudence. The beauty of pastoral scenes, support of clerical and political authority, and realistic English characters hint at Shakespeare's love of country and culture. While his drama alludes to many foreign settings and events, Shakespeare also laces his plays with many things English.

THE TUDOR DYNASTY

> *I am the Prince of Wales, and think not, Percy,*
> *To share with me in glory any more.*
> (*King Henry IV—First Part*, V.iv.63–64)

Henry VIII's break from the Roman Catholic Church fueled the reformist movement that was building momentum in sixteenth-century Europe. Spiritual and political ideologies clashed in conflicts that affected many facets of English life.

When Henry died, youthful Edward VI succeeded his ambitious father, but with little power over the realm. During his short reign, Edward, or, more often his cabinet, reiterated or revised existing policies.

Upon his death, Edward was succeeded by half-sister Mary, daughter of divorced Queen Catherine. Mary turned her attention to religious fervor by forcing England's return to Catholicism. Prosecuting dissenters, Mary earned the nickname "Bloody Mary" for the hordes who fell victim to her ruthless policies between 1553 and 1558. Queen Elizabeth took the throne after Mary died.

Tudor England reached the apex of its glory under the capable leadership of Queen Elizabeth I. A spirit of intellectual inquiry and religious tolerance replaced Mary's fanaticism and Edward's placidity, lighting the way for intellectual advancements in philosophy and science.

The Tudors performed real-life drama that impacted the world beyond England, leaving a rich legacy to nourish the creative minds of historians and playwrights. The English monarchy was complex and dangerous during this period, costing untold quarts of human blood as nobles fought for positions of authority. The Tudor story is perhaps best introduced from the fifteenth century.

The War of the Roses

Henry VII, grandfather of Elizabeth I, founded the Tudor dynasty in 1485 when he defeated Richard III at the Battle of Bosworth Field. This battle marked the end of the War of the Roses, the struggle between the houses of Lancaster (symbolized by a red rose) and York (symbolized by a white rose) for the English crown. The wars had commenced between John of Gaunt, duke of Lancaster, and Edmund Langley, duke of York, who were the third and fourth sons of Edward III.

In 1399 John of Gaunt's son Henry Bolingbroke took the crown from his cousin, the rightful King Richard II, to become Henry IV. His son Henry V ruled capably but died while his successor was still an infant. Henry VI was a weak ruler caught between rival factions, and he was overthrown by Yorkist descendant Edward IV. Henry Tudor's coronation as Henry VII and his marriage to Elizabeth of York (daughter of Edward IV) ended this longstanding feud.

Portrait of Henry VIII in his regal finery, by Hans Holbein the Younger, 1497–1543.

Henry VIII

In 1509 Henry's son was crowned Henry VIII who, following a papal dispensation, married the widow of his older brother Arthur who had died in 1508. In 1516 Henry and Catherine had a daughter, Mary, but no other children.

In 1527 Henry tried to divorce his wife by claiming the dispensation was invalid. Negotiations with Rome stalled, and in 1532 Henry's mistress Anne Boleyn became pregnant. Hoping for a male heir, Henry married her secretly the following January and in May 1533 the archbishop of Canterbury Thomas Cranmer dissolved Henry's marriage to Catherine of Aragon, making daughter Mary illegitimate. Shortly after, Anne Boleyn bore a daughter who would rule as Elizabeth I. Three years later Henry accused Anne of adultery (possibly a contrived charge) and had her executed.

Portrait of Anne Boleyn, second wife of King Henry VIII and mother of Queen Elizabeth I. © Bettmann/CORBIS

The day following the execution Henry betrothed Jane Seymour who died in 1536 giving birth to Henry's only son, Edward. Three more wives failed to provide additional heirs. Henry arranged a match with the German Anne of Cleves, but upon meeting her, decided she was unattractive and he refused to consummate the marriage. Later that year Henry wed Catherine Howard, who in 1542, like Anne Boleyn, was executed for adultery. In 1543 Henry married Catherine Parr in a union that lasted until his death in 1547.

After Henry defeated James IV at Flodden Field and denounced Martin Luther's reforms, the pope titled him "Defender of the Faith." But in 1533 Henry was excommunicated after divorcing Catherine of Aragon. He declared himself the Protector and only Supreme Head of the Church and Clergy of England, and a long period of conflict ensued between England's Catholics and Protestants. Government and church authorities were forced to acknowledge Henry as head of church and state by taking an oath of loyalty.

Edward VI

Following the death of Henry VIII, his sickly son Edward VI ruled in name only from 1547 to 1553, with the Lord Protector, the duke of Northumberland, as the power behind the throne. Northumberland tried to arrange a marriage between Edward and Lady Jane Grey, Henry VII's granddaughter, and declare her queen. Upon Edward's death Northumberland and Jane Grey were executed.

Mary I

Mary succeeded her half-brother Edward and ruled from 1553 to 1558. She married Philip II of Spain and severely persecuted Protestants in an effort to reinstate Catholicism as the state religion. Violence against non-Catholics was so extreme that she was given the nickname "Bloody Mary," and she died childless and unloved. Upon her death, her half-sister Elizabeth ruled England from 1558 until 1603 and restored Protestantism.

The Tudor Rulers

Henry VII, 1485–1509
Henry VIII, 1509–1547
Edward VI, 1547–1553
Mary I, 1553–1558
Elizabeth I, 1558–1603

The Stuart Rulers

James I, 1603–1625
Charles I, 1625–1649
Charles II, 1660–1685
James II, 1685–1688

QUEEN ELIZABETH I

Our radiant Queen hates sluts and sluttery.
(*The Merry Wives of Windsor,* V.v.46)

Daughter of Henry VIII and his second wife Anne Boleyn, Elizabeth was born at Greenwich Palace in 1533 and inherited the throne at age 25. A classical scholar, she ruled England by striking a balance between unstable factions. She was such a popular monarch that her accession day, November 17, was celebrated in England through the mid-nineteenth century.

Facing conflict on many fronts, Elizabeth proved herself courageous and capable. In 1559 a temporary peace was instituted among England, Spain, and France. When the French tried to stop a Scottish uprising, English troops intervened and the French withdrew, resulting in the 1560 Treaty of Edinburgh.

Though inflation increased at an unprecedented rate, Elizabeth spent frugally, maintaining a positive balance in the ordinary account that managed household expenses. She also established complementary relations between government and commerce.

During the summer Elizabeth and her court went on progress, a leisurely tour of outlying districts. She visited cities like Norwich and Bristol, as well as the university and cathedral centers, staying in district manors like Burghley's Theobalds and Leicester's Kenilworth. The Master of the Revels reviewed regal entertainments beforehand for possible offensive or seditious material.

In the last decade of her reign, England's strong position began to falter. One problem stemmed from several poor harvests between 1594 and 1597. Shakespeare's *King Henry IV—Part One,* produced about 1596, refers to the rising cost of oats, for example. In 1595 food riots forced Elizabeth to impose martial law. Shakespeare uses food riots in *Coriolanus* as a rationale for a public uprising. This play was written safely in the late years of his career when no one could accuse him of criticizing Elizabeth's government, and it does not appear that Shakespeare supported public uprisings; rather, as always, he provides insight into and understanding of people's motives, if not their means:

> We are accounted poor citizens, the patricians good. What authority surfeits [on] would relieve us. If they would yield us but the superfluity while it were wholesome, we might guess they reliev'd us humanely; but they think we are too dear. The leanness that afflicts us, the object of our misery, is an inventory to particularize their abundance; our sufferance is a gain to them. Let us revenge this with our pikes, ere we become rakes; for the gods know I speak this in hunger for bread, not in thirst for revenge. (I.i. 15–25)

England's enclosure system compounded the problem by permitting wealthy landowners to convert farmland into pasture, which displaced farm workers and limited the food supply. Yet Elizabeth finished her reign in good form, and her death was suitably mourned.

Elizabeth the Woman

Well educated and bright, Elizabeth knew how to manage people. In the 1580s the "cult of Gloriana" inspired nationalist sentiment by idealizing Elizabeth's public image as virgin, mother, and leader (Loades 1999, 245).

Elizabeth enjoyed drama and she favored Shakespeare's company of players. During her last decade, the Chamberlain's Men presented 32 known performances for the Queen as opposed to 33 performances by all rivals combined.

As a girl, Elizabeth's hair was red; later she wore a wig. She enjoyed sweets, which contributed to her black teeth and continual headaches. She wore black velvet and blue taffeta, black and white silk, and international styles that included Spanish sleeves and Flanders gowns. These were embroidered with black satin and vents with sleeves of lawn striped with purple silk and gold. She also wore French gowns and double bodices in the Italian fashion. Discarded shoes were given to the ladies-in-waiting.

Elizabeth valued older women as companions and counseled her maids of honor. The ladies were sent to the Queen's service by male relatives who paid for the privilege, hoping the girls might find husbands. To enter the Queen's service it was necessary to swear an oath of loyalty.

Suitors

Elizabeth flirted with many attractive men, including the earl of Oxford, and she entertained the idea of marriage for political reasons. She welcomed ambassadors from European courts who brought marriage suits and gifts. One of her earliest offers came from Archduke Charles von Hapsburg, the emperor's second son, who negotiated for her hand between 1564 and 1567. The kings of Sweden and Spain also were contenders.

Elizabeth made it policy not to favor her ministers, but a few received special attention. Robert Dudley, an early admirer, was suspected of murdering his wife to wed Elizabeth when Amy Robsart died suspiciously from a fall in 1560. Robert joined the Council in 1562 and in 1564 was created earl of Leicester; he cultivated Puritan leanings. Cecil opposed Elizabeth's marriage to Dudley because Dudley's father and grandfather had been executed for treason. For a time Dudley used his authority to keep Elizabeth from marrying anyone. When Elizabeth appointed Dudley head of the English army to support the Protestant Netherlands against Spain, the States-General made him governor, earning Elizabeth's displeasure, and he was called home. He died in 1588.

Robert Devereux, earl of Essex, came to court at age 20 in 1587. Talented and ambitious, he earned Elizabeth's affection though he lacked diplomacy. In 1590 he married Sir Philip Sidney's widow, inciting the Queen's anger. During a 1599 Irish uprising Essex led the English army against the rebels. When action was stalled by negotiations with the Irish Tyrone, Elizabeth removed Essex from most offices. She confined him to Essex House where he gathered other malcontents, including Henry Wriothesley, Shakespeare's early patron. In 1600 Essex led an insurrection against the government that resulted in his imprisonment, and in 1601, he was executed.

The Earl of Essex. "Robert DeVereaux, 2nd Earl of Essex," (1566–1601).
Soldier, favorite of Elizabeth I. Copy by Henry Bone, Enamel on copper.
Kingston Lacy, Dorset, Great Britain. © National Trust/Art Resource, N.Y.

ELIZABETH'S GOVERNMENT

> *Uneasy lies the head that wears a crown.*
> (*King Henry IV—Second Part*, III.i.31)

A pragmatist, Elizabeth strove for national unity through agreements like the Elizabethan Settlement, which sought to heal the religious breach caused by Mary's Catholic fervor. Realizing the precariousness of her rule as a woman considered a bastard by many, Elizabeth prudently accepted counsel from the men who advised her.

Advisers

Though a faction in the House of Commons opposed her, Elizabeth forged alliances between old Catholic loyalists and new Protestant nationalists.

She discarded two-thirds of Mary's counselors to appoint those who would serve her own interests, men like William Cecil (1520–98), First Baron Burghley (or Burleigh), who served as chief secretary of state. His son, Robert Cecil (1563?–1612) was first earl of Salisbury and first viscount Cranborne. William served as secretary of state from 1558 to 1572, and as Lord Treasurer from 1572 to 1598. These men could be counted on to support Protestantism. Other Privy Council advisers included Sir Francis Walsingham (c. 1530–90), an ardent Protestant and able ambassador who negotiated the 1572 Treaty of Blois with France. Walsingham and Cecil cultivated a spy network that alerted them to plots like the Babington conspiracy and enabled them to save the queen's life more than once.

The Privy Council

The Privy Council was the sovereign's select group of advisers who held high state positions. Usually they were members of the House of Lords or the House of Commons. The traditional areas of church, law, revenue, and navy remained largely under the direction of the archbishops and bishops, the Chancellor and the judges, the treasurer and the Chancellor of the Exchequer, the Steward, the Admiral, and their courts.

Local government, industry and trade, the colonies, Ireland, and diplomatic foreign relations came under the purview of the Secretary, who communicated vital information to the department chiefs, the Lords-Lieutenant, the Councils of the North and of Wales, to the Lord Deputy in Ireland, and to the foreign ambassadors. The Secretary kept minutes for the Council.

The Council supervised legal administration, regulated trade and wages, granted travel licenses, restricted the press, and monitored legal courts while keeping an eye on the church. The Council also coordinated military lists and supplies.

The Court System

Shakespeare's drama references many types of legal proceedings, suggesting a comfortable familiarity with the courts. Obviously the court system was instrumental in everyday life by monitoring laws and keeping the peace. Specialty courts ruled on regional issues in the north, Ireland, and Wales.

Parliament's two houses of government comprised elected or appointed officials from all over the kingdom: the House of Lords, represented by wealthy or powerful individuals who often opposed the crown, and the House of Commons, whose members were elected. Though only Parliament could vote on taxes, Parliament could meet only when summoned by the monarch, and then the monarch might summon only those members who favored his or her cause. The House of Lords met at Westminster Hall; the Commons met in St. Stephen's Chapel. Both remain today on the bank of the Thames River as part of the Westminster Palace complex.

The royal courts included the King's Bench and Common Pleas (or Common Bench), which supervised statute law and common law. The Court of Exchequer dealt with cases connected to the crown's financial rights while the High Court of Chancery specialized in cases not handled by Common Pleas. The Lord High Chancellor, the most powerful legal figure, presided over this court and was speaker of the House of Lords.

For those unable to travel to London for justice, assizes were held twice a year in each county where civil and criminal cases were tried, usually before a jury. Justices were high-ranking Londoners with legal standing. Quarter sessions were held four times yearly, over which local justices of the peace presided for minor issues.

Schisms

Poverty was a continuing challenge faced by all social classes. The Poor Law of 1563 issued a parliamentary tax for the poor rather than depend on old church order. Food riots ensued at the end of the sixteenth century. Government solutions included increasing food supplies, locking up vagrants, and shipping the unemployed to the colonies or pressing them into military service.

Political intrigue was a constant threat. In a 1569 rebellion, northern rebels gathered under the influence of Elizabeth's cousin Mary Stuart. As a Catholic and a member of the powerful Guise family, Mary challenged Elizabeth's right to rule but was defeated.

Despite the Elizabethan Settlement, religious uprisings continued to test the Queen's authority. Elizabeth responded with firm justice as anti-Catholicism increased. In 1580, propaganda appeared in pamphlets like *The English Roman Life*. Many considered the Prayer Book as too Catholic in nature. In 1581, four priests were executed, and in 1590, 89 were killed. In 1591 the Puritan faction established commissions to track priests.

Influenced by works like *A Mirror for Magistrates,* Elizabeth made it policy to reestablish the unquestioned authority of rulers. She balanced that authority by delegating duties to appropriate offices in a gesture of shared governance. Imprisonment without showing just cause remained a monarchial right.

Parliament

In the early 1500s, there were about 300 members of Parliament; both Elizabeth and James added to their numbers. Elizabeth called ten Parliaments during her reign, convening one nearly every three-and-one-half years with a total of 13 sessions. These Parliaments tended to pass new laws that impacted the government, religion, and society. Under James I, parliamentary sessions frequently defended these laws rather than pass new ones.

Bishops nominated by the monarch held one third of the House of Lords, or Upper House. Monarchs could also increase the number of members in the House of Commons, or Lower House. Elizabeth added 62 new members that included lawyers and merchants. Both houses generally were loyal to Elizabeth. A speaker was elected as each Parliament convened, and he would demand recognition of the three privileges: freedom from arrest, freedom of speech, and freedom of access to the sovereign.

England and Spain

In 1568 the English faced hostilities with Spain due in part to assaults on John Hawkins's slaving ships at San Juan de Ulloa. In retaliation the English seized a Spanish fleet carrying funds to the Spanish governor Alva in the Netherlands. As a result, England sought France as an ally and in 1572 enacted the Treaty of Blois. It was about this time that Elizabeth considered marrying a French noble, either the duke of Anjou or his brother, the duke of Alençon.

In 1573 de Requesens replaced Alva as the Spanish governor of the Netherlands and he made conciliatory overtures toward the English. Elizabeth attempted to balance the delicate interplay of authority in northern Europe. But by 1584–85, the fragile accord crumbled. In 1587 Sir Francis Drake attacked Spain, and in 1588 the Spanish Armada advanced on England, only to be defeated by violent storms, a short supply of powder, and the English ability to fight at a distance. This was Elizabeth's finest hour.

ELIZABETHAN ECONOMY

> *I thank my fortune for it,*
> *My ventures are not in one bottom trusted,*
> *Nor to one place; nor is my whole estate*
> *Upon the fortune of this present year:*
> (*The Merchant of Venice,* I.i.41–44)

Elizabeth's England witnessed tremendous growth in many areas, including population, architecture, and trade. Shakespeare's plays like *The Merchant of Venice* and *Timon of Athens* reflect mercantile interests and the dangers of a failed fortune.

In the sixteenth century, prices were more fixed and resistant to change than today. Yet the English economy was changing more rapidly than previously, due to a growing population, government spending, and the rate of coin circulation. With an increasing labor force, there was more dependence on real wages than before. Food prices rose markedly.

Inflation became problematic. In 1571 the usury laws were eased to help develop a healthy money market. Antwerp was the regional financial market center.

Commerce and Trade

England expanded international trade, increasing income from exports and even piracy. Between 1577 and 1580, Sir Francis Drake brought £600,000 to the crown from his circumnavigation voyage. Trading enterprises, like the

Muscovy Company established under Queen Mary I, were beginning to show profits, and in 1564, the Merchant Adventurers received a new charter that allowed the agency to control trade with northwestern Europe.

North and central Wales and the Lake District were less industrialized, while the newly enclosed counties of Northamptonshire, Leicestershire, and Buckinghamshire combined farming and industry. The lowland areas were mostly farming regions, while the highlands capitalized on mining.

Sheep and cattle provided a primary source of income, along with textiles such as flax, hemp, and wool. Dairy products, including cheese and butter, were brought to London from outlying regions. Coal was shipped to London and other parts of England (Ashton 1984, 4–6).

Robert Ashton estimates the total English population in 1603 was about four million, with 800 market towns by the mid-1600s.

Markets and Wages

Wages were low by today's standards due to the nature of seasonal employment, limited local markets, and ineffective communication. The expanding rural population increased rent and food prices. Most people struggled for food and shelter. Malnutrition was common, as were persistent health problems like tuberculosis.

Enterprising individuals created markets for luxury items such as glass windows and mirrors; Shakespeare's plays make several references to these commodities. The middle class enjoyed increased purchasing power. More homes were built, many with two floors, a few with attics.

Entrepreneurs sought government concessions, such as monopolies and export licenses, resulting in a new alliance between business and crown. Tourism grew as farmers, merchants, and foreign visitors came to see London attractions. Between 1590 and 1620 a "fashionable season" evolved, with town houses for the wealthy and hotels for the middle class. Entertainment including bull-baiting, plays, Westminster Abbey, the Tower of London, while St. Paul's Cathedral drew thousands.

Records show that dozens of people sometimes lived in a few rooms, and multiple families shared dwellings. Body lice were common, as were fleas and rats. Slums sprang up. Guilds provided training and employment for young men seeking jobs. Apprentices often lived with their masters and received moral instruction while learning a trade.

Concessions

The monarchy received revenue from royal lands, feudal rights, church tithes, and Star Chamber fines. This "ordinary" account was supposed to cover the monarchy's living expenses, but it grew increasingly inadequate during Elizabeth's reign. Sometimes Elizabeth borrowed money from merchants. She sold royal lands to finance wars and confiscated properties of criminal nobles.

Elizabeth also gave limited concessions. Between 1560 and 1589, she conferred 2,000 grants of arms conferring gentility. The College of Heralds provided income from fees for these grants and inspected the titles. In contrast, James I knighted 906 persons in the first four months of his reign. Baronetcies sold for £1,095 and after 1615, peerages and knighthoods likewise could be purchased.

Social gulfs widened, with stricter protocol. In the guilds, for example, glovers separated from leather sellers and apothecaries from grocers as the gap widened between members of the gentility and the middle class.

Portrait of James I King of England by Paul van Somer
(British portrait painter).

JAMES STUART I OF ENGLAND

> *From Scotland am I stol'n, even of pure love,*
> *To greet mine own land with my wishful sight.*
> (*King Henry VI—Part Three,* III.i.13–14)

James I (1566–1625) succeeded Elizabeth in 1603. The son of Mary Stuart, Queen of Scots, and her second husband Lord Darnley, James descended from Henry VII and was accepted by Catholics and Protestants.

Intelligent and sophisticated, James wrote poetry and crafted political treatises. He also was superstitious and weak-willed. A firm ruler of Scotland, he was unprepared for the intrigues of urban London. Under James, England experienced a weakened economy and religious factionalism that led to the civil conflicts of the 1640s during the reign of Charles I.

James was perhaps less skillful than Elizabeth in negotiating conflicts. In 1603 the Bye Plot engineered by William Watson was uncovered, and in 1605 the Gunpowder Plot, fostered by Robert Catesby, Sir Everard Digby, Francis Treasham, and Guy Fawkes, was discovered only at the last minute.

But James enthusiastically supported the arts. Shakespeare's company performed more court drama than all other performers combined. The former Lord Chamberlain's Men became known as the King's Men.

Queen Anne (1574–1619), wife of James I, also patronized the theater and arranged to see a revival of Shakespeare's *Love's Labour's Lost*. She hosted the Indian princess Pocahontas during her visit to London in 1616. The court enjoyed more glamour than before, but at cost.

SUMMARY

Elizabethan England moved people efficiently from the medieval world to a modern era. While early Tudors set the stage for this transition, Elizabeth performed much of the action as she skillfully negotiated volatile issues like religion and economy. James I cast a shorter shadow during his reign, though he likewise presided over several important advances that included English colonization of the New World.

Excerpt from the First Parliament
January 23–May 8, 1559

An Act restoring to the Crown the ancient jurisdiction over the State ecclesiastical and spiritual, and abolishing all foreign power repugnant to the same

> Most humbly beseech your most excellent Majesty your faithful and obedient subjects, the Lords spiritual and temporal and the Commons in this your present Parliament assembled, That where in time of the reign of your most dear father of worthy memory, King Henry the Eighth, divers good laws and statutes were made and established, as well for the utter extinguishment and putting away of all usurped and foreign powers and authorities out of this your realm and other your Highness' dominions and countries, as also for the restoring and uniting to the imperial crown of this realm the ancient jurisdictions, authorities, superiorities, and pre-eminences to the same of right belonging and appertaining; by reason whereof we your most humble and

obedient subjects, from the twenty-fifth year of the reign of your said dear father, were continually kept in good order, . . . until such time as all the said good laws and statutes by one Act of Parliament made in the first and second years of the reigns of the late King Philip and Queen Mary, your Highness' sister, intituled an Act repealing all statutes, articles, and provisions made against the See Apostolic of Rome since the twentieth year of King Henry the Eighth, and also for the establishment of all spiritual and ecclesiastical possessions and hereditaments conveyed to the laity, were all clearly repealed and made void, as by the same Act of Repeal more at large doth and may appear; . . .

The Oath required clerics to renounce the Church of Rome and acknowledge the Queen's authority over church and state:

I, A.B., do utterly testify and declare in my conscience, That the Queen's Highness is the only supreme governor of this realm and of all other her Highness' dominions and countries, as well in all spiritual or ecclesiastical things or causes as temporal, and that no foreign prince . . . hath or ought to have any jurisdiction, power, superiority, pre-eminence or authority, ecclesiastical or spiritual, within this realm; and therefore I do utterly renounce and forsake all foreign jurisdictions, powers, superiorities and authorities, and do promise that from henceforth I shall bear faith and true allegiance to the Queen's Highness, her heirs and lawful successors, and to my power shall assist and defend all jurisdictions, pre-eminences, privileges and authorities granted or belonging to the Queen's Highness, her heirs and successors, or united or annexed to the imperial crown of this realm: so help me God, and by the contents of this Book. (Prothero, G. W. ed. *Select Statutes and Other Constitutional Documents Illustrative of the Reigns of Elizabeth and James I.* 4th ed. Oxford: Clarendon, 1913.)

The Oath of a Privy Councillor

You shall swear to be a true and faithful councillor to the Queen's Majesty as one of her Highness' Privy Council. You shall not know or understand of any manner thing to be attempted, done or spoken against her Majesty's person, honour, crown or dignity royal, but you shall let and withstand the same to the uttermost of your power, and either do or cause it to be forthwith revealed either to her Majesty's self or to the rest of her Privy Council. You shall keep secret all matters committed and revealed to you as her Majesty's councillor or that shall be treated of secretly in council. And if any of the same treaties or counselors shall touch any other of the councillors, you shall not reveal the same to him, but shall keep the same until such time as by the consent of her Majesty or of the rest of the council publication shall be made thereof. You shall not let to give true, plain and faithful counsel at all times, without respect either of the cause or of the person, laying apart all favour, meed, affection and partiality. And you shall to your uttermost bear faith and true allegiance to the Queen's Majesty, her heirs and lawful successors, and shall assist and defend all jurisdictions, preeminences and authorities granted to her Majesty and annexed to her crown against all foreign princes, persons, prelates or potentates, whether by act of parliament or otherwise. And generally in all things you shall do as a faithful and true councillor ought to do to her Majesty. So help you God and the holy contents of this book.

Memorandum that the 12th day of December in the 13th year of the reign of our Sovereign Lady Elizabeth by the grace of God [&c.], I, George, Earl of Shrewsbury, have most humbly and obediently taken my corporal oath before God to observe and perform all the contents above written in every respect. In witness whereof I have subscribed my name and put my seal. G. Shrewsbury. (Prothero, G. W., ed. *Select Statutes and Other Constitutional Documents Illustrative of the Reigns of Elizabeth and James I*. 4th ed. Oxford: Clarendon, 1913.)

Excerpt from an Act for the Relief of the Poor

Be it enacted by the Authority of this present Parliament, That the Churchwardens of every Parish, and four, three or two substantial Housholders there, as shall be thought meet, having respect to the Proportion and Greatness of the Same Parish and Parishes, to be nominated yearly in *Easter* Week, or within one Month after *Easter,* under the Hand and Seal of two or more Justices of the Peace in the same County, whereof one to be of the *Quorum,* dwelling in or near the same Parish or Division where the same Parish doth lie, shall be called Overseers of the Poor of the same Parish: And they, or the greater Part of them, shall take order from Time to Time, by, and with the Consent of two or more such Justices of Peace as is aforesaid, for setting to work the Children of all such whose Parents shall not by the said Churchwardens and Overseers, or the greater Part of them, Be thought able to keep and maintain their Children: And also for setting to work all such Persons, married or un-married, having no Means to maintain them, and use no ordinary and daily Trade of Life to get their Living by: And also to raise weekly or oth-erwise (by Taxation of every Inhabitant, Parson, Vicar and other, and of every Occupier of Lands, Houses, Tithes impropriate, Propriations of Tithes, Coal-Mines, or saleable Underwoods in the said Parish, in such competent Sum and Sums of Money as they shall think fit) a convenient Stock of Flax, Hemp, Wool, Thread, Iron, and other necessary Ware and Stuff, to set the Poor on Work: And also competent Sums of Money for and towards the necessary Relief of the Lame, Impotent, Old, Blind, and such other among them being Poor, and not able to work, and also for the putting out of such Children to be apprentices, to be gathered out of the same Parish, according to the Ability of the same Parish, and to do and execute all other Things as well for the disposing of the said Stock, as otherwise concerning the Premisses, as to them shall seem convenient:

(http://users.ox.ac.uk/~peter/workhouse/poorlaws/1601frames.html)

Excerpt from the Act of Uniformity

An Act for the uniformity of Common Prayer and Divine Service in the Church, and the Administration of the Sacraments

Where at the death of our late Sovereign Lord King Edward the Sixth, there remained one uniform order of common Service and Prayer and of the administration of Sacraments, rites, and ceremonies in the Church of England, which was set forth in one book intituled the Book of Common Prayer and administration of Sacraments and other rites and ceremonies in the Church of England, authorized by Act of Parliament holden in the fifth and sixth years of our said late Sovereign Lord Kind Edward the Sixth, intituled an Act for the Uniformity of Common Prayer and administration of the Sacraments; the which was repealed and taken away by Act of Parliament in the first year of the reign of our late Sovereign Lady Queen Mary, to the great decay of the due honour of God and discomfort to the professors of the truth of Christ's religion: Be it therefore enacted by the authority of this present Parliament, That the said Statute of Repeal and everything therein contained, only concerning the said book and the service, administration of Sacraments, rites and ceremonies contained or appointed in or by the said book shall be void and of none effect from and after the Feast of the Nativity of St. John Baptist next coming; and that the said book with the Order of Service and of the administration of Sacraments, rites and ceremonies, with the alteration and additions therein added and appointed by this Statute, shall stand and be from and after the said Feast of the Nativity of St. John Baptist, in full force and effect, according to the tenor and effect of this Statute; anything in the aforesaid Statute of Repeal to the contrary notwithstanding. . . .

(http://www.fordham.edu/halsall/mod/1559actofuniformity.html)

SOURCES

Ashton, Robert. *Reformation and Revolution, 1558–1660*. London, UK: Paladin, 1985, c1984.

Frye, Roland Mushat. *Shakespeare's Life and Times*. Princeton, N.J.: Princeton University Press, 1967.

Hyland, Peter. *An Introduction to Shakespeare: The Dramatist in His Context*. New York: St. Martin's, 1996.

Loades, David. *Politics and Nation: England 1450–1660*. 5th ed. Malden, Mass.: Blackwell, 1999.

McMurtry, Jo. *Understanding Shakespeare's England*. Hamden, Conn.: Archon Books, 1989.

Prothero, G. W., ed. *Select Statutes and Other Constitutional Documents Illustrative of the Reigns of Elizabeth and James I*. 4th ed. Oxford: Clarendon, 1913.

QUESTIONS

1. How might Elizabeth's heritage have influenced her leadership style?
2. Which aspects of Mary Stuart's background may have prompted her to pursue control of England?
3. How did the leadership style of James I differ from that of Elizabeth I?

CRITICAL THINKING AND RESEARCH PROJECTS

1. Explore ways in which Elizabeth was able to navigate a relatively stable path between Protestantism and Catholicism.
2. Analyze the differences in the ways that Elizabeth and James patronized the arts.
3. Chart Elizabeth's leadership to evaluate her strategies in several key areas.
4. Compare varying responses of Elizabeth and James to similar issues, such as the economy, colonization, and religion.

FOR FURTHER READING

Barroll, Leeds. *Anna of Denmark, Queen of England: A Cultural Biography*. Philadelphia: University of Pennsylvania Press, 2001.

Brimacombe, Peter. *All the Queen's Men: The World of Elizabeth I*. New York: St. Martin's, 2000.

Dockray, Keith. *Henry VI, Margaret of Anjou and the War of the Roses*. Stroud, UK: Sutton, 2000.

Frye, Susan. *Elizabeth I: The Competition for Representation*. Oxford: Oxford University Press, 1993.

Guy, John. *The Tudor Monarchy*. London: Arnold, 1999.

Joughin, John J. *Shakespeare and National Culture*. New York: St. Martin's, 1997.

Loach, Jennifer. *Edward VI*, Ed. George Bernard and Penry Williams. New Haven, Conn.: Yale University Press, 1999.

Loades, David. *The Tudor Navy: An Administrative, Political and Military History*. London, UK: Scolar, 1992.

Lockyer, Roger. *The Early Stuarts: A Political History of England 1603–1642*. New York: Longman, 1999.

Marcus, Leah S., Janel Mueller, and Mary Beth Rose. *Elizabeth I: Collected Works*. Chicago: University of Chicago Press, 2000.

Morrill, John. *The Oxford Illustrated History of Tudor and Stuart Britain*. Oxford: Oxford University Press, 1996.

Neill, Michael. *Putting History to the Question: Power, Politics, and Society in English Renaissance Drama*. New York: Columbia University Press, 2000.

Pollard, A. F. *Tudor Tracts*. New York: E. P. Dutton, 1903.

Seward, Desmond. *The Wars of the Roses and the Lives of Five Men and Women in the Fifteenth Century*. London: Constable, 1995.

Weir, Alison. *Henry VIII: The King and His Court*. New York: Ballantine, 2001.

Wormald, Jenny. *Mary, Queen of Scots: Politics, Passion, and a Kingdom Lost*. London: Tauris Parke, 1988, 2001.

WEB SITES

http://www.britannia.com/bios/lords/leicesterrd.html

http://www.brittania.com/bios/lords/essex2rd.html

http://users.ox.ac.uk/~peter/workhouse/poorlaws/1601frames.html

http://www.fordham.edu/halsall/mod/1559actofuniformity.html

Pieter Bruegel, the Elder (active by 1551—died 1569), "The Harvesters." Oil on wood. H.
46½ in. W. 63¼ in. (118 × 160.7 cm). The Metropolitan Museum of Art, Rogers Fund, 1919.
(19.164). Photograph © 1998 The Metropolitan Museum of Art.

6

SHAKESPEARE'S SOCIETY

They bid us to the English dancing-schools,
and teach lavoltas high and swift corantos.
                    (*King Henry V,* III.v.32–33)

Like other European nations, England embraced the Renaissance during the
fifteenth and sixteenth centuries. Classical themes enjoyed revival in the arts
and education, while folkways and customs remained largely English, drawn
from a long tradition of Celtic lore.

William Shakespeare lived in London for most of his professional life as a host of developments were impacting society in a variety of ways. Shakespeare had access to thousands of books distributed by London's booksellers. Passing market stalls and street vendors selling goods from the Orient, Italy, and the Levant, he would have developed an appreciation of imports and commodities. He must have frequented alehouses and arenas where adventurers shared tales of outlandish horror and wild success. And perhaps Shakespeare took meals with women who boasted of breaching traditional male boundaries to lay bricks, write poetry, or fight in the militia, as some did.

While we know little of Shakespeare's day-to-day activities, we do know some things about the society in which he lived and about the people with whom he mingled.

"Winter Landscape" Lucas van Valckenborch (1535–1597), "Winter (February)," 1586. Oil on canvas. Cat 387. Inv. 1064. Kunsthistorisches Museum, Vienna. © Erich Lessing/Art Resource, NY.

ANCIENT HISTORY OF ENGLAND

In Shakespeare's time London already was rich in history. From Roman roots to the Norman conquest, ancient slumbering stories awakened to Shakespeare's nib.

Geoffrey of Monmouth's *Historia Regum Brittaniae* (A.D. 1136) connected modern England with ancient Troy. Allegedly, following the Trojan War, Brutus, grandson of the Trojan Aeneas, wandered through Europe and finally settled on the island of Albion. Defeating resident giants Brutus renamed the island "Britain" for himself and settled on the River Thames in a town he founded and called New Troy, later known as London. His descendents included the legendary King Arthur, founding the British line of kings. Such grandiose beginnings formed the stuff of literary dreams. Shakespeare's *King Lear* is set in an early period of English history and myth, evoking similar myths.

GAMES AND SPORTS

I love the sport well. (*The Merry Wives of Windsor,* I.i.290)

Despite the difficulties of everyday living and a relatively short life span, recreation played an important role in Shakespeare's society.

Hurling and wrestling were enjoyed on holidays or at community celebrations, along with shooting and archery, which utilized a "clout" as the target's nail or pin.

The upper classes pursued hawking and hunting along with fencing and dueling, Italian imports. Early forms of football and tennis were played, and in 1580, a work simply called *Discorse* outlined the strategic football that was played in Florence, Italy.

Rich and poor enjoyed fox hunting or shooting badgers, rabbits (or coneys), and squirrels. Queen Elizabeth had her favorite horses, including Grey Pool and Black Wilford. In 1591, Sir Thomas Cockaine published *A Short Treatise of Hunting* to join other works on the subject. Fishing the Trent and other rivers for salmon, trout, pike, and eels was popular for food as well as fun. The Nottingham fishery brought the town revenue. Small birds were caught by hunt, snare, net, lime, and by 1600, guns. Horse racing became a popular pastime.

Children enjoyed "All hid, all hid," an early version of blindman's bluff or hide-and-seek, which sometimes was called "Hodman-blind" or "Hide-fox-and-after-all."

Backgammon was called "tables" or "tick-tack." (Shakespeare refers to the game in *Measure for Measure*.) "Barley-break," sometimes called the "Last Couple in Hell," was played by three pairs of boys and girls. A piece of ground was marked into three areas, and one couple chased the others, trying to confine them to the spot called "Hell," holding hands until caught.

Many activities resemble those of today. Billiards was played, except the table was square with three pockets. Bo-peep was a nursery pastime similar to today's version. People played chess much as they do now. Bowls was a prototype of today's bowling. Fencing offered three degrees—a master's level, provost's, and scholar's. An early form of football drew King James's warning against its dangerous aspects: "From this Court I debarre all rough and violent exercises, as the football, meeter for laming than making able the users thereof." Shakespeare's Kent in *King Lear* uses the term in a disparaging manner.

Card games like Primero were universally popular, and all social classes liked to dance. Court and folk dances are noted in many period plays, especially morris dances (possibly of Moorish origin), the galliard, the pavan, the coronto, and the volta from Italy. Music, such as the earl of Oxford's March or the Gipsies' Round, was written or patronized by well-known figures.

By 1590, London's Bear Garden offered three bulls and at least five large bears, along with dancing dogs, another favorite. Men of all classes thrilled to blood sports like cock- or dogfights and bear- or bullbaiting.

Shakespeare liberally references sporting events and recreation in his drama. For example, tennis is mentioned in *King Henry IV—Part Two* and other history plays, with a notable scene in *King Henry V* based on the French Dauphin's gift of tennis balls, while bowling and dance appear in *King Richard II*. The tragic *Hamlet* includes pivotal scenes set on reading and fencing. Dancing occurs in comedies like *The Tempest* and tragedies like *Romeo and Juliet*. Play performance adds an important dimension to works like *A Midsummer Night's Dream* and *Hamlet*. Musical performance is found in many plays, an integral device for accenting characters' roles and the audience's mood. Clearly, relaxation and fun were important parts of Shakespeare's culture.

HOLIDAYS

Why then All-Souls' day is my body's doomsday. (*King Richard III*, V.i.12)

People celebrated customs and holidays that have since slipped out of usage. Mayday was a modern version of ancient fertility rites, when young girls danced in their finery around a maypole, catching the attention of young men.

Twelfth-Day (the source of Shakespeare's *Twelfth Night*) closed the traditional period of Christmas festivities with games of chance or masqued events.

St. Valentine's Day dated to Christian origins. It was believed that two single people meeting early in the day might end up romantically involved.

Shrove Tuesday (or Shrovetide) was a season of mirth or "shroving" which people, summoned by bell ringing from the church tower, celebrated by eating pancakes or "flap-jacks." The Welsh commemorated St. David's Day (March 1) for their patron saint by wearing a leek to recall St. David's strategy for distinguishing his men from Saxon enemies. Apprentices and other laborers had the day off.

Eastertide was the high point of the church year. Vendors sold hot cross buns, which were believed to offer curative powers and luck. On Easter Sunday people rose at dawn to watch the sun "dance for joy" at Christ's resurrection. Black Monday, or Easter Monday, recalled King Edward's siege of Paris on April 14, 1360, when cold and bitter weather killed many of his men.

St. George's Day was April 23; people wore blue for England's patron saint. Two weeks after Easter was hocktide, when money was collected for church repairs. Mayday Eve and Mayday were times of excitement, with a return to pagan festivities such as dancing in the streets and in and out of houses decorated with greenery.

At Midsummer Eve people gathered herbs and sought romantic revelations. Bonfires were lit, so-called due to their original purpose of burning bones. Harvest Home celebrated crop gathering, while the Michaelmas feast commemorated the paying of dues and rents.

Other holidays included St. Bartholomew's Day (August 24) for London's popular Smithfield Fair, and St. Crispin's Day (October 25) for the martyred French Christian shoemakers. All Saints and All Souls days or Hallowmas

Old Rabbi seated by an altar by Salomon Koninck (1609–1656).

(November 1 and 2) were times of bell ringing, which was thought to keep spirits away and to benefit souls is Purgatory. During plague or national unrest, bell ringing could reach such a height that Elizabeth issued an injunction against too much of it. Soul cakes were baked for the dead and given to children who caroled. Saint Nicholas (December 6) was the patron saint of children.

Christmas celebrations officially began on St. Thomas Day, December 21, when poor women temporarily permitted to beg went "a-gooding" from house to house. At New Years it was considered lucky to get a dark-haired man as the "first foot" to enter one's house. In some districts, the tradition called for a fair-haired man.

In 1605 Guy Fawkes led a plot to blow up King James and Parliament by planting gunpowder in a cellar under the House of Lords. The plot was discovered and the conspirators hung on Guy Fawkes Day, November 5, which is still celebrated with fireworks and children begging for pennies. Fawkes is burned in effigy as the central figure of intrigue. A "guy" meant a disreputable person, and a popular rhyme is still sung:

> Remember, remember, the Fifth of November,
> Gunpowder, treason, and plot;
> I see no reason why gunpowder treason
> Should ever be forgot.

Shakespeare's plays utilize holidays as memory devices or inspiration. In *Romeo and Juliet* (I.iii.17) the nurse reminds Lady Capulet that Lammas-eve will mark Juliet's fourteenth birthday, while Henry V breathes life into his troops with the famous St. Crispin's Day speech (IV.iii.18–67).

MUSIC

Marvelous sweet music! (The Tempest, III.iii.19)

Renaissance humanists gave special attention to the role of music in spiritual and secular society. An outgrowth of medieval church worship, music emerged in this time period with an emphasis on classical forms and instruments.

Collections of songs, rhymes, verses, and hymns circulated in the sixteenth and seventeenth centuries. John Dowland's "Come Again: Sweet Love Doth Now Invite" in his work, *The First Booke of Songes* (1597), makes use of the stylized complaint and melancholy. Many believed melancholy resulted from the soul's longing for its divine or celestial origins. A sample from Robert Jones' work, *O He Is Gone, A Musicall Dreamee: or The Fourth Booke of Ayres* (1609) illustrates this emotional theme:

No Grave for Woe

> No grave for woe,
> Yet earth my watrie tears devoures,
> Sights want ayre, and
> Burnt desires kind pitties showres,
> Stars hold their fatal course
> My joies preventing
> The earth, the sea, the aire,
> The fire, the heav'ns vow my tormenting.

The solo performance, with a single voice singing to musical accompaniment, was resurrected from classical music. A solo suggested supernatural or spiritual intervention, as implied by Ariel's song in Shakespeare's *The Tempest*.

Music often illustrated moral and spiritual harmony, or an individual's affinity with God or nature.

Thomas Morley's *A Plaine and Easie Introduction to Practicall Musicke* (London, 1597) parallels music to spiritual themes:

> You must have a care that when your matter signifieth ascending, high heaven, and such like, you make your musicke ascend: and by the contrarie where your dittie speaketh of descending loweness, depth, hell, and others such, you must make your musicke descend. (Morley, 1597, p. 178)

Stringed instruments were associated with the deity Apollo, while Dionysus was evoked in the wind instruments, reflected in Pan-like figures with horns. The Elizabethan lute recaptured Greek song. Often the lute was associated with love, or its semblance, and David's harp and lute prefigured the cross of Christ.

The lute also represented Islamic symbols for interpreting the universe, evolving from the Arabic 'ud. The lute's four strings signify both the four elements and the four bodily humors and often were dyed the parallel colors:

White = mucous
Red = blood
Yellow = bile
Black = black bile

The strings depicted zodiac signs and the seasons, while the lute was known as the philosopher's instrument and was connected to Pythagorean musical lore. Shakespeare's poetry and some of the plays reference a lute or lute playing.

As an important part of dramatic performance, musical accompaniment, study, or performance can be found in many of Shakespeare's plays, such as *Two Gentlemen of Verona, The Merry Wives of Windsor, Twelfth Night, Measure for Measure, A Midsummer Night's Dream, Love's Labour's Lost,* and many others. Following classical convention, Shakespeare realized the value and beauty of music that enhanced stage performance.

Shakespeare likens musical harmony to a lyrical tone or pleasing speech. An aging character in *Richard II* is described as silent, "his tongue now a stringless instrument" (*King Richard II,* II.i.149).

FOLK SAYINGS AND PRACTICES

> *Pitchers have ears.* (*King Richard III,* II.iv.37)

Everyone speaks in the vernacular at times, using proverbs and old saws that are passed from one generation to another, royalty included. Many sayings, beliefs, superstitions, and proverbs have come down to us from Shakespeare's era, some originating in his writings:

A black man is a jewel in a fair woman's eyes.
A beggar marries a wife and lice.
A curs't cur must be tied short.
A finger in every pie.
A fool's bolt is soon shot.
As thin as a whipping post.
As mad as a March hare.
As true as steel.
Barnes are blessings.
Be off while your shoes are good.
Better a witty fool than a foolish wit.
Death will have his day.
Give the devil his due.
Honest as the skin between his brows.
Marriage and hanging go by destiny.
Still waters run deep.
What can't be cured must be endured.

It was believed the seventh child of a seventh child held certain gifts. A baby born with a caul (or placenta) over its face would not drown; consequently, sailors bought cauls as special protection. Many believed that birth was associated with the tide coming in, and death, with its ebbing.

Carrying a bride over the threshold is a remnant of the time when women were captured by hostile tribes, while throwing rice is a fertility ritual.

Parents passed sick children through split ash trees to cure them, along with a host of other home remedies, as few could afford the skilled services of trained physicians.

Nursery rhymes like "Eena, Meena, Mina, Mo" from Celtic numbers, and "Hush-a-Bye-Baby" came into vogue during the sixteenth century. Ballads like "The Frog and the Mouse" from about 1580 and "Three Blind Mice" in 1609 remain with us today. Storybook figures like Mother Hubbard, Tom Thumb, Jack Sprat, and Tommy Tucker were popular then as now, along with "little folk" like pixies and fairies, originating in the Cornish mining district.

SHAKESPEARE'S ENGLISH

> *Write till your ink be dry.* (*Two Gentlemen of Verona,* III.ii.74)

Shakespeare's English is more modern than not, yet his dramatic language includes expressions from Old and Middle English that can be confusing to readers:

I come, anon.

(Romeo & Juliet II.ii.150)

"Anon" from Middle English means "immediately" or "right away." Word order and sentence structure likewise are arranged differently from today's usage:

> How now, Sir Proteus?
>
> *(Two Gentlemen of Verona III.ii.11)*

This expression parallels today's "What's up?" or "What's the matter?"

Characters' speech offers a good idea of the way people communicated in the sixteenth century. Other terms unfamiliar to twenty-first century readers might include to "give leave," as in allowing or permitting something, "mark you," meaning to note or pay attention to, and "to play at bowls" for the recreation of bowling.

Vocabulary

The growth of trade and transportation helped to spread new ideas and expand English vocabulary. Editors and printing houses contributed to the standardization of punctuation, spelling, and usage. By 1600 writings of Aristotle, Cicero, Seneca, Virgil, Ovid, Horace, and Terence had been translated into English. When church scholars switched to English from Latin texts, the role of English as a modern language became secure.

Spelling was surprisingly uniform, though discrepancies continue into our times. With the advent of printing, systems were created to standardize language use, evidenced in texts like *An A.B.C. for Children* (printed before 1558). Another work used by Shakespeare, Thomas Wilson's *Arte of Rhetorique* (1553), offers advice that the Bard seems to have taken:

> Among all other lessons this should first be learned, that wee never affect any straunge ynkehorn termes, but to speake as is commonly received: neither seeking to be over fine, nor yet living over-carelesse, using our speeche as most men doe, and ordering our wittes as the fewest have done. . . . (Baugh and Cable 1993, 217)

Sir John Cheke wrote in 1561 that "I am of this opinion that our own tung should be written cleane and pure, unmixt and unmangeled with borrowing of other tunges, wherein if we take not heed of tijm, ever borrowing and never paying, she shall be fain to keep her house as bankrupt" (Baugh and Cable 1993, 216–17).

William Shakespeare arguably demonstrated the most extensive vocabulary of his time, comparable to that of today's college graduate. Shakespeare not only created new words, he was also quick to draw others from a variety of sources.

Pronunciation

English pronunciation varied in sixteenth-century England. As Middle English shifted into a modern phase, the long vowels became shortened. A linguistic phenomenon known as the great vowel shift developed after A.D. 1500, resulting not only in throaty sounds moving upward and forward to reduce the gutteral pronunciation of many words, but also affecting the spelling of vowels and pronunciation today. Consider homonyms like *loan* and *lone*, which sound alike with differing silent vowels, *a* and *e*.

Many nouns dropped the final *e* that had become silent, for example, bedde (or "bed" as we know it today) became bedd and finally bed. Another characteristic to emerge was the addition of a final *s* to show possession; for example, shoon became shoes.

"Ye" and "you" replaced the informal second person in Middle English (thou, thee, thy). It was also in Shakespeare's time that the use of "ye," originally nominative case, changed to objective case; eventually it was used indiscriminately with "you" until it disappeared. The word "its" was introduced as a possessive pronoun, dating from the Old English "hit, his, him, hit," but occasionally Shakespeare's contemporaries used "it" as the possessive form. Another emergent feature was the use of "who" as a relative pronoun, as well as the gradual substitution of final *s* in place of the "th" endings in words like "blesseth" and "maketh."

Even with these changes, English remained dynamic and it continues to evolve in present-day usage.

PRINTERS

I'll to my book. (*The Tempest*, III.i.94)

The printing press impacted the modernization of language. By 1500, about 35,000 books had been printed in Europe. William Caxton's 1476 introduction of the printing press in England also helped. By 1640, over 20,000 books were published in England alone, including pamphlets and folios. The sharing of ideas was now available to the masses, and by the late sixteenth century possibly one-third to one-half of the English population was literate.

A wider reading audience led to a demand for the classics—but people wanted to read in their own language, English. Translations of old and newer works abounded. Some scholars frowned on reading the classics in translation, but many vigorously supported the notion of English as an elite language and a proper medium for classical literature, as noted by Richard Mulcaster, head master of the Merchant Taylors' School, whose *Elementarie* in 1582 promoted the use of a vernacular tongue:

> But why not all in English, a tung of it self both depe in conceit, and frank in deliverie? I do not think that anie language, be it whatsoever, is better able to utter all arguments, either with more pith, or greater planesse, then our English tung is, if the English utterer be as skilfull in the matter, . . . I love Rome, but London better, I favor Italie, but England more, I honor the Latin, but I worship the English. (Baugh and Cable 1993, 199–200)

Elizabethan playwrights held little control over the publication of their work. A printer who wished to publish a popular play did not need the writer's permission. All that was required was for the printer to meet requirements of the national censorship and of the Stationers Company of London. Publishers sometimes paid authors for their work and occasionally authors cooperated by writing prefaces or dedications; they might even proofread in the print shop. It was not until a hundred years after Shakespeare's time that Parliament instituted a statute on authors' rights.

The potentially volatile nature of print media influenced the Tudors to divert all publishing through the Stationers' Company, except for a privileged few in Oxford and Cambridge. This company was the guild of printers, publishers, and booksellers and it regulated all publishing activities and punished infringements with fines, confiscation of books, destruction of presses, and imprisonment.

Printers were required to ensure that a published work would not offend the monarchy, and if it were a significant work, have it certified by the archbishop of Canterbury, the bishop of London, the Lord Chamberlain, and other members of the Privy Council. A panel of 12 London clergy named by the archbishop examined less important writing. If a work seemed inoffensive, the publisher took it to the headquarters of his guild, Stationers' Hall, on Paternoster Row behind St. Paul's Cathedral in London. At Stationers' Hall one or both wardens inspected the manuscript to be sure it was approved, checked to see that no other company member had registered rights to it, and certified the publisher to print and sell it. The publisher next took the manuscript to the company clerk for entry in the Stationers' Register. The publisher was authorized as the official printer of the work, and subsequent editions had to be approved through him or violators faced punishment by the Stationers' Company.

To avoid competitors buying and producing a popular play, acting companies sometimes tried to prevent the printing of their drama. But neither playwrights nor companies had clear legal rights before 1709.

Shakespeare's sonnets circulated privately before 1600, and in 1609 were first published for mass reading. It wasn't until 1623, seven years after his death, that his plays were collected and printed in a single volume by fellow sharers of his theater troupe.

PLAYHOUSES

As in a theatre the eyes of men,
After a well–graced actor leaves the stage,
Are idly bent on him that enters next. (*King Richard II,* V.ii.23–25)

An early attempt in 1567 to build a public playhouse at a Stepney farmhouse failed due to construction problems. The builder was John Brayne, brother-in-law to James Burbage, who went on to open England's first permanent playhouse called the Theater in 1576 in Shoreditch, a northern London suburb.

Figure I-1. **William Shakespeare, 1610.** Artist Unknown,
Oil on canvas. National Portrait Gallery, London.

Figure 1-2. **Elizabeth I.** Gheeraerts, Marcus the younger,
1562-1636, Flemish National Portrait Gallery, London/
SuperStock Inc.

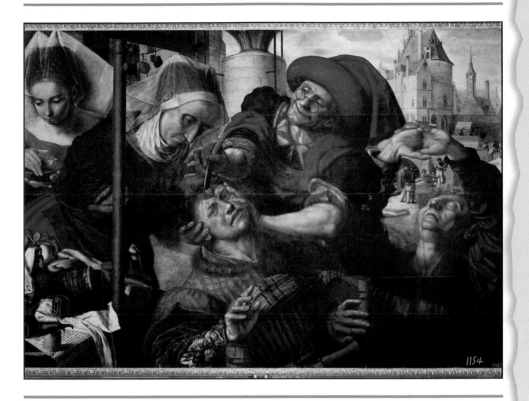

Figure 1-3. **The Surgeon: the Extraction of the Fool's Stone.** Jan Sanders van Hemessen (ca. 1504-1566), "The Surgeon: The Extraction of the Fool's Stone." Museo del Prado, Madrid, Spain. © Erich Lessing/Art Resource, New York.

Figure 1-4. **The Fortune Teller.** Michelangelo Merisi da Caravaggio (1573-1610), "The Fortune Teller." Musei Capitolini, Rome, Italy. © Nimatallah/Art Resource, New York.

This circular, open-air structure took advantage of sunlight for daytime performances, which often began between 2:00 and 4:00 P.M. People milled around the platform stage as they ate, drank, smoked, and conversed with each other and sometimes with the performers in a mode that was far more interactive than today. Actors typically were called "players" and entertained audiences with juggling, singing, dancing, and wrestling in addition to performing drama.

Puritans disliked theaters, believing that plays caused riots and public disturbances, and they associated drama with the Roman Catholic Church—though the Church had officially discouraged theater since the sixth century A.D. London playhouses were limited to operating outside city boundaries, usually in neighborhoods with brothels, gambling houses, and animal-baiting arenas.

After 1606 the players weren't allowed to take the names of God or Jesus in vain under penalty of a £10 fine. Instead, playwrights interjected names of the ancient Greek and Roman gods like Jove or Mars.

Shakespeare's plays frequently mention drama performance, with references to plays, players, stage, and speech. Acting was a metaphor close to Shakespeare's heart, an occupation that mirrored everyday existence.

LONDON IN THE SIXTEENTH CENTURY

Methought I sate in seat of majesty
In the cathedral church of Westminster. (*King Henry VI—Part Two*, I.ii.36–37)

London remained England's primary commercial and social center. By 1600, London's population had increased to 200,000 residents, rendering it Europe's largest city. Bounded by the Thames River on the south, the city was accessed by London Bridge, which at that time held numerous shops and dwellings. The Thames provided for local, national, and even international trade. But the Thames also was a sewer.

Frequent travel and crowded conditions bred outbreaks of plague and other diseases. The worst plague epidemics in Shakespeare's lifetime were the outbreaks of 1592–93 and 1603, the latter claiming over 20 percent of London's residents.

Six walls that no longer remain surrounded London, with many postern gates that allowed pedestrians to enter and depart. Landmarks included Westminster Abbey, consecrated on December 28, 1065 by Edward the Confessor. The Abbey is the final resting place of many famous men and women. On Christmas in 1066, William the Conqueror began a tradition of crowning rulers in the Abbey. Since then, all English rulers except Edward V and Edward VIII have been crowned there. In the thirteenth century, Henry III replaced the original building.

The Tower of London was constructed by William the Conqueror in the eleventh century, and he connected it to the city wall. Edward I added walls and towers to the original structure. Used as a place of torture, imprisonment, and death, the Tower is referenced in many history plays as the site of political intrigue and gloom. Its gruesome fascination lured visitors from all over the realm. In modern times the Tower guards the Crown Jewels and houses a museum of weaponry and armor.

In A.D. 314 Restitutus became London's first bishop, though the location of his church is unknown. In 604 the first St. Paul's Cathedral was built, but it burned in A.D. 675. Following reconstruction, Vikings sacked the cathedral in the tenth century, necessitating additional restoration. Between the eleventh and fourteenth centuries the cathedral was yet again restructured, this time in the Norman style. In 1561 after being struck by lightening, Queen Elizabeth donated funds for repairs. The cathedral remains a popular visitors' site in present-day London. Shakespeare's history plays sometimes reference Paul's or St. Paul's as a social and spiritual center.

Private dwellings often were solid and well built; others were shanties. Streets could be narrow and winding as outgrowths of former footpaths. Drinking water was obtained from the Thames or from natural springs and man-made conduits.

The excitement of fair days when people sold and exchanged goods was perhaps paralleled in more grisly fashion by public executions. Following hanging, criminals' bodies sometimes were disemboweled or beheaded, with body parts displayed at the Tower or on London Bridge as a warning. Bloodshed fascinated Elizabethans, which accounts for their interest in bull- and bearbaiting rings. At times, more than a hundred dogs were kept for this purpose.

The Lord Mayor and two sheriffs were elected annually to govern London, although Elizabeth's Privy Council could issue orders that were binding.

In Shakespeare's history plays, sites like the Inns of Court or Temple Hall make additional references to hallmarks of London.

Bankside

The south side of the Thames River, or Bankside, lay outside the city parameters in Shakespeare's time. As the chief entertainment district, the area was famous for bullbaiting, cockfights, and dogfights. From 1560 on the Master of the Royal Game kept bears and dogs in ready availability.

There were several prisons, including the Clink, the Counter, the Marshalsea, and the White Lion. Prisoners sometimes strolled outdoors with their keepers and a few came to see plays. The south bank of the Thames became a haven for fugitives and soldiers who, with the elite, frequented taverns, playhouses, and brothels. In the late 1500s, all but two playhouses were temporarily closed due to concerns about seditious and immoral material; the Globe was allowed to remain open.

Shakespeare is believed to have lived in Bankside at a location now partially obscured by Blackfriars Bridge, and he probably attended religious services at Southwark Cathedral where his brother's funeral service was held.

MEDICINE

What I can do can do no hurt to try,
Since you set up your rest 'gainst remedy. (*All's Well That Ends Well,* II.i.134)

Medical practice remained largely a hit-or-miss effort. While the study of human anatomy and animal experiments had begun to increase understanding about the body, diagnoses and treatments were largely inaccurate. A few widespread diseases were treated in ways that helped to address symptoms or limit contamination. For example, though the causes or spreading of the plague were not understood, houses where sick people lived were quarantined.

The Human Body

Many misunderstandings about science persisted through the Renaissance period. It was believed the body consisted of four elements:

Fire = hot
Air = cold
Earth = dry
Water = moist

Combinations of the elements produced "complexions" or "humors":

Sanguine = hot and moist
Phlegmatic = cold and moist
Choleric = hot and dry
Melancholic = cold and dry

Diseases occurred from an imbalance. The bodily humors reflected one's basic temperament as well as the planetary orbits. Sailors navigated by this system and doctors prescribed medical treatment accordingly. Blood represented character, especially passion or courage. Low blood suggested cowardice. Bodily functions were discussed more openly than now; some woodcuts and prints from this period depict urination, usually by lower-class figures.

Organs represented emotions as much as bodily functions. People believed the brain was divided into three parts, with memory at the distant boundary. Some thought the brain housed the soul. Eyes provided glimpses into a person's spirit and revealed love (or its lack) in blueness, or witchcraft, as in the "evil" eye.

"Choler" reflected passion or anger while "melancholy" suggested a reflective or sorrowful nature. The liver was thought to be the seat of passions, especially love, a tradition that may have come from Arabian physicians, while the spleen was the seat of laughter. Shakespeare's plays make frequent use of this primitive "psychology," with many characters identified principally by a personality orientation. For example, the merchant Antonio in *The Merchant of Venice* is described as melancholy early in the play, a designation that helps to prepare us for his near execution later on.

Personal Features

Physical features played a role in external perceptions. Red hair was considered unattractive. Tradition claims Judas had red hair, while it also betokened the invading Danes. At one point yellow hair was not only considered unfashionable, but also a deformity, which some traced to the biblical Cain. Having a lot of hair implied a lack of intellect.

Skin moles were suspicious, considered by some to have supernatural origins. Special attention was given to the face and hands, as they were often the only visible parts of the body when dressed. A skeleton was called an "anatomy."

Personal identification through fashion was popular. Clothing such as decorative or perfumed gloves, ruffs, masks worn by both genders, face patches in the 1590s, cosmetics, and wigs were in style. Wigs not only promoted fashion, they also covered hair loss and helped to control lice. Dyeing beards was popular in Shakespeare's day, and to mutilate a beard was an outrage. Swearing by one's beard was a custom for evoking truth. Certain cuts of beard reflected occupations or standing, such as a general's cut, the clown's beard, or a cathedral beard.

Clothing was washed, beaten, and brushed regularly. While the body was not immersed in water on a regular basis, people washed the face and hands consistently. Many drowning deaths were recorded because people did not know how to swim. Some feared water as the dwelling place of evil spirits or demons.

Surgeon-Barbers

Surgeon-barbers, like today's hair stylists and sports doctors, were much frequented and more of a masculine than feminine domain. Services like bloodletting, teeth drawing, teeth cleaning, nail paring, and picking or syringing the ears were offered and provided with soap and perfume. After 1600, many sold tobacco, which was thought to cure diseases, including those that were sexually transmitted, despite King James's adverse views of the substance.

Syphilis was common, as indicated by Shakespeare's lower-class characters like Falstaff. Then as now, sexually transmitted diseases were associated with immorality and sometimes referred to as gout or sciatica. Such diseases were contracted by personal conduct or by congenital inheritance. Traditional treatments included mercury or other heavy metals, sweat baths, and guaiacum, an imported wood derivative. Informational literature included a 1579 pamphlet by William Clowes entitled *The Cure of the Disease Called Morbus Gallicus by Unctions*. Surgeons did most of the hands-on work that is performed in triage today.

"The Toothpuller." Michelangelo Merisi da Caravaggio (1573–1610), "The Toothpuller." Galleria Palatina, Palazzo Pitti, Florence, Italy. © Scala/Art Resource, NY.

Physicians

Health shall live free, and sickness freely die. (*All's Well That Ends Well,* II.i.168)

In 1518, Henry VIII granted a charter to physicians for establishing a Royal College in London. Physicians used medical skill to treat internal illnesses, assisted by surgeons who received basic medical training during an apprenticeship. Surgeon-barbers handled tasks like shaving and bleeding patients or drawing teeth. Apothecaries, or pharmacists, also contributed to general medical care. Midwives and wet nurses often tended upper-class births and nurseries.

Few sick people consulted physicians because trained doctors were scarce and few patients could afford them. Between 1547 and 1553, five hospitals opened (or reopened) in London to serve the sick. Nurses and surgeons rather than physicians treated patients. Outside London, local practitioners treated the ill. These healers, including aristocrats and clergy, had studied folk medicine or relied on family recipes as cures.

A doctor's training began at Oxford or Cambridge, and upon graduation the candidate received a license to practice. However, more training could be sought at Edinburgh, noted for advanced medical classes, or on the Continent. The Royal College monitored medical practice in and around London, but due to need, many medics practiced without licenses or even adequate training.

Some physicians followed Galen's logic of curing by opposites and herbs with phlebotomy and purging. Doctors commonly studied astrology and practiced magic. Public health concerns resulted in pamphlets distributed to the public, for example, in 1583, when plague regulations were enacted. Legislation sometimes followed, as in 1603 when infected households in many London parishes received financial support.

Shakespeare's drama includes many references to treating illness. In addition, son-in-law John Hall was a physician who practiced in Stratford from about 1600 to 1635.

Medical Discoveries

William Harvey (1578–1657) was born in England and educated at Canterbury. He studied medicine at Cambridge in 1593. In 1600 he went to the University of Padua in Italy to study with Fabricius, professor of anatomy, and in 1602, Harvey graduated as a Doctor of Medicine. In 1604 he was admitted to the Royal College of Physicians.

Based on dissection experiments, Harvey pursued his theory of the blood's movement throughout the body, despite the prevailing medical practice that adhered to theories espoused by ancient Galen. In 1628 Harvey published *The Motion of the Heart and Blood in Animals*, and the next year he was appointed physician to the royal family. Later he moved to Oxford, and in 1645 he was named warden of Merton College at Oxford. Here is an excerpt from his studies:

> In the first place, then, when the chest of a living animal is laid open and the capsule that immediately surrounds the heart is slit up or removed, the organ is seen now to move, now to be at rest; there is a time when it moves, and a time when it is motionless. . . . From these particulars it appeared evident to me that the motion of the heart consists in a certain universal tension—both contraction in the line of its fibres, and constriction in every sense. It becomes erect, hard, and of diminished size during its action; the motion is plainly of the same nature as that of the muscles when they contract in the line of their sinews and fibres; for the muscles, when in action, acquire vigour and tenseness, and from soft become hard, prominent, and thickened: in the same manner the heart. (From William Harvey on the Motion of the Heart and Blood in Animals (1628) Chapter II.n.p. www.fordham.edu/halsall/mod/1628harvey–blood.html)

Discoveries like these contributed to understanding the body and in turn, to better diagnoses and treatment for a variety of conditions. Harvey's study of embryology led to his publication *Essays on the Generation of Animals*.

Gabriello Fallopio (1523–62) was the first writer to explain the Fallopian tubes in his 1560s description of the female genitalia, although ovaries were not well understood until the nineteenth century. Ambroise Pare (1517?–90), a French surgeon, introduced the concept of arterial ligature. Thomas Vicary published *The Englishman's Treasure; or, the True Anatomy of Man's Body* in 1586.

Apothecaries, or what we call pharmacists, dispensed many types of drugs. Those too ill to afford a doctor might consult an apothecary. Medicine could be obtained from grocers, as the apothecaries' society was part of the Grocers' Company. Today's parallel would be buying aspirin at the drug store.

John Hester ran one of London's largest apothecaries from 1570 to 1593 and published tracts in translation from the continental followers of Paracelsus, with new recipes.

Many folks dosed themselves for common ailments, like constipation or arthritis, seeking medical assistance only when necessary. In 1609 a man named Arthur Throckmorton under the care of Dr. Chenell of Oxford was dissatisfied with 8 stools per day, so he took a "physic" (a purging potion) to obtain 12. Miscarriage was called "a shift" and abortion was achieved with medicinal herbs or physical blows.

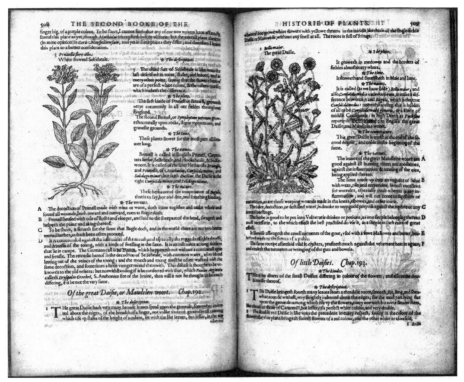

John Gerarde, "The herball or Generall historie of plantes . . . " 1597.

A popular medicine/recipe book was *The secretes of the reverende Maister Alexis of Piedmount, Containyng excellent remedies against diuers diseases, woundes, and other accidents, with the manner to make distillations, perfurmes, confitures, diynges, fusions, and meltynges . . .* (1558). In 1597 a gardener named John Gerard published a large text simply titled *Herbal.*

Many women of wealthy households felt it a duty to learn something about medical treatments to help the poor. Thomas More's daughter Margaret was respected at Canterbury for medical knowledge. Queen Elizabeth often prescribed for herself rather than rely on physicians. Elizabeth Grey, countess of Kent (1581–1651) published *A Choice Manual, or Rare Secrets in Physic and Chyrurgery* (2d ed., 1653).

Mental Illness or Insanity

The most influential classical writers on mental illness were Soranus (translated in 1567) and Aretaeus (translated in Latin in 1552 and Greek in 1554), both second-century writers. Aretaeus describes mental patients with humane and sympathetic accounts in great detail. He was first to distinguish between senility ("a torpor of the senses") and mania.

Psychiatry of the day was a mix of physic, astrology, and the occult. A popular practitioner of the late 1500s was Simon Forman, who "cast questions" for rich and poor.

The most common diagnoses for mental illness during the Renaissance were phrenitis or "phrenesy" (frenzy), mania, melancholy, and other disorders that might be considered neurological, such as epilepsy, "apoplexy," tetanus, and degenerative senility. Mania and melancholy were considered chronic rather than acute disorders; many believed excessive choler caused mania. Passionate, irritable, and active persons—those ruled by choler—were most subject to mania.

Melancholy was of great interest to Renaissance dramatists and believed to stem from three causes: (1) primary brain affection or disturbance; (2) disturbances in the hypochondria or lower abdomen (source of vapors or malignant fluids); and (3) a disorder affecting the brain by "sympathy."

As with medicine, the study and treatment of mental illnesses and personality disorders were imperfect sciences. Several of Shakespeare's characters suffer from melancholy, like Hamlet, or lunacy, like Ophelia. King Lear adopts a form of madness that contributes to the drama's plot development. This little-understood condition was an important and difficult part of Elizabethan life.

DEATH AND BURIAL

Come from that nest of death, contagion, and unnatural sleep.
(Romeo and Juliet, V.iii.151–152)

Death stood at the center of Shakespeare's world. Symbolically, cemeteries were placed in the center of the village, with open pits reflecting mass graves for the poor. Common causes of death included plague, smallpox, childbirth, and dysentery.

Omens of impending death were common. It was believed the dying person revived briefly (called "lightening") and experienced any number of symptoms that foreshadowed death, including prophecy, mirth, supernatural voices or noises, or unearthly peace.

Death was thought to occur at tide's ebb, and it was considered unlucky to keep a corpse aboard ship. Flowers decorated the body, and graves were strewn with fresh blossoms. In Denmark, male nobles were buried in their armor, while in Italy the dead were interred in suits of clothes. In England a winding sheet was customary.

Death chamber practices included removing a pillow from under the head of the dying to facilitate death, since many believed that pigeon feathers particularly or featherbeds generally increased the tortured resistance of the dying person.

Church bells rang for the deceased, often a certain number based on the departed's gender or age. Afterlife beliefs were based on Catholic teachings about purgatory, heaven, and hell. Literature refers to places of icy cold, scorching heat, or frenzied, wind-swept habitats as abodes of the soul, although many hoped for the biblical Heaven.

Death proliferates in period drama. In *Hamlet,* the murdered king's ghost urges his son to revenge after alluding to the horrors of Purgatory, while Ophelia's questionable suicide leads to a flower-strewn burial and tender regrets. In Shakespeare's history plays, a host of key and support characters experience violent death, a plot device that apparently appealed to Elizabethan audiences. Certainly death is the tragic pinnacle in works like *Othello, King Lear,* and *Julius Caesar,* among others.

The Black Plague, Bubonic Plague, or Black Death

The Black Plague paralleled the great flu epidemic of the early twentieth century. The worst episode from 1348–50 reduced Western Europe's population by a third. Plague outbreaks in the sixteenth and seventeenth centuries decimated Europe's cities, killing as much as 10 percent of the population. England experienced five major outbreaks between 1563 and 1665. Between June 1592 and May 1594, London's theaters were closed most of the time; 11,000 died in London alone. Images of death proliferated on church walls and in woodcuts, personifying the Grim Reaper as a crowned ruler.

The term "Black Plague" derived from skin hemorrhages close together or a black abscess in the groin, armpit, or palm of the hand. Death came within three days—sometimes within 24 hours—as a 55 percent mortality rate followed the pestilence. The plague was highly contagious and often claimed several victims within a residence. Two strains were dominant: bubonic or pneumonic. In the former, large, painful swellings called buboes appeared, but the latter, resulting in inflamed lungs, was more lethal.

Outbreaks flourished in unsanitary conditions during the summer months; 80 degrees was the ideal temperature. But exceptions occurred during the Russian winter and in the clean Italian cities. Doctors could do little but prescribe preventive measures such as basic hygiene, airing out homes, and quarantining infected residences.

One theory was that "bad air" or the south wind caused the plague; consequently, bells were rung, guns shot, and music played to stir the heavy atmosphere. Small birds and spiders were placed in rooms before people entered, and disinfectant-like herbs were burned for their odors—fir, laurel, oak leaves, wormwood, and lavender. Even bad smells were thought to help, so people kept goats inside and burned leather and human refuse. Tobacco was considered useful. Amulets from precious stones to animal bones were worn to ward off the disease.

In truth, fleas carrying the bacteria lived on black rats that infested structures of rich and poor. The rats were brought by ship from the Levant, arriving in Britain during the fourteenth century. As opposed to the common house rat that climbed all over, the black rat preferred cellars and drains and stayed near ground level, thereby claiming more poor victims in single-story dwellings, though the disease spread to people of all social classes.

Those in households where the plague had struck at least one victim wore white armbands or carried a whitened stick. Some stayed in specially constructed hospitals for 40 days. Travelers suspected of carrying the plague were turned away from towns 15 or 20 miles outside the city limits.

During the worst epidemics, bodies were too numerous to bury decently, so corpses were thrown into the streets for cart drivers who called "Bring out your dead." Bodies then were buried en masse without ceremony by freed galley slaves and condemned criminals. They sometimes took advantage of their duty to spread the disease and steal possessions.

GHOSTS AND WITCHCRAFT

Take heed o' th' foul fiend. (*King Lear*, III.iv.80)

Throughout recorded history humans have maintained a belief in ghosts and other supernatural beings. The ancient Greeks believed that a person denied funeral rites was doomed to wander the earth. Many people believe that ghosts cannot bear daylight and will disappear before sunrise. Allegedly, ghosts of the departed returned to homes or families, often with an important message, as depicted in Shakespeare's *Hamlet*.

An early work that influenced Elizabethan supernatural beliefs was the *Malleus Maleficarum*, published in 1486 by Jacob Sprenger and Henrich Kramer. Although witch hunts grew out of periods of persecution like the Inquisition, the idea of witches was still fairly new in Shakespeare's time. By the seventeenth century, however, virtually everyone believed in magic, which was closely associated with religion and astrology. Witches were believed to fly on broomsticks by night and to keep familiars.

Dr. John Dee, a Welshman of good family and a learned mathematician, dabbled in magic, astrology, and alchemy. He forecast the best day for Elizabeth's coronation. Dr. Dee defined astrology as "an art mathematical, which demonstrateth reasonably the operations and effects of the natural beams of light and secret influence of the stars and planets." His clients included the queen, who gave him a hundred angels (or coins) to keep Christmas and consulted him May 3, 1594, in the Privy Garden where he gave her a written "heavenly admonition" which she received with appreciation. Dr. Dee and his associate Edward Kelley, an apothecary, conducted séances at Cracow, Prague, and Triban between 1583 and 1588, establishing a European reputation built on crystal-gazing, summoning spirits, and changing metals to silver and gold. Considered a necromancer by the Catholic Church, Dee left a diary that provides intriguing details of his patients and treatments.

Simon Forman was a magician, astrologer, physician, and necromancer. Like Dr. Dee's , his notes and diaries described his practices. Born in 1552, he was a well-known fortuneteller in London by the 1590s. Many clients became paramours, and Forman records liaisons with some like Annie Young, who was his mistress from 1584 to 1585. He purportedly seduced 12 or more women, most of whom were married, including Mrs. Flower, a seaman's wife, and Mrs. Hipwell, whose husband practiced sodomy. In 1599 at age 47 he married a 19-year-old girl.

Some authorities mistrusted astrology, including John Chambers, who in 1601 published *A Treatise against Judicial Astrology*. This drew Sir Christopher Heydon's reply in 1603 entitled *A Defence of Judicial Astrology*. Astrology was also popular on the Continent, with Nostradamus, a French Jew, the favorite astrologer of Catherine de Medici and her son Charles IX.

Demonology became another popular topic. It was believed Satan or his demons could take a variety of shapes, such as human or animal forms, to torment or manipulate humans. Burton's *Anatomy of Melancholy* and Harsnet's *Declaration of Egregious Popish Impostures* categorize various spirits and demons such as Modo (the prince of darkness), Amaimon (ruler of the north side of the "infernal gulf"), and Flibbertiggibet, a fiend.

In 1584 Reginald Scot published *The Discoverie of Witchcraft*. Taking a compassionate view of accused witches as one who did not believe in them, Scot, a moderate Anglican, offers a patient and reasonable approach to interpreting the so-called confessions by the accused.

In 1597 James VI of Scotland published *Daemonology,* which reflected typical superstitions. Witchcraft trials were not uncommon. Shakespeare uses ghosts or witchery as key features in several plays, including *King Henry VI, Macbeth, Hamlet,* and *The Tempest*. Often such visitants reveal truth or foretell the future, especially to stubborn or confused protagonists.

Many innocent people were accused of practicing sorcery or witchcraft, often for revenge by accusers. Church courts, requiring only repentance confirmed by witnesses, were more lenient than the courts of common law where witchcraft was considered a felony deserving death. Those most likely to be accused of witchcraft were deviants from social norms, demonstrating birthmarks, questionable morals, physical deformities, or poverty.

Other works of the period include Puritan George Gifford's *Discourse of the Subtle Practices of Devils by Witches and Sorcerers,* and in 1593, *A Dialogue Concerning Witches and Witchcrafts*.

MILITARY SERVICE

> *He hath done good service, lady, in these wars.*
> (*Much Ado About Nothing*, I.i.49)

Elizabeth and her Privy Council made many important military decisions. Enlisted men could not be promoted through the ranks and often were "pressed" (impressed) into military service; some were volunteers. Men between the ages of 16 and 60 were eligible, though only a few actually received training in weapons or strategies.

"Portrait of a Man in Armour with Gold Decoration" by Tintoretto, c. 1550.

These men continued to work at a trade until called up for active duty, much like today's reserves. Vagrants and released convicts also enlisted, especially in the 1580s when Spain posed a serious threat. Lieutenants appointed muster masters, many without experience. Provost marshals supervised soldier discipline, which could be difficult to enforce over vagrants or untrained troops.

Weapons were provided by each person's shire or borough. Typically, 100 to 200 men served under a captain who clothed and fed them. Officers sometimes were aristocrats or businessmen looking for opportunities.

There was no standing army in Elizabethan England, though the navy continued to build and maintain ships under the direction of the secretary of the navy, who built new and more maneuverable vessels and adapted older ships.

England built a good supply of artillery, though early in the reign there were few supplies and little preparation for war. Sir Thomas Gresham directed that large amounts of arms, armor, gunpowder, and saltpeter be imported from the Low Countries and Germany. Local arsenals held a combination of private and town arms in part funded by military taxes. By the 1590s, however, many refused to pay the military tax. Absentee landlords were not assessed for taxes based on property they did not inhabit, a practice many citizens viewed as unfair.

In the 1588 war with Spain, a mix of royal and impressed private ships prepared for battle. Heavy storms off the English coast coupled with Spain's powder shortage led to the defeat of the Spanish Armada. The Spanish fleet's global authority was broken, but its treasure ships of the 1590s were better armed against English pirates.

Weaponry included the longbow, while firearms entailed use of muskets, calivers, and pistols. Cannon and other artillery had been available since the early fifteenth century; gunpowder was composed of sulfur, charcoal, and saltpeter. Swords primarily were used by the upper classes. Foot soldiers fought with pikes, spears, and daggers. Armor and horses remained in wide use.

While the longbow helped win medieval victories, by 1600 the rapier was more widely used. Works like Grassi's *The True Art of Defense* (published in 1570) appeared in translation by 1594.

As the revenge tradition grew in the Elizabethan Age, the duel form of combat appeared, where a man who felt insulted would "call out" or issue a written or oral challenge to his opponent. Attended by "seconds," a time was set for the two to meet and square off before firing; the survivor "won."

Military offenses appear in numerous history and tragedy plays, delighting audiences with dazzling swordplay and staged confrontations between battalions.

Chivalry

Chivalry was the code of ethics practiced by warring factions comprising noble and military classes. Chivalric values included courage, honor, fidelity to authorities, mercy, and generosity. Nurtured by the Catholic Church and encouraged by "courtesy books" such as Baldassare Castiglione's *The Courtier* (1528), these ideals inspired Europe's social and political development during the Renaissance.

Shakespeare would have become familiar with this code through his reading of historians Holinshed and Hall and the humanist English writers.

PUNISHMENTS

> . . . *the knave constable had set me i' th' stocks, i' th' common stocks,*
> *for a witch.* (The Merry Wives of Windsor, IV.v.120)

Period drama alludes to many types of punishment. Records reveal torture and cruelty designed to elicit confessions or provide examples for would-be criminals.

Boiling a person to death, searing the eyes by holding them close to a basin of boiling water, or whipping and stewing in brine were three popular horrors. The strappado was a military punishment that fastened ropes under the criminal's arms, drew him by a pulley to a high beam, and released him suddenly with a jerk—resulting in a dislocated shoulder blade.

Hanging someone by the heels was reserved for errant knights who also might have their spurs chopped off, called "hacking." Traitors' faces and limbs might be defaced or removed. Prisoners were restrained in stocks or fetters by a bilboes, or an iron bar, or perhaps the pillory. A rack still stands in the Tower of London, though its use is questioned. Stocks served as a common punishment in both the Old and New Worlds.

Perjurers were branded while the whipping of schoolboys was called "breeching." Authorities whipped vagrants and stripped them of most clothing, perhaps beating them "until bloody."

A wisp of straw could be applied to a woman of loose morals or loose tongue (a harlot or a gossip/scold) as a mark of public censure. Verbally loose women were carted about the streets of town in a cucking-stool. Witches were drowned, burned, or hanged.

SUMMARY

From London's theater district to the outlying villages, glimpses of holidays, games, sayings, customs, and laws fill gaps about the everyday world of Elizabethan culture. Historic events and recorded language detail the black–and–white text of Shakespeare's plays, adding vivid hues that enhance our understanding of the scenes and images recorded on dusty pages.

Studying English life allows us to share the minds and emotions of Shakespeare's characters, and perhaps to recognize the backdrop against which he juxtaposes spectacular scenes of literary drama.

SOURCES

Baugh, Albert C., and Thomas Cable. *A History of the English Language*. 4th ed. Englewood Cliffs, N.J.: Prentice Hall, 1993.

Beier, A. L., and Roger Finlay, eds. *London 1500–1700*. New York: Longman, 1986.

Bentley, Gerald Eades. *Shakespeare: A Biographical Handbook*. New Haven, Conn.: Yale University Press, 1961.

Bradbrook, M. D. *Shakespeare in His Context: The Constellated Globe*. The Collected Papers of Muriel Bradbrook, Vol. IV. London: Harvester Wheatsheaf, 1989.

Chamblerin, E. R. *Everyday Life in Renaissance Times*. New York: Capricorn 1965.

Dyer, T. F. Thiselton. *Folk-Lore of Shakespeare*. New York: Dover, 1966.

Fox, Levi. *The Shakespeare Handbook*. Boston: G. K. Hall, 1987.

Frye, Roland Mushat. *Shakespeare's Life and Times*. Princeton, N.J.: Princeton University Press, 1967.

Hale, John. *The Civilization of Europe in the Renaissance*. London: HarperCollins, 1993.

Hall, Kim F. *Things of Darkness: Economies of Race and Gender in Early Modern England*. Ithaca, N.Y.: Cornell University Press, 1995.

Harvey, William. *On the Motion of the Heart and Blood in Animals*. www.fordham.edu/halsall/mod/1628harvey-blood.html

Hoeniger, F. David. *Medicine and Shakespeare in the English Renaissance*. Newark: University of Delaware Press, 1992.

Hyland, Peter. *An Introduction to Shakespeare: The Dramatist in His Context.* New York: St. Martin's, 1996.

McMurtry, Jo. *Understanding Shakespeare's England.* Hamden, Conn.: Archon Books, 1989.

Meron, Theodor. *Bloody Constraint: War and Chivalry in Shakespeare.* New York: Oxford University Press, 1998.

Morley, Thomas. *A Plaine and Easie Introduction to Practicall Musicke.* London, n.p., 1597.

Prothero, G. W., ed. *Select Statutes and Other Constitutional Documents Illustrative of the Reigns of Elizabeth and James I.* 4th ed. Oxford: Clarendon, 1913.

Rowse, A. L. *The Elizabethan Renaissance.* London: Macmillan, 1971.

Wells, Robin Headlam. *Elizabethan Mythologies: Studies in Poetry, Drama, and Music.* Cambridge: Cambridge University Press, 1994.

Wells, Stanley. *Shakespeare: A Life in Drama.* New York: Norton, 1995.

QUESTIONS

1. Why would London lure a young man like William Shakespeare?
2. Based on England's geography, why was London the capital of this country?
3. Why might the liver be viewed as the seat of human passions?
4. Why did the supernatural play such a key role in this time period?
5. What were some of the medical developments taking place at this time?

CRITICAL THINKING AND RESEARCH PROJECTS

1. Although earlier efforts were made to establish theaters in England, the first permanent theater opened in 1576, enabling drama performance to grow and flourish. Which facets of English life (and London, in particular) might have fostered the development of theater during this time?
2. Explore the use of games and holidays in several of Shakespeare's plays. What do such references add to the plot? Research the origins and traditional celebration of one such holiday.
3. In several of Shakespeare's plays, younger heroines lack mothers or sisters (Ophelia in *Hamlet*; Jessica in *The Merchant of Venice*). Consider possible reasons as you analyze the roles of older women (or lack of such roles) in Shakespeare's plays.
4. Draw a sixteenth-century man or woman modeling Elizabethan fashions. Label each item (including shoes, hat, and jewelery) and explain its function.
5. Take the position of an apothecary, surgeon, or physician. Write a detailed report diagnosing a particular injury or disease; then indicate the prescribed treatment and expected results, as well as any follow-up that will be needed.
6. Make a chart of female characters in one of Shakespeare's plays studied by your class. Categorize women by age, occupation, marital status, social status, and character type (hero v. villain, etc.). Look for other ways to categorize them as

well. Compare them (when applicable) to the male characters. Summarize your findings.

7. As you study plays with death-related themes (*Romeo and Juliet, Hamlet*), prepare a report about what you believe to be Shakespeare's view of death. Compare events from his life to the time these tragic plays were written to look for influential factors.

8. Compare the monarchy of Elizabeth I with a European counterpart. Why would a European ruler be eager to annex England via marriage with Elizabeth?

FOR FURTHER READING

Archer, I. W. *The Pursuit of Stability: Social Relations in Elizabethan London.* Cambridge: Cambridge University Press, 1991.

Fumerton, Patricia, and Simon Hunt, eds. *Renaissance Culture and the Everyday.* Philadelphia: University of Pennsylvania Press, 1999.

Mahood, M. M. *Shakespeare's Wordplay.* London and New York: Methuen, 1957.

Manley, I., ed. *London in the Age of Shakespeare: An Anthology.* London and Sydney: Croom Helm, 1986.

Paster, Gail Kern. *The Idea of the City in the Age of Shakesepeare.* Athens: University of Georgia Press, 1986.

Salkeld, Duncan. *Madness of Drama in the Age of Shakespeare.* Manchester, UK; Manchester University Press; New York: Distributed by St. Martin's, 1993.

Sawday, Jonathan. *The Body Emblazoned: Dissection and the Human Body in Renaissance Culture.* London and New York: Routledge, 1995.

Smith, D. L., R. Strier, and D. Bevington, eds. *The Theatrical City: Culture, Theatre and Politics in London, 1576–1649.* Cambridge: Cambridge University Press, 1995.

Stow, John. *Survey of London (1598/1603),* ed. C. L. Kingsford. 2 Vols. Oxford: Oxford University Press, 1908, 1968.

WEBSITES

http://www.britannia.com/travel/top/westmin.html
http://www.britannia.com/travel/shakespeare.html
Mr. William Shakespeare and the Internet

http://daphne.palomar.edu/shakespeare/
(Terry Gray, Palomar College, California, USA)

" The Artist's Father" by Albrecht Durer.

7

CHRISTIANITY

One sees more devils than vast hell can hold.
(A Midsummer Night's Dream, V.i.9)

TUDOR REFORM

Despite chronic anxiety over foreign wars and economic concerns, religion was the greatest source of conflict in Elizabethan England because it stirred domestic strife as well as international tensions. Religious violence stemming from clashes between Catholicism and Protestantism tore apart families and led to persecution.

Though Catholicism had been England's state faith for centuries, King Henry VIII broke with the Church of Rome when Pope Clement VII refused to annul his marriage to Catherine of Aragon. Henry had married Catherine, widow of his deceased brother Arthur, to maintain her dowry and unity with Spain. When no sons were born after several years, Henry urged Cardinal Wolsey, archbishop of York, to procure a divorce for him from the Pope. But Pope Clement VII owed a debt of allegiance to Charles V, the Holy Roman Emperor who was Catherine's nephew. Instead of divorcing Henry, the pope excommunicated him.

Henry refused to give up. In 1529 he called the Reformation Parliament, which passed 137 statutes involving political and church issues. Henry mandated small, incremental reformist steps in the transition of the state faith from Catholicism to Protestantism. Thomas Cranmer, archbishop of Canterbury, supervised the monasteries' dissolution and distribution of church property. Supporters of reformers like Luther, Zwingli, and the Lollards increased in number and received the king's favor.

Queen Elizabeth I at prayer ("Christian Prayers," 1569).
© Bettmann/CORBIS.

When Henry's daughter Mary I came to the throne in 1553, she tried to re-unite England with the Church of Rome. But five years later when Mary died, Elizabeth worked to return the country to the Protestant faith and Puritan influence. The switch was not accomplished without a struggle that gnawed into the realms of diplomacy and colonialism. Elizabeth walked a fine line between upholding Protestantism while offering cautious tolerance to Catholics.

Weekly worship was mandatory. Those who failed to attend church could be prosecuted and fined. William Shakespeare would have worshipped at Trinity Church with his family in Stratford and probably attended the church at Southwark during his residency there.

Many facets of Catholic worship remained embedded in Anglican Church rites. Immoral behavior was punishable by civil law, though clerical laws were less stringently enforced.

In 1542 the Convocation of the Archbishopric of Canterbury issued 12 homilies, or sermon texts, for untrained clergy. Based on personal faith and public obedience to state rule, the *Homilies* provided guidelines for everyday living on topics like "Of the True and Lively Faith," "Of Good Works," and "An Exhortation to Obedience." During Elizabeth's reign, a second book of homilies added 21 topics, including "Against Rebellion" following the 1569 northern rebellion of the earls. Religious pamphlets and printed sermons became popular reading for England's increasingly literate populace. Shakespeare gleaned drama material from moral dilemmas and church-state conflicts. He used the political threat of divorce to secure proof of Helena's validity as Bertram's deserving wife in *All's Well that Ends Well:*

> If it appear not plain and prove untrue,
> Deadly divorce step between me and you!
>
> *(V.iii.317–318)*

Religious practice could not be separated from state affairs and people's lives, unlike the clear-cut distinctions in Western culture today. It is useful for Shakespeare scholars to have some knowledge of the Bible to fully appreciate his symbols and allusions.

VERSIONS OF THE BIBLE

For centuries following Jesus Christ's ministry, written Scriptures were preserved in their languages of origin, Hebrew and Greek, and later translated into Latin by church scholars. In the sixteenth century, a series of church reforms led to the Bible's translation into English.

John Wycliffe (1330–1384), born in Yorkshire, England, received bachelor's and master's degrees at Oxford where he became a renowned professor. In 1366 he served as the king's chaplain, and in 1372 he earned a doctorate of divinity degree. Wycliffe inspired the translation of the Bible into Middle English and denied the doctrine of transubstantiation, for which he was labeled a heretic. Supporters included John of Gaunt and his Oxford colleagues.

Though Pope Gregory XI condemned his work in 1377 and sought to have him arrested, Wycliffe's political connections protected him. The Lollards followed Wycliffe's teachings after his death in a movement that was blamed for the Peasants' Revolt. Some of Chaucer's friends were Lollards.

William Tyndale (c. 1494–1536) translated the Bible from Hebrew and Greek. Born near the Welsh border, Tyndale attended Oxford where he studied languages, liberal arts, and the Scriptures. He also studied at Cambridge and then tutored the children of Lord Welch in Glouchestershire. Tyndale translated Erasmus' *The Manual of a Christian Soldier* and gave a copy to Lord and Lady Welch, but local priests began to complain that Tyndale's works were heresy. He went to London, and unable to secure a position, left for Germany. His English New Testament was printed at Worms in 1526, followed by the Pentateuch in 1530. Despite criticism from those who believed Scripture ought to remain in the classical languages, Tyndale defended his actions in the 1535 edition:

> These things, I say, to know, is to have all the scripture unlocked and opened before thee; so that if thou wilt go in, and read, thou canst not but understand. . . . And now, because the lay and unlearned people are taught these first principles of our profession, therefore they read the scripture, and understand and delight therein.
> (http://www.williamtyndale.com/0pathway.htm)

The authorities disagreed, and on October 6, 1536, Tyndale was strangled and burned at the stake.

The Matthews Bible, compiled by Tyndale's associate John Rogers, was the first licensed by Henry VIII after his break from the Church of Rome, followed in 1539 by the Great Bible intended for use by Church of England clergy. Both drew heavily on Tyndale's work.

The Geneva Bible followed, preferred by laypersons and widely read. Translators working in Geneva revised Tyndale's English New Testament into a new edition by 1557, with John Calvin's brother-in-law William Whittingham providing much of the work. In 1560 a complete revised Geneva Bible was dedicated to Queen Elizabeth. The Geneva Bible enjoyed such widespread use that it was reprinted in several editions by 1600. Shakespeare probably read this version more than any other.

Here a passage from the Geneva Bible (1560) is compared to the King James version (1611):

GENEVA, FROM GENESIS 3	KING JAMES, FROM GENESIS 3
1: Now the serpent was more subtle than any other wild creature that the LORD God had made. He said to the woman, "Did God say, 'You shall not eat of any tree of the garden'?"	Now the serpent was more subtle than any beast of the field which the LORD God had made. And he said unto the woman, Yea, hath God said, Ye shall not eat of every tree of the garden?

2: And the woman said to the serpent, "We may eat of the fruit of the trees of the garden; 3: but God said, 'You shall not eat of the fruit of the tree which is in the midst of the garden, neither shall you touch it, lest you die.'"

4: But the serpent said to the woman, "You will not die. 5: For God knows that when you eat of it your eyes will be opened, and you will be like God, knowing good and evil."

2 And the woman said unto the serpent, We may eat of the fruit of the trees of the garden: 3 But of the fruit of the tree which is in the midst of the garden, God hath said, Ye shall not eat of it, neither shall ye touch it, lest ye die.

4 And the serpent said unto the woman, Ye shall not surely die: 5 For God doth know that in the day ye eat thereof, then your eyes shall be opened, and ye shall be as Gods, knowing good and evil.

Triumph of Death by Pieter Brueghel the Elder, c. 1525–69.

The Bishops' Bible, prepared by a group of learned bishops in 1568, generally was used in churches. In 1611, King James organized 47 scholars at Westminster, Oxford, and Cambridge to prepare the "Authorized, or King James Version" of the Bible. Protestants still read it today and it is considered by some the most authoritative and accurate translation. (An excerpt from its dedication to the king follows this chapter.)

CATHOLICISM AND THE ANGLICAN CHURCH (OR CHURCH OF ENGLAND)

After Henry VIII separated from the Roman Catholic Church following his divorce from Catherine, England established the Anglican Church, a move that led toward Protestantism. However, the Church of England continued to use a number of Catholic-related rituals and practices. Ministers of Henry's son, Edward VI, sought more Protestant reforms.

When Henry's daughter Mary, who married King Philip of Spain, came to the throne in 1553, she switched state allegiance to the Church of Rome, resulting in widespread violence, persecution, and bloodshed. Her premature death in 1558 allowed her half-sister Elizabeth to rule.

Elizabeth sought to reconcile the two factions by establishing the Elizabethan Settlement. Though neither side was fully appeased, the country enjoyed relative peace for a time. Elizabeth hoped to win over the Catholics gradually by providing a tolerant environment.

The Counter-Reformation brought English priests home from abroad, resulting in renewed tensions. In 1581 the government passed an act that labeled treasonous the withdrawing of monarchy and church support. Fines were raised for recusants—those who did not attend church—to £20 per month. As anti-Catholic momentum increased, a 1585 act declared Jesuits or seminary priests to be traitors and they were banished from England on pain of death. English subjects studying Catholicism abroad were required to return to England to take the Oath of Supremacy or be declared guilty of high treason. By 1593, Catholic laypersons could go no further than five miles from their residence and marriages had to be performed in parish churches to be recognized.

Being charged with illegal Catholic practice could result in a harsh sentence from Elizabeth's Lord Chief Justice:

> You must go to the place from whence you came, there to remain until ye shall be drawn through the open City of London upon hurdles to the place of execution, and there hanged and let down alive, and your privy parts cut off, and your entrails taken out and burnt in your sight; then your heads to be cut off and your bodies divided into four parts, to be disposed of at her Majesty's pleasure. And God have mercy on your souls! (Sams 1995, 36)

After 1603 James wanted to improve conditions for English Catholics, but the Gunpowder Plot revealed the danger of leniency. In an act of 1606, Polish recusants were required to attend the Church of England and receive the sacrament. Recusants were barred from court and the city of London except for special circumstances, and they were banned from the legal, medical, and military professions. Anyone caught using marriage, baptismal, or burial rites other than those of the Church of England was punished. Justices of the peace could search homes for Catholic books and relics. Protestant extremists faced more lenient penalties.

ELIZABETH'S ACTS OF SUPREMACY AND UNIFORMITY

Elizabeth waived further ecclesiastical change in an effort to reclaim peace for England. Her Acts of Supremacy and Uniformity revived the antipapal statutes of Henry VIII, confirming the crown's authority over the national church, but she did not restore the title of "Supreme Head" to the monarchy.

The Act of Uniformity returned widespread use of the second prayer book that Mary had repealed. Ministers using other books were to be punished. Bishops and secular judges were assigned the duty of regulating these policies. In general, Elizabeth's parliaments supported her stand against the Roman church, with a substantial number of spiritual peers represented in the upper house.

The Convocation was the Church of England's legislative body. It met when the monarch summoned it, and sittings coincided with those of Parliament. Convocation rulings were validated by royal assent.

Providing instruction on clerical rights, ceremonies, and duties, the Injunctions of 1559 included token acceptance of married clergy, though this was not legalized by statute until 1604. Additional articles in 1583 required all ministers to use the prayer book and to adhere to the original 39 articles.

PURITANS

Marry, sir, sometimes he is a kind of puritan. (*Twelfth Night*, II.iii.139)

The High Commission was the church court assigned to carry out orders. The monarch nominated seventeen commissioners to judge complaints against offenders. Six of these could act with or without jury assistance. The commission could punish disturbers of public worship, vagrants, and quarrelers and deal with morality issues. Punishments included fines or imprisonment, and the Act of 1587 allowed the crown to take two-thirds of an offender's property under certain conditions. Some government-mandated articles of faith went against Puritan conscience.

In 1582 Calvinist ministers adopted a second Book of Discipline. In 1583, John Whitgift became archbishop of Canterbury at a time when efforts were being made to establish a Presbyterian organization of churches in which deacons and church leaders determined ecclesiastical order. Such orders were called "classes" when connected to a larger system in other parts of the country. This directly challenged the episcopalian order of the rule of bishops within the Church of England.

Parliament complained that the commission exceeded fine limits and used temporal as well as spiritual penalties; it also protested the lack of an appeals process. In 1610, James I added an appeals system and mandated that five or more officials must contribute to final decisions.

Protestants gained seats in the House of Commons and became a dominant force in challenging the Anglican Church over issues such as the vestment controversy and the bishops' abuse of power.

Many Puritan leaders trained at colleges and universities. Their writings demonstrated a reasonable, scholarly response to emotional issues. Puritans wished to remove barriers between man and God by encouraging believers to pray directly to God rather than through priests or saints. They believed God could forgive humans without clerical intervention, as mandated in confession or the sale of indulgences. Puritans who had studied the classical writers incorporated those views in their sermons.

Puritans disdained the ornate Anglican style, feeling it overwhelmed or distracted the congregation who would then become complacent about the nature of sin and miss the needed conversion. Some Puritans felt stained glass windows, incense, and decorous vestments drew attention to earthly objects rather than to God, the focus of worship.

Puritan Demands

Brought to the Lower House of Convocation on February 13, 1563, the following Puritan demands were rejected by a majority of one vote (58 for, 59 against).

- That all the Sundays in the year and principal holidays be kept holy days, with all other holydays to be abrogated.
- That in all parish churches the minister in common prayer turn his face toward the people read the divine service appointed, where all the people assembled may hear and be edified.
- That in ministering the sacrament of baptism the ceremony of making the cross in the child's forehead may be omitted to avoid the appearance of superstition.
- That in cases of age, sickness and infirmities, the practice of kneeling be left to each person's discretion.
- That ministers wear a surplice and simple vestments.
- That the use of organs be removed from church services.

It wasn't until 1571 that Queen Elizabeth ratified these changes and others drawn from the Thirty-Nine Articles of the 1563 Convocation.

PROTESTANTISM

The group that called themselves Puritans or "Precisians" included moderate political figures like Secretary of State Sir Francis Walsingham, the Dudley family, and the earls of Warwick and Leicester, along with the queen's relations and reformist bishops like Edmund Grindal.

As early as 1563 the Puritan faction objected to certain ceremonies in the Church of England and brought a proposal to the convocation for debate. Although the proposal was defeated by one vote, dissidents stopped using those parts of the Anglican service.

Practices such as licensing pastors to minister to more than one parish, using organ music during the service, wearing elaborate clerical vestments, and mandating celibacy were opposed. Protestants argued against using cake over bread in the Eucharist and the sign of the cross in baptism.

In 1613 James's daughter married the Elector Palatine, confirming the English King's tolerance of Protestantism. James also helped to mediate tensions between Denmark and the Dutch. These and other events supported a movement toward international Protestantism, although James arranged Catholic marriages for his sons to balance religious influence.

On September 16, 1620, a group of 102 settlers which included at least 35 separatist Puritans departed on the *Mayflower* from Plymouth, which is the name given to their New World colony in what now is known as Massachusetts.

THE REFORMATION

Though you and all the kings of Christendom
Are led so grossly by this meddling priest,
Dreading the curse that money may buy out,
And by the merit of vild gold, dross, dust,
Purchase corrupted pardon of a man
Who in that sale sells pardon from himself;
Though you, and all the rest so grossly led,
This juggling witchcraft with revenue cherish,
Yet I alone, alone do me oppose
Against the Pope, and count his friends my foes.
(King John, III.i.162–171)

Although reforms and heretical movements had surfaced during the Middle Ages, including the twelfth-century Waldenses in Lyons, the thirteenth-century Inquisition, and the fifteenth-century burning of Bohemian John Hus, the Reform movement caused most alarm under sixteenth-century leaders like Luther and Calvin.

The impact of church reform can be seen in art works of the northern painters at Bruges, Ghent, the Hague, and Augsburg by artists like Albrecht Durer (1471–1528) and Hans Holbein the Younger (1497–1543). Humanism played a role in this movement by promoting the image of universal man to challenge the traditional focus of God and church.

Puritanism began as an intellectual manifestation of church reform in response to the split of the Anglican Church from the Church of Rome. The movement grew steadily after 1550, and by 1558 the Church of England, or Anglicanism, had become Protestant rather than Episcopal. Puritanism focused on issues of morality and sin, taking a sober view of life. Calvinism taught that people are generally sinful, requiring divine salvation. Reformists sought to purify the faith, remolding practice after the simplicity of the first-century church.

It wasn't until the 1560s that reformers were called Puritans. The movement had no set goals or structural organization but was based on beliefs. The Elizabethan Settlement satisfied some of the early reformers, while others continued to press for more changes.

In many respects the Puritans and Anglicans were similar. Both were Protestant and emphasized salvation by faith over works, believing the Bible should be followed literally. Puritans agreed that Anglicans could be saved, and some Anglican sermons were printed in the New World.

John Foxe (1516–87), born in Lincolnshire, attended Oxford University. He received a Bachelor of Arts degree in 1537 and became a professor, completing a master's degree in 1543. Friends included Hugh Latimer and William Tyndale, and at Oxford he embraced Protestantism. In 1545 he left the university when his views were deemed extreme. He married and moved to London.

Foxe was ordained a Church of England deacon and worked for the Reformation by writing tracts and a history of Christian martyrs. In 1553 he left England when Queen Mary came to the throne. The first part of his book was published in 1554 in Strassburg, France. He then went to Frankfurt to support John Knox's Calvinist movement and from there to Basel, Switzerland, serving as a printer's proofreader.

Manuscripts and eyewitness accounts of the Protestants' persecution under Queen Mary were forwarded to Foxe in Basel where he completed his book in 1559. He returned to England and published his work in March 1563 under the title *Actes and Monuments of These Latter and Perillous Days*. The book became popularly known as *The Book of Martyrs*. Foxe was ordained an Anglican priest in 1560. He preached and published his sermons, and ministered to plague victims in 1563. He petitioned Queen Elizabeth not to execute Anabaptists in 1575 nor the Jesuits in 1581.

His book was used in English churches, read to Francis Drake's shipmates, and studied by Puritan families. When he died, Foxe was buried at St. Gile's Church in London.

Richard Hooker (1554–1600), English cleric, created a philosophy for the Church of England. His *Ecclesiastical Polity* of 1594 supported the following of nature or reason, which Hooker paralleled to God's law. In his positive outlook, Hooker believed in evidence of a logical design in the universe.

Thomas Hobbes (1588–1679), another reformer, was educated at Oxford, he traveled through Europe and witnessed English and French uprisings, met Galileo, and developed an interest in science. *Leviathan* (1651) was his chief work. Unlike Hooker, Hobbes was a pessimist, believing nature is full of strife but that humans need to work with natural laws to create order and preserve property. His views resemble Machiavelli's practicality and demonstrate a secular rather than divine view of kingship.

EUROPEAN PROTESTANTISM

Many European figures played a role in the Reformation and the Counter-Reformation. Some traveled to England. Others published work that eventually reached many European countries. Reformers identified abuses in the Catholic Church and developed a more simple worship system that came to be known as Protestantism.

Desiderius Erasmus Roterodamus

Erasmus (1466?–1536) was a key figure of the northern Renaissance. A Dutch theologian, he studied classical literature and accepted the teachings of Jesus as central values. Erasmus did not join a specific branch of Protestantism but sought changes that would result in a simple scriptural message presented to the masses.

The Praise of Folly in 1509 and the *Novum Instrumentum* of 1516, a translation of the New Testament with the original Greek on facing pages, are probably Erasmus's best-known works. Here is an excerpt from the *Paraclesis*, or preface, of the translation.

> Indeed, I disagree very much with those who are unwilling that Holy Scripture, translated into the vulgar [common] tongue, be read by the uneducated, as if Christ taught such intricate doctrines that they could scarcely be understood by very few theologians, or as if the strength of the Christian religion consisted in men's ignorance of it. The mysteries of kings perhaps are better concealed, but Christ wishes his mysteries published as openly as possible. I would that even the lowliest women read the Gospels and the Pauline Epistles. And I would that they were translated into all languages so that they could be read and understood not only by Scots and Irish but also by Turks and Saracens. . . .
> (www.galileolibrary.com/history/history_020601/history_page_121.htm)

Erasmus's work played a key role in turning the minds of prominent leaders to the need for clerical reforms.

John Calvin

Born in 1509 in Noyon, northeast of Paris, Jean Cauvin, Anglicized as John Calvin, studied theology and law before converting to Protestantism in the 1530s. Geneva became the site of reformist protests in the sixteenth century, and in 1536 nuns and priests were banished. William Farel asked 27-year-old John Calvin to help lead a reform movement. In 1536 Calvin wrote *Institutes of the Christian Religion* with a preface to the French king. The work was expanded and republished several times between 1536 and 1559, and served as an important tool in the reform movement. Calvin became a leader and pastor, founding Geneva Academy in 1555, which later became the University of Geneva.

Although Calvin believed in the separate jurisdictions of church and state, he supported the notion that humans could serve God anywhere, from public office to private domain. In August 1540 Calvin married Idelette de Bure, widow of a reformist follower. Their one child was born prematurely and soon died. Idelette died in the spring of 1549. Calvin lived frugally, working hard until he developed tuberculosis. He preached his last sermon on February 6, 1564, dictating notes until just eight hours before his death on May 27, 1564. An excerpt from *The Institutes* is at the end of this chapter.

Martin Luther

Martin Luther was born in Saxony in 1483 and attended the University of Erfurth where he studied Christian writers like Augustine, Aquinas, and Scotus.

In 1508 he began teaching at the University of Wittenberg and three years later received his doctorate. His adherence to St. Paul's doctrine of faith over works forced him to disagree with many Catholic practices, including selling indulgences (forgiveness of sins) and making pilgrimages. In 1516 Pope Leo X assigned a Dominican friar named Tetzel to collect money from people eager to purchase pardons for loved ones.

On September 30, 1517, Luther posted his objections on the church door annexed to the castle of Wittenberg. Leaders including the German emperor and King Charles of Spain asked Duke Frederick of Saxony to silence Luther. The duke conferred with several advisers, including Erasmus, and cautioned Luther, though no action was taken.

On August 7, 1518, the Pope ordered Luther to Rome. Luther agreed to obey the pope as long as he followed Scriptural teachings. But when the pope, being fallible, departed from Scripture, it remained the Christian's duty to disagree. Luther also insisted that anyone receiving the sacrament must believe the Scriptures.

In 1519 Pope Leo sent two cardinals to burn Luther's works and either kill him or send him to Rome. In 1520 Luther wrote his *Appeal to the Christian Nobility of the German Nation:*

> Grace and power from God, Most Illustrious Majesty, and most gracious and dear lords.
>
> It is not from sheer impertinence or rashness that I, one poor man, have taken it upon myself to address your worships. All the estates of Christendom, particularly in Germany, are now oppressed by distress and affliction, and this has stirred not only me but everyone else to cry out time and time again and to pray for help . . . Often the councils have made some pretense at reformation, but their attempts have been cleverly frustrated by the guile of certain men, and things have gone from bad to worse. With God's help I intend to expose the wiles and wickedness of these men, so that they are shown up for what they are and may never again be so obstructive and destructive . . . The Romanists have very cleverly built three walls around themselves. Hitherto they have protected themselves by these walls in such a way that no one has been able to reform them. As a result, the whole of Christendom has fallen abominably.
>
> . . . Therefore just as those who are now called "spiritual," that is, priests, bishops, or popes, are neither different from other Christians nor superior to them, . . . The pope has broken the agreement and made the annates a robbery to the injury and shame of the whole German nation. He gives them to his friends, sells them for huge sums

of money, and uses them to endow offices. In so doing he has lost his right to them and deserves punishment. . . . The pope should have no authority over the emperor, except the right to anoint and crown him at the alter just as a bishop crowns a king . . .

We also see how the priesthood has fallen, and how many a poor priest is overburdened with wife and child, his conscience troubled . . . So then, we clearly learn from the Apostle that it should be the custom for every town to choose from among the congregation a learned and pious citizen, entrust to him the office of the ministry, and support him at the expense of the congregation. He should be free to marry or not.

(http://www.lsma.edu/bmcbride/History/Reformation/luthadrs.htm)

In 1521 Luther attended the Diet of Worms with assurance of safe conduct. On the fourth day he appeared before the emperor and German nobles and was then sent home. Near age 40, Luther married former nun Katherine von Bora on June 27, 1525. Their union produced three boys and three girls. He continued to write and preach until his death at 63.

The Counter-Reformation

Angels and ministers of grace defend us! (Hamlet, I.iv.39)

The Catholic Church reacted to the Reformation, which occurred largely in northern Europe, in a movement that became known as the Catholic Reformation or the Counter-Reformation. Conservative Catholics took steps to reform and stabilize the church against Protestantism and secularism.

One cause of instability was the Great Schism (1378–1417) that, due to political competition, resulted in two papal lines. It ended when Martin V was elected pope, but the conflict delayed the much-needed reforms. Pope Paul IV, along with a number of priests and laypersons, formed a small reform party that was helped by outsiders like Sir Thomas More, Erasmus, and Cardinal Jimenez. The ensuing Council of Trent conducted a series of meetings between 1545 and 1563, forming the hub of the reform movement.

Ignatius Loyola and the Jesuits

Ignatius Loyola, born in 1491 to a Basque family, began his career as a soldier. Wounded during the siege of Pamplona, he spent his convalescence reading Saxony's *Life of Christ* and Jacopo de Voragine's *The Golden Legend*, a collection of stories about the saints. In 1524 he commenced study at the universities of Alcala, Salamanca, and Paris.

In 1540 Loyola and six followers received papal authority to organize a religious order called the Society of Jesus; members were called Jesuits.

Jesuits advocated education and were deeply committed to the Catholic Church. They successfully sought reforms within the Church. When Loyola died in 1556, more than a thousand Jesuits were serving as missionaries and educators on several continents. (See at chapter's end a letter dated March 26, 1553, from Rome to Portugal in which Loyola reiterates the importance of Christian obedience.) Loyola and the Jesuits helped to reinstate support for the Catholic Church.

OTHER FAITHS

But then I sigh, and, with a piece of scripture,
Tell them that God bids us do good for evil (Richard III, I.iii.333–334)

Judaism

Edward I banned Jews from England in 1290. Later, following the Spanish pure blood laws, they were expelled from Spain in 1492, and from Portugal in 1497. Iberian Jews who remained were forced to convert and called Marranos or New Christians, or they had to keep their religious views private. In Shakespeare's time most were quietly tolerated when they assimilated or did not call attention to themselves. Jews believed in the biblical God, followed the Ten Commandments and Levite law, and preserved racial purity in part by avoiding intermarriage with non-Jews. Their main holy work was called the Torah, comprising the first five books (sometimes called the Pentateuch) of the Old Testament, and the Talmud. Judaism traces its roots to the biblical Abraham (see Genesis, Chapter 11 and following), as do the other world religions of Christianity, Islam, and the Baha'I faith. Basic Jewish beliefs include the following:

- There is one God who created everything.
- God communicated with the Jews through the writings of Moses and the prophets.
- God will reward humans' good behavior and punish wrongdoing.
- The Jews do not believe Jesus Christ is the Messiah.

(Source: http://www.religioustolerance.org/jud_desc.htm)

Islam

Muslims remained suspect in Elizabethan society and were considered "outsiders" by most European nations, due in part to Turkish invasion of southern Europe and Muslim control of Jerusalem's Christian sites. Muslims follow the teachings of seventh-century prophet Muhammad (A.D. 570–632) who taught complete submission to Allah, or God, based on five pillars of faith:

- The existence of one God with Muhammad as key servant and messenger.
- The need to pray five times daily, facing Mecca in the East.

- The call to fast during the month of Ramadan, abstaining from food, beverages, and sex between dawn and sunset.
- The responsibility of "Zakah," or contribution of the wealthy for the care of the needy and benefit of society.
- The goal of "hajj," or pilgrimage to the Ka'bah in Mecca at least once for those who have the means.

    (Source: http://www.understanding-islam.com/related/text.asp?type=question&qid=808)

The teachings of Islam through the revelation of prophet Muhammad are found in the holy book called the Qur'an (or Koran), which teaches "There is no compulsion in religion" (Qur'an 2:256). Moslems generally accept the Christian Jesus as a prophet but not as the Son of God. Shakespeare's protagonists refer to Moslems as "infidels" or "pagans," along with other terms that describe them as beyond the realm of Christendom and mainstream society. Between August 1600 and February 1601, a Moroccan embassy of sixteen "noble Moors" visited the English court, contributing to more widespread understanding of and appreciation for Islamic culture and fashion.

Turks sometimes captured Christian vessels and sold captives as slaves or held them for ransom. Occasionally Christians converted to Judaism or Islam from force or choice.

Shakespeare's writing, like that of his contemporaries, reflects a certain amount of anxiety about religious conflicts between Protestants and Catholics and about the role of Jews and Turks in Christian Europe. His writing utilizes Christian symbols and themes, suggesting the pervasive nature of religious faith to Shakespeare himself or to his audience. From the use of generic references like "devil" in pagan drama like *The Tempest* and *Timon of Athens*, to specific Christian allusions such as "Saint Anne" in *The Taming of the Shrew* or "Noah's flood" in *The Comedy of Errors*, Shakespeare seems to have found the Christian faith a mainstay and a credible prop for many of his characters.

SUMMARY

Few issues disturb people more than religion. England became a seat of religious controversy for a number of reasons, notably Henry VIII's secession from the Church of Rome, the printing of the Bible in English for mass readership, and the question of Elizabeth's religious support. These factors and others paved the way for the Reformation and the Counter-Reformation, resulting in competing branches of a leading world faith.

Protestantism flourished during the sixteenth and seventeenth centuries and was brought to America by Puritan settlers who established colonies under the banner of religious freedom.

Other worship systems such as Judaism and Islam survived Christian revival of this era but were forced to practice clandestinely or to make a public show of conversion, despite private practice.

The Act of Supremacy (1534)

Albeit, the King's Majesty justly and rightfully is and oweth to be the supreme head of the Church of England, and so is recognised by the clergy of this realm in their Convocations; yet nevertheless for corroboration and confirmation thereof, and for increase of virtue in Christ's religion within this realm of England, and to repress and extirp all errors, heresies and other enormities and abuses heretofore used in the same, Be it enacted by authority of this present Parliament that the King our sovereign lord, his heirs and successors kings of this realm, shall be taken, accepted and reputed the only supreme head in earth of the Church of England called *Anglicana Ecclesia,* and shall have and enjoy annexed and united to the imperial crown of this realm as well the title and style thereof, as all honours, dignities, preeminences, jurisdictions, privileges, authorities, immunities, profits and commodities, to the said dignity of supreme head of the same Church belonging and appertaining. And that our said sovereign lord, his heirs and successors kings of this realm, shall have full power and authority from time to time to visit, repress, redress, reform, order, correct, restrain and amend all such errors, heresies, abuses, offences, contempts and enormities, whatsoever they be, which by any manner spiritual authority or jurisdiction ought or may lawfully be reformed, repressed, ordered, redressed corrected, restrained or amended, most to the pleasure of Almighty God, the increase of virtue in Christ's religion, and for the conservation of the peace, unity and tranquillity of this realm: any usage, custom, foreign laws, foreign authority, prescription or any other thing or things to the contrary hereof notwithstanding. (From: *Statutes of the Realm,* III; *spelling modernized*)

Dedication of the King James Bible to the King

To the Most High and Mighty Prince
James
By the Grace of God
King of Great Britain, France, and Ireland
Defender of the Faith &C.

The Translators of the Bible wish Grace, Mercy, and Peace Through JESUS CHRIST our Lord

Great and manifold were the blessings, most dread Sovereign, which Almighty God, the Father of all mercies, bestowed upon us the people of England, when first he sent Your Majesty's Royal Person to rule and reign over us. For whereas it was the expectation of many, who wishes not well unto our Sion, that upon the setting of that bright Occidental

Star, Queen Elizabeth of most happy memory, some thick and palpable clouds of darkness would so have overshadowed this Land, that men should have been in doubt which way they were to walk; and that it should hardly be known, who was to direct the unsettled State; the appearance of Your Majesty, as of the Sun in his strength, instantly dispelled those supposed and surmised mists, and gave unto all that were well affected exceeding cause of comfort; especially when we beheld the Government established in Your Highness, and Your hopeful Seed, by an undoubted title, and this also accompanied with peace and tranquility at home and abroad.

But among all our joys, there was no one that more filled our hearts, than the blessed continuance of the preaching of God's sacred Word among us; which is that inestimable treasure, which excelleth all the riches of the earth; because the fruit thereof extendeth itself, not only to the time spent in this transitory world, but directeth and disposeth men unto that eternal happiness which is above in heaven. . . .

From John Calvin's Institutes *of the Christian Religion*

. . . The miserable ruin, into which the rebellion of the first man cast us, especially compels us to look upward. Thus, not only will be, in fasting and hungering, seek thence what we lack; but in being aroused by fear, we shall learn humility. For, as a veritable world of miseries is to be found in mankind, and we are thereby despoiled by divine raiment, our shameful nakedness exposes a teeming horde of infamies. Each of us must, then, be so stung by the consciousness of his own unhappiness as to attain at least some knowledge of God. Thus, from the feeling of our own ignorance, vanity, poverty, infirmity, and—what is more—depravity and corruption, we recognize that the true light of wisdom, sound virtue, full abundance of every good, and purity of righteousness rest in the Lord alone. To this extent we are prompted by our own ills to contemplate the good things of God; and we cannot seriously aspire to him before we begin to become displeased with ourselves . . .

What help is it, in short, to know a God with whom we have nothing to do? Rather, our knowledge should serve first to teach us fear and reverence; secondly, with it as our guide and teacher, we should learn to seek every good from him, and having received it, to credit it to his account . . . Here indeed is pure and real religion: faith so joined with an earnest fear of God that this fear also embraces willing reverence, and carries with it such legitimate worship as is prescribed in the law. And we ought to note this fact even more diligently: all men have a vague general veneration for God, but very few really reverence him; and wherever there is great ostentation in ceremonies, sincerity of heart is rare indeed. (http://www.smartlink.net/~douglas/calvin/bk1ch01.html)

From Loyola's Letter to the Members of the Society in Portugal
March 26, 1553

"It gives me great consolation, my dear brothers in our Lord Jesus Christ, when I learn of the lively and earnest desires for perfection in His divine service and glory which He gives you, who by His mercy has called you to this society and preserves you in it and directs you to the blessed end at which His chosen ones arrive.

And although I wish you perfection in every virtue and spiritual gift, it is true (as you have heard from me on other occasions) that it is in obedience more than in any other virtue that God our Lord gives me the desire to see you signalize yourselves. . . . :"
(http://www.cin.org/jesuit.html)

SOURCES

Ali, A. Yusuf, Transl. and commentary. *The Holy Qur'an*. Brentwood, MD: Amana Corp., 1983.

Ashton, Robert. *Reformation and Revolution 1558–1660*. London: Paladin, 1985.

Bartlett, Kenneth R., and Margaret McGlynn. *Humanism and the Northern Renaissance*. Toronto: Canadian Scholars' Press, 2000.

Holy Bible, Authorized King James Version. (Giant Print Reference). Grand Rapids, Mich.: Zondervan, 1994.

Loades, David. *Politics and Nation: England 1450–1660*. 5th ed. Malden, Mass.: Blackwell, 1999.

Marx, Steven. *Shakespeare and the Bible*. Oxford: Oxford University Press, 2000.

Prothero, G. W., ed. *Select Statutes and Other Constitutional Documents Illustrative of the Reigns of Elizabeth and James I*. 4th ed. Oxford: Clarendon Press, 1913.

Sams, Eric. *The Real Shakespeare: Retrieving the Early Years, 1564–1594*. New Haven, Conn.: Yale University Press, 1995.

The Geneva Bible: A Facsimile of the 1560 Edition. Madison: University of Wisconsin Press, 1969.

Zophy, Jonathan W. *A Short History of Renaissance and Reformation Europe: Dances over Fire and Water*. Upper Saddle River, N.J.: Prentice Hall, 1996.

QUESTIONS

1. What were some of the problems of the Catholic Church cited by Protestant reformers?
2. Why did men like Tyndale risk their lives for the sake of the Bible?
3. How has Protestantism changed since its beginnings?

4. Which faith seems more dominant in the world today, Protestantism or Catholicism? Why? Which is more dominant in the United States?
5. Does modern society still discriminate against Jews?

CRITICAL THINKING AND RESEARCH PROJECTS

1. Research the worship practices of a leading figure from Shakespeare's era, such as Queen Elizabeth.
2. Study one or more of Shakespeare's plays to speculate about his religious views.
3. How and why have today's Christian practices changed? Research the development of one Protestant denomination since the seventeenth century and analyze causes and effects of its evolution. (Calvinism, Lutheranism, the Amish, etc.)
4. What role does Judaism play in global affairs today?
5. How does the western world view Islam in the 21st century?

FOR FURTHER READING

Alter, Robert. *The World of Biblical Literature*. New York: Basic, 1992.

Brigden, Susan. *London and the Reformation*. Oxford: Clarendon, 1989.

Collinson, Patrick. *The Elizabethan Puritan Movement*. London: Jonathan Cape, 1967.

Cottret, Bernard. Trans. Peregrine Stevenson and Adriana Stevenson, with afterword by Emmanuel Le Roy Ladurie. *The Huguenots in England: Immigration and Settlement c. 1550–1700*. Cambridge: Cambridge University Press, 1991.

Doran, Susan. *England and Europe in the Sixteenth Century*. London: Macmillan, 1999.

Gilley, Sheridan, and W. J. Sheils, eds. *A History of Religion in Britain*. Oxford: Blackwell, 1994.

Hamilton, Donna B., and Richard Strier. *Religion, Literature, and Politics in Post-Reformation England, 1540–1688*. Cambridge: Cambridge University Press, 1996.

Harris, Stephen L. *Understanding the Bible*. 4th ed. Mountain View, Calif.: Mayfield, 1997.

Mahmud, S. F. *A Short History of Islam*. Oxford: Oxford University Press, 1988.

Milton, Anthony. *Catholic and Reformed: The Roman and Protestant Churches in English Thought 1600–1640*. Cambridge: Cambridge University Press, 1995.

Milward, Peter. *Shakespeare's Religious Background*. Bloomington: Indiana University Press, 1973.

Porter, H. C. *Puritanism in Tudor England*. London: Macmillan, 1970.

Porterfield, Amanda. *Female Piety in Puritan New England*. Oxford: Oxford University Press, 1992.

Prestwich, Menna, ed. *International Calvinism 1541–1715*. Oxford: Clarendon, 1985.

Shaheen, Naseeb. *Biblical References in Shakespeare's Comedies*. Newark: University of Delaware Press, 1993.

WEB SITES

http://etext.lib.virginia.edu/etcbin/toccer-

http://www.understanding-islam.com/related/text.asp?type=question&qid=808

new2?id=RsvGene.sgm&images=images/modeng...

http://www.religioustolerance.org/jud_desc.htm

http://britannia.com/history/monarchs/mon41.html

http://www.williamtyndale.com/Opathway.htm

http://www.johnwycliffe.org/background/index.html

http://icg.harvard.edu/~chaucer/special/varia/lollards/lollards.html

http://www.cin.org/jesuit.html

http://www.lsma.edu/bmcbride/History/Reformation/luthadrs.htm

http://www.smartlink.net/~douglas/calvin/bk1ch01.html

http://www.galileolibrary.com/history/history_020601/history_page121.htm

8

THE ELIZABETHAN SOCIAL ORDER

(I may call him my master, look you, for I keep his house; and I wash, wring, brew,
bake, scour, dress meat and drink, make the beds, and do all myself) —
(*The Merry Wives of Windsor,* I.iv.94–97)

Everyday life in the sixteenth century reflected medieval and modern characteristics, as England's boundaries were shaped and redefined. Minorities
were identified and placed within a social hierarchy as English society came to
terms with new and existing cultural differences. Values and mores gradually
shifted to accommodate revision and expansion.

Living in London for most of his theater years, William Shakespeare represented entrepreneurship as someone who had left family and home in the Midlands to seek—and find—a fortune in urban drama. He must have had countless opportunities to observe the many changes sweeping over English shores from Europe and beyond. Periodically Shakespeare visited Stratford, where life carried on much as it had for hundreds of years. After traveling between these two lifestyles for perhaps 20 years, Shakespeare returned to Stratford after retiring from the theater.

While issues like land enclosure and property disputes claimed Shakespeare's attention, he must also have enjoyed Stratford's quiet life beyond London's dirt and clamor. Many of his plays describe homely scenes with middle-class characters and simple lifestyles. Fathers share wisdom with children venturing into the world, masters scold servants for idleness or foolery, and teenagers rebel against parents in stories that made Shakespeare famous. Though rural families provided many of their own household needs, a brisk economy began to build throughout England.

THE FARMLANDS

Then did the sun on dunghill shine. (The Merry Wives of Windsor, I.iii.63)

By 1600 farms were managed by what was left of the medieval feudal system in which the lord (not necessarily a noble) ran his farm by administering justice and providing work to locals who came under his protection. Villages composed of workmen and their families sprang up near these farms and offered amenities like bakeries, breweries, blacksmiths, schools, and churches. When the landowner lived away, an agent monitored operations and collected rents.

Workers planted fields in strips of half an acre, separated by grassy lengths known as balks, allowing people to travel across fields without pushing through the grain. An average holding might be 18 acres of farmable land.

Many villages held pastureland for grazing in common until the issue of enclosure stirred controversy, forcing landowners to consolidate land holdings and fence off individual properties. England was largely an agrarian country, providing farm products to tenant farmers and city dwellers.

HOUSEHOLDS

*Neither press, coffer, chest, trunk, well, vault, but he hath an abstract for
the remembrance of such places. (The Merry Wives of Windsor, IV.ii.52–53)*

Homes were designed to meet a family's basic living needs, with minimal dependence on external sources. Living conditions were what most of us consider plain. Middle-class household goods included mattresses and sometimes pillows, pewter rather than wooden eating utensils, and occasional rugs on wooden floors, though a structure's lower levels were covered with rushes or straw that had to be freshened. Later, rush mats replaced loose rushes. Sometimes housewives strewed herbs to absorb odors.

Furniture included wooden cupboards, tables, and seats. Homes boasted wooden chairs, not very comfortable but often ornate. Furniture design from the early 1500s through the mid-1600s was termed the Age of Oak in Tudor or Jacobean style. Henry VIII used oak or pine furnishings as did the Catholic churches of his day, some with painted decoration. Household pieces became larger and more elaborate, often featuring the Tudor rose emblem. The Jacobean style incorporated "Puritan" designs, smaller with detailed ornamentation. Padding was added to chairs.

Stools provided seats, while chests offered storage. Tapestries and embroidered hangings brightened wall space and restricted drafts of damp air. Windows were diamond-paned while ceilings often had ornamental plaster. Heating and cooling depended on the large central fireplace that also was used for cooking.

Decorations took the form of tapestries, glassware, pictures, and books. Eating utensils consisted of knives, spoons, metal or glass mugs, and wooden or clay plates. Country dwellers raised much of their own food; city residents bought theirs from vendors or street markets. Bread was a daily staple. The household ate in the great hall, or simply "hall." In smaller homes the kitchen doubled as a dining area. Male servants slept there at night on palettes, or bedrolls. Privacy was scarce; there were no bathrooms as we know them today. Rather, chamber pots were placed discreetly behind screens, but more often tucked under beds or left in corners. People bathed from bowls or pots of water, or infrequently, wooden bathtubs.

Glass windows became popular, some with lead panes. Shutters covered windows for insulation and protection. Enclosed stoves replaced an open hearth. Since bedrooms opened into each other, privacy was attempted by hanging a curtain about the bed. Side rooms provided closet space for activities like reading or sewing. Wainscoting was popular. Paneling divided the boards into frames, sometimes adorned with sketches or artistic designs.

Aristocratic homes included two or three stories enclosing one or more courtyards. A grand hall stood at the home's center, with a large central staircase replacing the narrow circular steps of previous centuries. Upstairs, a long gallery allowed exercise in bad weather while a library provided indoor recreation.

Gardens included herbs, fruits, vegetables, and flowers, often organized in geometric patterns. Housewives and gardeners tended roses, lilies, and cabbages, along with flowers like carnations, marigolds, or pansies. Cooking herbs included basil, chamomile, marjoram, and hops. Others, including violets, lavender, and rose petals, served as room deodorants.

Foods and Beverages

> . . . *we have a hot venison pasty to dinner.* (*The Merry Wives of Windsor,* I.i.195)

While Italians ate large quantities of fruit, the English consumed more meat. Menus featured dark bread, beef, ale, mutton, lamb, pork, bacon, fowls, and eggs. Before 1500 the English drank ale rather than beer. When the preservative nature of hops was discovered, people brewed beer. Stratford was one of many malting or brewing towns.

Nobles ate well. First and second courses offered meats such as boiled beef, roast veal, rabbits, and pigeon pie. Later courses included lamb, kid, chicken, pork, and tarts. Also served were fresh salmon, venison, white herrings, and green pottage, with butter and salt for seasoning. Salads of lettuce with oil and sugar were popular. In summer, cooks served fruits like strawberries, oranges, and cherries.

Dulcets, or sweets, included jellies, marmalade, Florentine (a custard or sweet pie), and gingerbread. A popular dish found all over England was frumenty, hulled wheat boiled in milk and seasoned with sugar. Numble pie from deer entrails or game birds was another delicacy.

By 1580 the lucrative spice trade with Asia introduced exotic flavorings, including pepper, cloves, mace, sugar, cinnamon, ginger, nutmeg, and liquorice. Several of Shakespeare's plays reference such treats.

The queen's household servants were light eaters, consuming items like larks, partridges, and pheasants, and sweets such as custard, fritter, tarts, and dulcets.

Friday was a fish day, a Catholic legacy. By 1595, Wednesday was made another fish day, probably to help the Navy and to preserve cattle.

In Shakespeare's plays the alehouse leveled distinctions between social classes to provide an earthy common ground where men would meet to share pastimes like drinking, dicing, and wenching. Usually owned, tended, and frequented by lower-class figures like Shakespeare's Mistress Quickly Pistol, and Doll Tearsheet as well as royalty like Prince Hal, the alehouse is woven into the fabric of Shakespeare's plays to present a slice of life from the entertainment district. Here duty was exchanged for fun and shared with those who could not be acknowledged beyond the establishment's doors.

SOCIAL RANKS

> *. . . there dwells one Mistress Quickly, which is in the manner of his nurse—*
> *or his dry nurse—or his cook—or his laundry—*
> *his washer and his wringer.* (The Merry Wives of Windsor, I.ii.2–5)

Although England retained a largely feudal agricultural system, complex social strata emerged during the sixteenth and seventeenth centuries in urban areas.

The chain of being dictated that the monarchy govern all levels of society. Next were the nobles, including peers like knights, who usually were granted the title following military or economic service. Other gentry included esquires, gentlemen, landholders, and the wealthy. Gentry could govern at the local level.

Gentleman landowners often rented land for hire. Yeomen farmed their own land. Townsmen of similar rank were known as burgesses and held important local positions as members of the rising middle class.

Tenants who worked other people's lands were called husbandmen. Next were craftspersons like tailors and carpenters whose occupations were regulated by the guilds and apprenticeships. Boys entered a trade at 14, remaining in the master's household for seven years until they mastered a skill and could support themselves.

The lowest level of society included the poor, farmhands or day laborers, and vagabonds. Everyone was expected to work; those who didn't were punished by whipping or imprisonment.

TITLES AND RANKS

> *. . . there is no sin but to be rich.* (King John, II.i.594)

Monarchs ruled England. Although the monarchy maintained absolute rule, Parliament and church leaders, especially the archbishop, helped to guide the ruler. Monarchial authority was viewed as the "divine right of kings," instituted by Holy Scripture. A ruler held rank just below God and was viewed as God's weapon to curse or scepter to bless. Documents were signed with Christian names followed by "R" for the Latin "Rex," meaning "king," or "Regina" for "queen." Surnames were not used much before the fourteenth century.

While kings ruled individually, under certain conditions several queens might exist contemporaneously:

- The king's wife
- The king's widow
- The king's mother
- The queen dowager (like a widow, especially with a successor on the throne)
- The queen mother (if her son became monarch)

Conflicts arose when rulers left no male or legitimate heirs or left infant heirs. In such cases ambitious nobles could seize control.

Peerages

> *The Earl of Douglas is discomfited.* (King Henry IV—Part One, I.i.67)

William Harrison, clergyman and topographer, defines ranks and titles in his *Description of England,* which was published during the 1570s and 1580s as part of Raphael Holinshed's *Chronicles of England, Scotland, and Ireland.*

A "peer" held one of the five highest titles and might sit in the House of Lords. A "nobleman" served as a model of chivalrous behavior. An "aristocrat" was a more general term than "peer" and often referred to a privileged person born into a high social status. Peers could not be arrested except for treason, felony, or breaking the peace—terms which applied to U.S. Congress members until 1995.

The term "gentleman" included nobles who were addressed in specific ways:

- The king was saluted as "Your majesty."
- Dukes were greeted as "Your grace."

- Marquises were called "Lord" plus the name of the specific title in lieu of a family name.
- Earls, also called "Lord," owned extensive lands and formed connections with other earls. They sometimes banded to challenge a ruler's authority.
- Viscounts were termed "Lord so-and-so."
- Barons used the "Lord" designation. Though barons once held great power, by Shakespeare's time they generally were peers.
- The knights were honorary titles earned by special positions (like Lord Mayor) but also awarded for military skills. They were addressed as "Sir" followed by their Christian name, not the family name. For example, Walter Raleigh, when knighted, was addressed as "Sir Walter."
- A Knight of the Shire was a member of the House of Commons. He represented a particular shire, which was a territorial division such as Derbyshire or Lancashire (much like the states in America).

The Knights Templar and Knights Hospitalers were crusader remnants. Knights were not noble and they varied in rank. They might hold seats by election or by appointment in the House of Commons. An unspecified knight was a "Knight Bachelor." A "Knight Banneret" performed military service before the monarch on the battlefield. A "Knight of the Garter" was the highest rank. By 1560 there were only about six hundred knights in England.

- Esquires originally were knights' attendants. Later they held a coat of arms and came from good families.
- Gentlemen were addressed as "Mister" which was a title of rank. Their wives were known as "Mistress."
- Citizens or burgesses were tradesmen with privileges, such as serving on councils or as members of guilds, classifications which set occupational standards and divided the districts.
- Yeomen, sometimes called "husbandmen," farmed as overseers or employers.
- The artificers or laborers had no voice or authority. They served; they did not rule. They used "Mister" with surnames. Higher-level yeomen were addressed as "Goodman" or "Goodwife." "Sir" was a term of respect, while "sirrah" showed contempt.

Women took titles from husbands and fathers, and often were addressed as "Lady so-and-so" if they married men at or above the level of knight.

Children called their parents "Sir" and "Madam," while a child born to nobility addressed parents as "my lady mother" and "the lord my father."

WOMEN

Song

> *Who is Silvia? what is she,*
> *That all our swains commend her?*
> *Holy, fair, and wise is she;*

The heaven such grace did lend her,
That she might admired be. (*Two Gentlemen of Verona,* IV.ii.39–43)

Women generally were identified in roles as daughters, wives, and mothers with surnames deriving then as now from fathers or husbands. Women couldn't testify in court against their husbands. They could not vote on public issues or hold office, except for the monarch, as in Elizabeth's case.

Sixteenth-Century Views

Elizabethan views of women appeared in many print sources, including the Bible and popular writings like *The Nobilitie and Excellencie of Womankynde* (London, 1542) and an English translation of Agrippa of Nettesheim's defense of women, which emphasized the right of common property and opposed patriarchal control. Claude de Taillmeont's *Discours de Champs faez a l'honneur . . . des dames* (Lyons, 1551) criticized men for using women as objects of marital commerce.

Other male writers presented negative opinions of women, including Joseph Swetnam's *The Arraignment of Lewde Idle Froward and Inconstant Women* (London, 1615). Hamlet's invective against women reflects such a view:

> I have heard of your paintings, well enough.
> God hath given you one face, and you make yourselves
> another. You jig and amble, and you [lisp,] you nickname
> God's creatures and make your wantonness
> [your] ignorance. (III.i.142–146)

Society considered it immoral and sometimes unlawful for women to wear men's clothing or behave in a masculine manner, although dramatists used the cross-dressing convention with great success in female roles like Shakespeare's Viola in *Twelfth Night* and Jessica in *The Merchant of Venice*. Girls did not customarily receive the same opportunities for education as their brothers. Employment outside the home was uncommon for women in the professions such as law or business, but sometimes women managed farm products or harvests, especially if they were widowed or remained in their father's households.

Women and Literature

Some women did find ways of entering the trades and exploring the arts. Anne Vaughan Lock (ca. 1534–ca. 90) published translations of John Calvin's sermons and shared exile in Geneva with other reformers during Queen Mary's reign. Elizabeth Weston (1581–1612), daughter of alchemist Edward Kelley, lived a good part of her life in Bohemia. She published *Poemata* (1602) and a revision of that work, *Parthenicon* (ca. 1607–10).

Some women received a formal education and used it to good advantage. Joanna Fitzalan Lumley (1537–1616) was the first English person to translate a Greek drama, *The Tragedy of Euripides,* though it remained unpublished until 1909.

Mary (Sidney) Herbert (1561–1621), countess of Pembroke, was the sister of Sir Philip Sidney and Sir Robert Sidney, both poets. She came to court in 1575, married Henry Herbert, the second earl of Pembroke, in 1577, and had four children. She patronized the arts and was praised by male contemporaries Edmund Spenser and Michael Drayton. Upon her death she was buried in Salisbury Cathedral. Her works include an edition of Philip Sidney's *Arcadia* and she completed his verse translation of the psalms, contributing 107 of 150. She prepared a translation of Garnier's tragedy *Antoine* (1590) and Duplessis-Mornay's *Discours de la vie et de la mort* in 1592. She influenced later poets like George Herbert and John Donne and became involved with Protestant politics.

The first Englishwoman to write a tragic drama was Lady Elizabeth Cary who wrote *The Tragedy of Mariam* between 1602 and 1604, although it was not published until 1613. A translator, she had studied Latin, Spanish, French, and Hebrew and retained Catholic tendencies, which later alienated husband Henry Carey.

Aemilia Lanyer (1569–1645) was the daughter of Baptista Bassano, Queen Elizabeth's court musician, who came from Venice and may have been a converted Jew. Aemilia became the mistress of Lord Hunsdon and in 1592, at age 23, married her cousin by marriage, Alphonse Lanyer, also a court musician. He was given a monopoly for weighing straw and hay in London and died in 1613. In 1611 Aemilia published *Salve Deus Rex Judaeorum* (Hail God King of the Jews) in which she proposes a feminist perspective of Christianity:

> I have written this small volume . . . for the general use of all virtuous Ladies and Gentlewomen of this kingdom; . . . And this have I done, to make known to the world, that all women deserve not to be blamed though some forgetting they are women themselves, and in danger to be condemned by the words of their own mouths, fall into so great an error, as to speak unadvisedly against the rest of their sex . . . and therefore could wish . . . they would refer such points of folly, to be practiced by evil disposed men, who forgetting they were born of women, nourished of women, and if it were not by the means of women, they would be quite extinguished out of the world, . . . As also in respect it pleased our Lord and Savior Jesus Christ, without the assistance of man, . . . to be begotten by a woman, borne of a woman, nourished of a woman, obedient to a woman; and that he healed women, pardoned women, comforted women: . . . after his resurrection, appeared first to a woman, sent a woman to declare his most glorious resurrection to the rest of his Disciples. . . .   (http://www.pinn.net/~sunshine/march99/lanyer2.html)

When her husband died, Aemilia supported herself by teaching in a London suburb.

Elizabeth Hoby (née Cooke) (1540–1609), corresponded with Queen Elizabeth and entertained the queen at Bisham in 1592. Her first husband, Sir Thomas Hoby, translated Castiglione's *Courtier* and died as an ambassador to France. With her second husband came the title "Lady Russell." She wrote mostly epitaphs, like this one:

An epicedium by ELIZABETH HOBY, their mother, on the death of her two daughters ELIZABETH and ANNE

> ELIZABETH lies here (alas for my heart), thus fated:
> You lie here, scarcely mature, a tender virgin
> When you lived, you were a daughter dear to her mother
> Now, live dear to God and your [dead] father.
> Your death was cruel, but there was one still crueler:
> The one which cut down your younger sister ANNA with you.
> ANNA, you were the glory of your father and mother; after your
>   Sister's end
> And after your mother's grief, here you lie, golden virgin!
> There was one mother, one father, one death, for the pair
> And this one stone hides both their bodies.
> Thus I, their mother, wanted to unite them in a single tomb,
> Weeping, whom I once carried in the same happy womb
>
> These two noble and most hopeful sisters
> In the same Year, i.e. 1570
> In the same Month, i.e. February
> Only a few days apart,
> Slept in the Lord.
>
> *(Stevenson and Davidson 2001, 44–45; 47)*

Women like these made quiet but valuable contributions to the arts.

MARRIAGE AND FAMILY

Fathers, from hence trust not your daughters' minds. (Othello, I.i.170)

The English viewed marriage as a pillar of the social structure. Families perpetuated genetic lines, protected individuals, and contributed new citizens, and preserved reputations, honor, and morality. Couples who engaged in premarital sex often did so with plans to marry. Those lacking a dowry or with limited incomes sometimes cohabited before the wedding.

Sons received legacies and heritages, though daughters sometimes did as well. Often a daughter's portion would be entailed on the nearest male relative. A girl's share usually was paid as a dowry upon her marriage. Sometimes a will stipulated the daughter could maintain control of her dowry through marriage and pass the residue on to her daughters. In other cases a husband took control of the wife's dowry. If a woman didn't marry, she might live with her brother's family and he would get control or she might enter a religious order and take her dowry there.

Wealthy or powerful persons could divorce. The median age for middle-class marriage was about 24 for girls and 27 for boys. Often the couple had grown up together and knew each other well; many married for love, though parents held authority to make practical marriages for their children. Dowries for women and jointures for men were contractual conditions of the binding agreement.

Engagements and Weddings

> *I got possession of Julietta's bed:*
> *You know the lady; she is fast my wife,*
> *Save that we do the denunciation lack*
> *Of outward order. This we came not to,*
> *Only for propagation of a dow'r.*
> (*Measure for Measure*, I.ii.146–150)

Engagements or betrothals were binding, so couples taking vows before witnesses were considered legitimately espoused and could call each other "husband" and "wife," though all expected a church ceremony to follow. There were a number of pregnant brides but fewer illegitimate children during this era.

Then as now, couples exchanged rings and kisses following pledges of love and faithfulness, and afterwards they shared a "bowl of wine." Sunday was a popular marrying day. Flowers, music, and dancing were common, with the bride expected to dance with every wedding guest. Many brides wore knives at their girdles, and veils were simpler than today's versions. Honeymoons were virtually unknown.

Children's games, by Pieter the Elder Bruegel (b. 1525–1569), "Children's Games," 1560. Oil on oakwood, 118 × 161 cm. Kunsthistorisches Museum, Vienna, Austria. © Copyright Erich Lessing/Art Resource, NY.

The bridal bed would be decked with flowers and should be blessed. Friends and family might accompany the couple to the bedchamber and visit for a time. The next morning the couple would be serenaded. Sometimes wedding sheets were saved as proof of the bride's purity in case of later claims of infidelity.

Child Marriage

Child marriage was not rare and when it occurred, it could be nullified. Records show that Sir Thomas Gerard, age 12, was forced to marry Alice Worsley, 17, but he refused to live with her. William Poole, age 11, was married to Elizabeth Tilston, age 8. John Bridge, 11, married Elizabeth Ramsbotham, 13, to seal a bargain between his grandfather and her father, who paid a sum to buy them a piece of land.

John Somerford, age three, was wed to Jane Brereton, age two; both were carried to their wedding. Families arranged such unions to link noble families or rich estates.

Pregnancy

The Queen your mother rounds apace. (The Winter's Tale, II.i.16)

Marriage and childbirth were considered the highest calling for most women. Yet many died in childbirth due to ignorance and poor hygiene. Bathing was viewed as unhealthy because it could relax the womb and cause miscarriage.

Many believed the moon could affect gender. Windows and doors were kept closed to bar evil spirits during the birth, and the fire was stoked to give additional heat. Women sometimes had a dozen children or more, depending on their health and the longevity of their marriages. Birth control was primitive at best, consisting largely of abstinence or withdrawal before ejaculation.

Infertility resulting from genetic disorders, poor hygiene, or inadequate medical care was not uncommon, as evidenced in Henry the Eighth's marital woes.

Church courts licensed the midwives upon presentation of six testimonials and a sworn oath that included, among other things, a promise not to smother unwanted babies, not to use witchcraft, and to ensure Anglican baptism (Morrill 1996, 100).

Babies were swaddled, or wrapped tightly, to keep their limbs from flailing and to help them retain warmth and strength. Diapers were called "clouts" and often were made of worn clothing or rags. Most mothers breast-fed their children, though some upper class women chose a "wet nurse" for the baby. Breast-feeding helped prevent ovulation, which could delay pregnancy, a benefit appreciated by many new mothers.

Extramarital Relationships

She is persuaded I will marry her, out of her own love and flattery, not out of my promise. (Othello, IV.i.127–129)

Prostitutes of both sexes worked the streets and taverns or inns. Establishments called brothels (in London known as the "stews") offered sex along with other entertainments like cards or ale. Many made good profits. A prostitute, also termed a meretrix or harlot, might work as an individual, with or without a male or female manager. Or she might work as part of a small group, usually with a manager who arranged accommodations and fees.

Midwives were called in at the moment of birth so that unmarried women might be compelled to name fathers of illicit offspring at the height of labor pains. The Quarter-Session records show that efforts were made to locate illegitimate fathers, as the parishes could not afford to support many such children:

> Jane Shepherd of Elford, found in the cow-house of Alice Smith, widow, made known to Isabel Baillie, midwife, that John Draper, a fiddler, born deaf and dumb, was the father of her child. (Rowse 1971, 156)

Other women present at the birth witnessed the event with their names. In another record, punishment is levied against the unmarried parents:

> The father is to pay 10d weekly [about a day's wage] towards its maintenance for two years, and then to take charge of the child, receiving 1d weekly from the said Alice, until it shall be able to get its own living. Further, the said John Sabin shall sit by the heels [in the stocks] the next Sunday for the space of three hours, immediately after 1 o'clock in the afternoon, if found in Walsall, or else the next Sunday after his coming there. The like for Alice after her churching [the post-childbirth purification rite]. (Rowse 1971, 156–57)

Independent women—those who never married or who lost or abandoned their husbands—sometimes were protected in an institution created for such purposes. Hospitals for the syphilitic or elderly, homes for young girls in danger of entering prostitution, and residences for repentant harlots became available. Frequently, women who participated in extramarital sexual activity were viewed as witches and came to be associated with magic and witchcraft; when caught, they were punished accordingly.

There also were many happy marriages at this time. Most folks made do with their spouses, since the canon law of the English Church allowed divorce only for adultery, though separation was tolerated in cases of abandonment or abuse.

A. L. Rowse claims it was believed that a man who married a woman in her shift, or smock, was not liable for her debts, as indicated in this church register of 1547:

> Here was wedded early in the morning Thomas Munslow, smith, and Alice Nycols, which wedded to him in her smock and bareheaded.
> (Rowse 1971, 157)

Extramarital sex was considered immoral, and in many cases, illegal, although the aristocracy often got away with it. Queen Elizabeth, however, jealously guarded her ladies-in-waiting and court members and punished indiscretions.

MINORITIES

> *You do remember this stain upon her?* (*Cymbeline*, II.iv.138–139)

Minority groups drew increased attention in Elizabethan England as nationalism evolved, promoting a distinctive English culture with clear boundaries. Negroes, Jews, Gypsies, Catholics, Protestants, Moslems, homosexuals, and the disabled drew suspicion and often discrimination from authorities who sought to protect national interests by imposing special uses for, or limitations on, nonmajority groups of people.

Little People

> *I had rather, forsooth, go before you like a man than follow him like a dwarf.*
> (*The Merry Wives of Windsor*, III.ii.5–6)

Dwarves were of special interest to royalty and were retained in numbers by monarchs throughout Europe during the Renaissance.

In the 1560s and 1570s one of Elizabeth's attendants was a dwarf called Ippolita the Tartarian, whom Elizabeth referred to as "our dearly beloved woman." More than a showpiece and less than a companion, Ippolita reflected the Queen's interest in diverse peoples and lands. In 1574 the Queen added a Negro attendant who wore a gaskin coat of white taffeta with gold tinsel and trousers. In the 1580s Ippolita was succeeded by Thomasina, a richly dressed dwarf, and later an Italian jester named Monarcho, who drew notice in his red grogram chamlet and hat of blue taffeta.

Period writing references dwarves as not holding enviable social positions. Sometimes Shakespeare's use of the term implies a person who is not particularly tall. In *A Midsummer Night's Dream*, for example, one of the female leads—Hermia—apparently is of slight build and short stature. When repudiated by a lover who is under the spell of a misguided love potion, she exclaims to her rival,

> And are you grown so high in his esteem,
> Because I am so dwarfish and so low?

> *(III.ii.294–295)*

Potion-blinded Lysander sends her away with the taunt

> Get you gone, you dwarf;
> You minimus, of hind'ring knot-grass made.

> *(III.ii.327–328)*

Portrait of a dwarf included in royal progress. Juan van der Hamen y Leon (1596–1631), Portrait of a dwarf, possibly "Bartolo" or "Bartolillo," a dwarf who was included in the royal progress during the Prince of Wales' visit to El Escorial in 1632. 122 × 87 cm. Location: Museo del Prado, Madrid, Spain. Erich Lessing/Art Resource, NY.

Like other countries of this period, England gradually came to terms with exposure to diverse peoples who did not fit the mainstream social pattern.

People with Disabilities

> *He is as disproportion'd in his manners*
> *As in his shape.* (*The Tempest,* V.i.291–292)

Disabled people often lived normal lives and learned to cope with physical challenges. Shakespeare's 1590s play about Richard III, born with a deformed back, emphasized the king's evil character. The implication was that Richard's twisted body reflected his distorted inward character.

Robert Cecil (1563–1612), first earl of Salisbury, was England's Secretary of State (1558–1572), and then Lord Treasurer (1572–1598). Born with a hunched back, he proved an able administrator under both Tudor and Jacobean reigns. His later decline from power fed speculation that a crooked back reflected crooked policies.

Disabled persons sometimes were subject to unusual rulings. For example, a deaf-mute man required the bishop's permission for a special marriage ceremony in 1576:

> The said Thomas [Tilsey] for the expressing of his mind instead of words, of his own accord used these signs. First, he embraced her [Ursula Russell] with his arms and took her by the hand, put a ring upon her finger, laid his hand upon his heart and then upon her heart, and held up his hands toward heaven. And to show his continuance to dwell with her to his life's end, he did it by closing of his eyes with his hands and digging out of the earth with his foot, and pulling as though he would ring a bell, with divers other signs. (Rowse 1971, 158)

In the sixteenth century vagrancy and poor laws grew increasingly stern in enforcing punishments against "masterless men" who would not work. In 1572 the government passed a vagabond act that insisted "common players" and "jugglers" be whipped back to their parish of origin unless licensed by two justices of the peace or employed by a noble household. Anyone able to work was expected to hold a job.

Reconstructive surgery, treatment, prostheses, therapy, and counseling did not exist for disabled persons. People were expected to do the best they could, with or without their family's help. Those with deformed or missing limbs might travel with a company of players to earn money by showing their unusual features or by begging assistance.

At the close of *A Midsummer Night's Dream* Oberon's final song celebrating the couples' nuptials includes a blessing that precludes "blots of Nature's hand":

> Never mole, hare-lip, nor scar,
> Nor mark prodigious, such as are
> Despised in nativity,
> Shall upon their children be.
>
> *(V.i.411–414)*

Women and men accused of witchcraft could be convicted on the basis of a mole, birthmark, or other disfigurement that some interpreted to be the mark of the devil.

Negroes

You bloody Negroes, ripping up the womb of your dear mother England, blush for shame. (*King John*, V.ii.152–153)

Throughout history the concept of blackness has been interpreted as the opposite of enlightenment and goodness. Some cultures viewed darkness as suggestive of evil or ignorance. People of "black" or dark complexions were viewed suspiciously as "the other" against whom northern Europeans refined their self-image. Those of African, Indian, and Arab descent were considered inferior or even dangerous. Society termed "outsider" groups such as Jews, Moors, and even the Irish as "black." Yet Moors or African figures embody some positive features in plays like Shakespeare's *Othello*. Though tragic and even murderous, the title character models positive qualities like courage and leadership.

Slavery

Had you rather Caesar were living, and die all slaves, than that Caesar were dead, to live all freeman? (*Julius Caesar,* III.ii.22–24)

When the Portuguese tried to dominate global trade, they sold captured African slaves at the Italian markets of Venice, Pisa, and Genoa and supplied slaves to the West Indies. Other captives, such as Turks and Tartars, likewise became merchandise at these markets until the Turks gained control of the slave trade.

The first Africans sold as slaves were purchased in Lisbon in 1510. By 1555, John Lok brought five Africans to Britain from West Africa, not as slaves, but to learn English and to help Africa.

In 1562 Sir John Hawkins (1532–95) obtained 300 African slaves by piracy from Guinea whom he sold to Spaniards in the West Indies. At this point England actively entered the slave trade. In 1585 the Barbary Company was founded. In 1618, the West Africa Company opened for trade in Guinea and Benin. Elizabeth tacitly supported slave-based enterprises by funding private and commercial ventures.

By 1618, London's Company of Adventurers was trading in Africa and had built the first English factory. A year later, 20 slaves landed in Jamestown in August 1619.

Written narratives about Africa began to appear in the late sixteenth century. In 1597 Abraham Hartwell's *A Reporte of the Kingdome of Congo* appeared in print. In 1600 John Pory published an English translation of Johannes Leo Africanus' *A Geographical Historie of Africa,* a definitive travel guide for the next three centuries.

Africans in England

In her book *Things of Darkness* (1995), Kim Hall underscores the limited role of blacks in Elizabethan culture. Like exotic pets and imported luxuries, Africans functioned as marginalized staples in works of art, serving as jewelry adornments and servants in portraits of famous figures. Their chiaroscuro posture reflects white supremacy.

Literary references to Africa or the Orient represented metaphors of religious and foreign difference as evidenced in poems like *A Fair Nymph Scorning a Black Boy Courting Her* by John Cleveland, Edward Herbert's *Sonnet of Black Beauty,* and Eldred Revett's *One Enamour'd on a Black-moor.* Some women in Shakespeare's sonnets reveal dark attributes, with darkness suggesting an unruly, oversexed nature evidenced in women like Penelope Rich who mothered illegitimate children, and Frances Howard, who poisoned her husband.

Moors

> *O, tell me, did you see Aaron the Moor?* (*Titus Andronicus,* IV.ii.52)

A Moor is a Moslem of mixed Arab and Berber bloodlines living in northwest Africa. Expelled by Spain in 1492, Moors were viewed with suspicion throughout Europe. Nearly a century later Elizabeth expelled the Moors from England in 1596 and 1601, reflecting popular fear of their evil influence. While some Moors were dark-skinned, others were tawny or even light, which made it difficult for mainstream culture to sort them from its midst.

Islam was viewed as a symbol of sexual and moral depravity, especially in the wake of the Ottoman advance into Europe. Travelers' tales of the Turkish court and stories of cruelty and plunder made their way into English society, leading Elizabeth to take rigid measures to prevent Moorish uprisings or plots.

Jews

> *I am a Jew. Hath not a Jew eyes? Hath not a Jew hands, organs, dimensions, senses, affections, passions; fed with the same food, hurt with the same weapons, subject to the same diseases, heal'd by the same means, warm'd and cool'd by the same winter and summer, as a Christian is? If you prick us, do we not bleed? If you tickle us, do we not laugh? If you poison us, do we not die? And if you wrong us, shall we not revenge? If we are like you in the rest, we will resemble you in that.* (*The Merchant of Venice,*
> III.i.58–68)

When Jews were banned from England in 1290, leaving only a remnant in London, they were unable to build a unified identity that would allow them to merge completely with the dominant culture or to separate successfully as a minority cluster.

While few medieval Jews willingly converted to Christianity, early modern Jews assimilated more easily. But with assimilation, the Jews became obvious targets for segregation and discrimination. Reasons included condemnation of Jews who had rejected Christ, the close-knit nature of Jewish families and communities, and envy of successful business practices, often in banking and money lending. Usury at low interest rates was legal, but many Christians were suspicious of Jewish financial success and the funding of foreign ventures.

Popular literature questioned the nature of Jewish people. Dramas like Christopher Marlowe's *The Jew of Malta* in 1589 and Shakespeare's *The Merchant of Venice,* along with Thomas Nashe's *The Unfortunate Traveler* feature Jews as victims of society. Barabbas in Marlowe's work is boiled alive for poisoning a nunnery. It is unclear whether the play satirizes Christian society for hypocrisy or reflects Marlowe's anti-Semitism. Shakespeare's Shylock is stripped of his fortune and forced to accept Christianity. Nashe's Zadoch is impaled and roasted alive.

Plays like these may have drawn audiences partly because of the discovery of an alleged plot by Queen Elizabeth's physician, Rodrigo Lopez, to poison her. During his torture and execution it was learned that Lopez was a Marrano, or Jew of Iberian descent. Marranos often made public conversions to Christianity but maintained a private Jewish identity, much like closet Catholics of the late 1500s. It wasn't until 1649 under Oliver Cromwell that Jews were legally permitted to settle in England. Translations of the old Testament scriptures into English and interest in mystic studies like the cabala helped to promote greater understanding and tolerance of Jews during this period.

Gypsies

> . . . *Like a right gipsy, hath at fast and loose*
> *Beguil'd me to the very heart of loss.* (Antony and Cleopatra, IV.xii.28)

Because Gypsies wrote or kept few records, what we know of them from the sixteenth century is largely based on European accounts. Scholars link the Gypsy people to origins in India, in part because their language—Romany or Romani—appears to be a Hindu variant. Legends abound about their migration through Asia, the Middle East, and finally Europe. A common story in several cultures is that their people fell away from Christian worship, and after repenting, were sentenced to wander the earth for a time for their sin, as indicated in this 1550 account from Sebastian Munster in his *Cosmographia universalis:*

> [They] had formerly abandoned for some years the Christian religion and turned to the error of the pagans and that after their repentance, a penance had been imposed upon them that, for as many years, some members of their families should wander about the world and expiate in exile the guilt of their sin. (Fraser 1995, 65)

Widely recognized as smiths, the Gypsies settled for brief periods in the countries they traveled. In some cases, their stay lasted just a few weeks. In other places they remained for years, quietly working in their own small communities. Having spent some time in Egypt, they came to be called "Gypsies," or inhabitants of "Little Egypt." Their dress was distinctive, with women and sometimes men wearing turbans, often supported with wicker, and draped with cloaklike garments that tied at one shoulder.

In the Peloponnesian peninsula Gypsies settled in a Venetian coastal community called Modon, as indicated in 1497 by Arnold von Harff of Cologne who noted about two hundred huts in an area called "Gype":

> This district was taken by the Turkish Emperor within the last sixty years, but some of the lords and counts would not serve under the Turkish Emperor and fled to our country, to Rome, to our Holy Father the Pope, seeking comfort and support from him. Wherefore he gave them letters of recommendation to the Roman Emperor and to all the princes of the Empire, that they should give them safe conduct and support, since they were driven out for the Christian faith. They showed these letters to all princes, but none gave them help. They perished in misery, leaving the letters to their servants and children, who to this day wander about these lands and claim to be from Little Egypt... Wherefore these vagabonds are knaves and spy out the land. (Fraser 1995, 54)

Johannes Cinganus, or John the Gypsy, was a military leader at Nauplion in 1444 and seems to have received certain privileges. But most European accounts were critical, as exemplified in this excerpt from Bernhard von Breydenbach in 1483, who claimed they were "nothing but traitors and thieves, who say they come from Egypt when they come to German lands" (Fraser 1995, 53).

Branded as Saracens, Tartars, or spies, Gypsies were condemned as fortunetellers and horse thieves. Another legend says that after serving penance, they returned to their homeland, so that remaining "Gypsies" actually were bands of robbers or vagrants.

In 1539, Francis I expelled Gypsies from France. But within five years he was referring to Antoine Moreul as the "well-loved captain of Little Egypt" and he allowed them free travel. As more European countries began to expel Gypsies, perhaps associating them with the growing Turkish threat, people traveled in smaller groups and increasingly lost their noble titles.

In England, a 1530 edict complained that the Gypsy people

> By Palmestre coulde telle Menne and Womens Fortunes and so many tymes by crafte and subtyltie had deceived the People of theyr Money and also had comytted many and haynous Felonyes and Robberies. . . . (Fraser 1995, 113)

After 1550, stringent laws were passed against vagrants with language that specifically included the Gypsies. In 1596 nearly 200 Yorkshire Gypsies were condemned to death, though only 9 who were foreign-born were actually executed (Fraser 1995, 133). Persecution of the Gypsies, like other minorities, persists into modern times.

SUMMARY

Elizabethan England came face to face with diversity at a time when "difference" was not valued. Those who deviated from the normative structure often paid a steep price. Personal freedom was rare and costly; anyone convicted of thriving beyond the pale of society might be subject to persecution, conviction, or even death. This was a time of expansion and a growing awareness of the outside world, which eventually offered enlightenment as much as treasure. The spiraling Elizabethan social order helped to create a unique system that introduced many new peoples and cultures to Western civilization and contributed to a growing tolerance for unknown nationalities and customs.

SOURCES

Beier, A. L., and Roger Finlay, eds. *London 1500–1700*. New York: Longman, 1986.

Chamblerin, E. R. *Everyday Life in Renaissance Times*. New York: Capricorn, 1965.

Fox, Levi. *The Shakespeare Handbook*. Boston: G. K. Hall, 1987.

Fraser, Angus. *The Gypsies*. 2d ed. Oxford: Blackwell, 1995.

Hall, Kim F. *Things of Darkness: Economies of Race and Gender in Early Modern England*. Ithaca, N.Y.: Cornell University Press, 1995.

"Life in Elizabethan England. Secara, Maggie Pierce." http://ren.dm.net/compendium/23.html

McBride, Kari Boyd. "Biography of Aemilia Lanyer." http://www.u.arizona.edu/ic/mcbride/lanyer/lanbio.htm

McMurtry, Jo. *Understanding Shakespeare's England*. Hamden Conn.: Archon, 1989.

Morrill, John. *The Oxford Illustrated History of Tudor and Stuart Britain*. Oxford: Oxford University Press, 1996.

Rowse, A. L. *The Elizabethan Renaissance*. London: Macmillan, 1971.

Shyllon, Folarin. *Black People in Britain 1555–1833*. London: Oxford University Press, 1977.

Stevenson, Jane, and Peter Davidson, eds. *Early Modern Women Poets*. Oxford: Oxford University Press, 2001.

Turner, James Grantham, ed. *Sexuality and Gender in Early Modern Europe*. Cambridge: Cambridge University Press, 1993.

QUESTIONS

1. What might have led to such an extensive array of peerage titles and positions in Elizabethan society?
2. What were some of the rights and privileges enjoyed by the aristocracy and denied other classes?
3. What are some reasons for the short life expectancy at this time?

4. Why were women barred from certain kinds of public positions?
5. Explain why child marriage was tolerated.
6. Why were Jews persecuted?
7. How were Blacks viewed in Elizabethan England?
8. Could someone practice a religious faith other than that of the Anglican Church?
9. How did single women get by in this patriarchal society?
10. How were people with disabilities treated? Why?

CRITICAL THINKING AND RESEARCH PROJECTS

1. Research the life of an English aristocrat and explain the stages of his or her training to hold a position of privilege.
2. Describe court life during Elizabeth's reign. How would influences there impact the life of a young person entering government service (much like today's Congressional page in the U.S.)?
3. Examine England's role in the development of the western world's slave culture.
4. Research a particular disability in Elizabethan England, explaining diagnosis and treatment, if any.
5. Investigate the stereotypes and myths associated with an "outsider" people group, such as the Jews, Moors, Gypsies, or others. Describe the public and private lifestyle of a member of this group.

FOR FURTHER READING

Alexander, Catherine M. S., and Stanley Wells, eds. *Shakespeare and Race.* Cambridge: Cambridge University Press, 2000.

Amussen, Susan. *An Ordered Society: Gender and Class in Early Modern England.* Oxford: Blackwell, 1988.

Barthelemy, Anthony Gerard. *Black Face, Maligned Race.* Baton Rouge and London: Louisiana State University Press, 1987.

Bennett, Judith, and Amy Froide, eds. *Single women in the European Past.* Philadelphia: University of Pennsylvania Press, 1998.

Chew, Samuel. *The Crescent and the Rose: Islam and England during the Renaissance.* New York: Oxford University Press, 1937.

Fryer, Peter. *Staying Power: The History of Black People in Britain.* London: Pluto, 1984.

Hannaford, Ivan. *Race: The History of an Idea in the West.* Baltimore, Md.: Johns Hopkins University Press, 1996.

Harris, Tim. *Popular Culture in England c. 1500–1850.* London: Macmillan, 1995.

Hendricks, Margo, and Patricia Parker, eds. *Women, "Race," and Writing in the Early Modern Period.* New York and London: Routledge, 1994.

Katz, David S. *The Jews in the History of England 1485–1850.* Oxford: Clarendon, 1994.

Orlin, Lena Cowen. *Elizabethan Households: An Anthology.* Washington, D.C.: Folger, 1995.

Porter, R. *London: A Social History*. London: Hamish Hamilton, 1994.

Ramdin, Ron. *Reimaging Britain: Five Years of Black and Asian History*. London: Pluto, 1999.

Rappaport, S. *Worlds Within Worlds: Structures of Life in Sixteenth Century London*. London: Cambridge University Press, 1989.

Said, Edward W. *Orientalism*. London: Routledge and Kegan Paul, 1978.

Sedgwick, Eve Kosofsky. *Between Men: English Literature and Male Homosexual Desire*. New York: Columbia University Press, 1985.

Shapiro, James. *Shakespeare and the Jews*. New York: Columbia University Press, 1996.

Singman, Jeffrey L. *Daily Life in Elizabethan England*. Westport, Conn.: Greenwood, 1995.

Tokson, Elliot H. *The Popular Image of the Black Man in English Drama 1550–1688*. Boston: G.K. Hall, 1982.

Weisner, Merry E. *Women and Gender in Early Modern Europe*. Cambridge: Cambridge University Press, 1993.

Yaffe, Martin D. *Shylock and the Jewish Question*. Baltimore, Md.: Johns Hopkins University Press, 1997.

WEB SITE

http://www.pinn.net/~sunshine/march99/lanyer2.html

Map of Europe c. 1570.

9

THE EUROPEAN EFFECT

For know, my lords, the states of Christendom,
Mov'd with remorse of these outrageous broils,
Have earnestly implor'd a general peace.
(*King Henry VI—Part One*, V.iv.96–98)

Under Queen Elizabeth, England nurtured relationships with European neighbors despite conflicts over issues like religion and trade. Elizabeth's diplomacy was tested in the strained relations between England and Spain and with the uncertainty of French and Scottish support. Many English travelers toured European cities, while England drew visitors from all over the Continent.

Moneychanger and his wife. Quentin Metsys (c. 1466–1530), "The Moneylender (Banker) and His Wife," 1514. Louvre, Paris, France. © Erich Lessing/Art Resource, NY.

Shakespeare's writing shows keen awareness of England's interest in European affairs. With over two hundred references to European cities and peoples in his drama, at least a third of the plays are based in ancient or modern European locales. Though creative artistry can "blur "geographical boundaries, Shakespeare's drama reflects laws and customs of distant regions, undoubtedly gleaned from travelers passing through London's entertainment district or from tales narrated by traveling troupe members like Will Kempe.

While it is unknown whether Shakespeare ever left England, it is certain he would have had contact with foreign visitors at the Globe and neighboring establishments. With court connections like Henry Wriothesley and the Lord Chamberlain's patronage, Shakespeare may have enjoyed close views of diplomatic life. A student of human nature, Shakespeare must have studied foreign relations and visitors' mannerisms, perhaps sketching in his mind's eye voice inflections, fashions, and beliefs that later would be instilled in his characters. Cultural distinctions in his plays mirror insight, humor, and tension, as seen, for example, in Portia's visiting suitors from far-flung regions in *The Merchant of Venice.*

Elizabethan theater reproduced continental figures that brought Europe to the general populace. The stage became a window to the world for patrons from all social classes. Places like Elsinore in *Hamlet,* Vienna in *Measure for Measure,* and Navarre in *Love's Labour's Lost* came to life on stage for those who could afford no other means of travel.

European Commerce

Commercial enterprises among European countries increased substantially at this time. Drama includes themes and scenes based on mercantilism and trade, such as Antonio's wealth-laden ships in Shakespeare's *The Merchant of Venice* and passing references to commerce in works like *The Comedy of Errors.*

Trading companies formed under Tudor and Jacobean rule. The Merchant Adventurers controlled trade with northwestern Europe, while the Muscovy Company created under Mary I fostered a relationship with Russia.

In the 1570s Baltic and Spanish trade increased. By the 1580s, the Levant and Barbary companies engaged in eastern Mediterranean and North African trade by exporting English lead, tin, and fabrics. Although Mediterranean piracy menaced some expeditions, English ships were defensible, while Spanish and Italian vessels were more prone to attack. English ships sometimes carried cargoes for these countries. In 1601 England established company control of trade with the Orient via the East India Company, a joint-stock enterprise with public investors. Chartered companies conducted trade with prominent European cities such as Rotterdam and Hamburg. England sent merchants to these and other cities for luxury items like jewelry, glass, and clocks. Entrepreneurs made and lost fortunes in voyages that carried livelihoods as well as cargo, reflected by Shakespeare's Salarino in *The Merchant of Venice:*

> . . . Should I go to church
> And see the holy edifice of stone,
> And not bethink me straight of dangerous rocks,
> Which touching but my gentle vessel's side
> Would scatter all her spices on the stream,
> Enrobe the roaring waters with my silks,
> And in a word, but even now worth this,
> And now worth nothing?
>
> *(I.i.29–36)*

After the 1604 Treaty of London, peace with Spain facilitated overseas commerce. Without war expenses, trade increased with southern Europe, especially with the demand for new English draperies, resulting in part from the enclosure laws.

The Holy Roman Empire

By 1500 the Holy Roman Empire included much of central Europe, especially the German states, the majority of the Netherlands, all of Lorraine, Savoy, and northwestern Italy as far south as the Papal States, Bohemia, Moravia, and part of Polish Silesia. Perhaps 300 states and 15 to 20 million people comprised the Empire.

In theory the Holy Roman Emperor was accountable only to God, sharing temporal authority with the pope. But in reality the emperor's authority was dispersed among European heads of state. Structurally the emperor had no standing army and no specific revenue. The Habsburgs of Austria took a leading role in European politics in Vienna, the setting for Shakespeare's *Measure for Measure,* which questions the nature of governmental authority:

> Thus can the demigod, Authority,
> Make us pay down for our offense by weight
> The words of heaven: on whom it will, it will;
> On whom it will not, so; yet still 'tis just.
>
> *(I.ii.120–123)*

Charles V   Charles V (1500–58) was Holy Roman Emperor between 1519 and 1556. Nephew of Catherine of Aragon, the first wife of Henry VIII, Charles fathered Philip of Spain who married Mary I, Catherine's daughter. Charles studied Spanish, Italian, French, and German to forge connections to the peoples he governed.

Grandson of Isabella of Castile and Ferdinand of Aragon, Charles V became King Charles I of Aragon, Catalonia, Valencia, and other lands in 1516. The country we know today as Spain was then referred to in plurality as "the Spains" just as Germany was called "the Germanies." Charles ruled New World territories like Mexico and Peru and several Mediterranean islands, as the most powerful European ruler of the early 1500s.

Charles patronized the arts and enjoyed science. When he retired, his son Philip inherited the Spanish territories and New World holdings. Central European lands and title were bequeathed to his brother Ferdinand, from whence they passed into the Austrian Habsburg line. Charles held the Roman Empire together in a series of victories, including the defeat of the Protestant League at Muhlberg in 1543, while his illegitimate son Don John of Austria defeated the Turks at Lepanto in 1571.

AUSTRIA

> . . . 'tis most credible; we here receive it
> a certainty, vouch'd from our cousin Austria. . . .   (*All's Well That Ends Well,* I.ii.4–5)

The land we call Austria today changed boundaries many times as a result of war and political intrigue. Bohemia included the kingdoms of Hungary, Austria, Transylvania, and Moravia. The term "Bohemian," meaning one free from conventional traditions or a gypsy-type wanderer, dates to about 1570.

Shakespeare's drama makes good use of the region, with the Bohemian theme evidenced in *The Winter's Tale* when the king's daughter becomes a shepherdess following her exile. "Bohemian" is mentioned in *The Merry Wives of Windsor,* while the clown in *Twelfth Night* alludes to the hermit of Prague in a philosophical vein. In this work Shakespeare seems to have confused locales in a scene direction describing Bohemia as a desert country near the sea in act III, scene iii.

Hamlet references the important city of Vienna as a murder site, *Pericles* alludes to a brothel customer killed by pleasure as "the poor Transylvanian," and *Cymbeline* mentions "Dalmatian," once an Austrian crown land, as at war with the Romans. In *King John,* the archduke of Austria is a French ally against the English. Vienna gained renown as a cultural center during the Renaissance.

The year 1526 saw the beginning of Habsburg (or Hapsburg) rule of Bohemia under the leadership of Archduke Ferdinand. He brought Jesuits to the area and restored Roman Catholicism as the state religion. In 1529 the Turkish Ottomans advanced on Vienna to stake a claim in Europe, but they were defeated. Rudolf II (1552–1612) governed Europe as Holy Roman Emperor from 1576 to 1612. He ruled Hungary from 1572 to 1608 and was king of Bohemia from 1575 to 1611. Rudolf was born in Vienna, son of Emperor Maximilian II. Fits of insanity compromised his leadership. Intensely interested in science, he was the patron of Tyco Brahe and Johannes Kepler.

An art collector, Rudolf II brought many artists to the Prague court, including painters like Hans von Aachen. Josef Heintz the Elder was named court artist in 1591. Composers Orlando di Lasso and coppersmith Aegidius Sadeler served at court from 1597, along with Dutch artists Bartholomaus Spranger and Joris Hoefnagel.

Rudolf reversed Protestantism to support the Counter-Reformation. In 1604–06, Stephen Bocskay led a revolt against Roman Catholicism and in 1608, Matthias pressured his brother Rudolf to transfer authority over Hungary, Austria, and Moravia to him. In 1609 Rudolf authorized religious freedom, though Matthias disregarded the ordinance. Members of the Bohemian ruling body threw two imperial counselors out the window of Hradcin Castle on May 23, 1618, contributing, with other events, to the Thirty Years' War that destroyed much of Bohemia, which never regained its former glory.

Perhaps the brothers' divided rule and uncertain religious orientation form the backdrop of Shakespeare's *Measure for Measure* with its Vienna setting. When the lax duke transfers authority to his deputy Angelo who is, at least on the surface, a firmer ruler, subjects face harsh penalties for behavior that seems to have been tolerated previously, and confusion results until the rightful duke again assumes control.

HUNGARY

Heaven grant us its peace, but not the King of Hungary's! (*Measure for Measure,* I.ii.4–5)

Shakespeare's *Measure for Measure* alludes to a conflict between Austria and Hungary, and boundary disputes in that region continue today. By the late fifteenth century Hungary reached its peak to become the dominant power in Eastern Europe under the rule of Matthias Corvinus. A Renaissance prince and patron of humanism, literature, and art, Corvinus brought Italian scholars and artists to Buda, which became the most enlightened court after Italy.

Following Corvinus's death, Hungary's influence declined. In their quest to invade Europe, Ottoman Turks defeated the Hungarians at Mohacs in 1526 and Hungary was divided into three parts in 1541. The Turks retained control of the central portion. The Hapsburgs ruled a northwestern strip, called the Kingdom of Hungary. The eastern region of Transylvania, considered an autonomous principality, remained under Turkish influence. Lutheranism was popular until Calvinism took root. Hungary and Serbia helped block Turkish expansion into the Balkans.

Italy

> ... To see fair Padua, nursery of arts,
> I am arriv'd for fruitful Lombardy, ...
> The pleasant garden of great Italy. (*The Taming of the Shrew*, I.i.2–4)

The city-states comprising Italy provide scenic backdrops for many Renaissance dramas. Nine of Shakespeare's plays are set wholly or partially in Italian settings, including *Two Gentlemen of Verona, Romeo and Juliet*, and *The Taming of the Shrew*. Many allude to classical writers like Ovid or to Renaissance themes like art or learning. Writings by Italian writers like Tasso and Ariosto were translated into English by the late sixteenth century and influenced Shakespeare and his peers who borrowed devices such as mistaken identity and role substitutions in *Twelfth Night, Measure for Measure*, and *The Comedy of Errors*.

Ruled by great families like the Medici, the Borgia, and the Sforza, places like Florence, Venice, and Padua, along with the Papal States, hosted the rebirth of the classical arts and the establishment of institutes of learning.

The pope in Rome governed the Catholic Church. By the end of the fifteenth century Rome was second only to Florence in artistic expression. A series of popes, including Alexander VI (Borgia), Julius II (della Rovere), and Leo X (Medici), created a powerful papal state with Rome as the political capital of Europe. The Catholic Church enjoyed unprecedented power and influence. Shakespeare revives Rome's bloody past in tragedies like *Coriolanus, Titus Andronicus*, and *Julius Caesar*.

By 1500 Florence and Venice had become republics while Naples remained a kingdom. Cities like Verona, Padua, Genoa, Pisa, Siena, Assisi, and Urbino gave birth to artists and writers who earned lasting fame with unique contributions.

For the first time in Western culture, visual art claimed a position in the arts equal to that of poetry, evidenced in religious themes, mannerism, and the baroque movement. Michelangelo Buonarroti's *David* (1501) and the Sistine Chapel ceiling (1508–12), Leonardo da Vinci's *Last Supper* (1495), and Titian's (Tiziano Vecelli) *Venus of Urbino* (1538) help to define art of this period. Literature celebrated similar themes, including Shakespeare's narrative poem *Venus and Adonis*.

SOUTHERN EUROPE

The senators of Athens greet thee, Timon. (*Timon of Athens,* V.i.136)

Southern Europe was well traveled, its ancient history and sites drawing many visitors, including the English. With Greece as birthplace of the classics, tourists came to enjoy its culture and the climate. Shakespeare set several plays in ancient places, such as *A Midsummer Night's Dream* in Athens, and *Twelfth Night* in Illyria.

Yugoslavia and Serbia

Yugoslavia received that name only in the twentieth century. In Shakespeare's time southern Europe (or the Balkans) was a boiling pot of warfare and wavering boundaries among lands known as Serbia, Bosnia, Hercegovina, Bulgaria, and Albania. Grecian and Turkish empires bordered these countries. In the fifteenth and sixteenth centuries the Ottomans swept across this region to advance on Europe. *Twelfth Night* pays passing tribute to middle eastern influence with two mentions of the Persian sophy (ruler) and another to the niece of Gorboduc.

King Henry VI—Part Two references "Bargulus the strong Illyrian pirate" (IV.i.108). Illyria became part of the Byzantine Empire in A.D. 395. In 1168, Stefan Nemanja organized the first kingdom of Serbian people, a grouping reinforced by King Stefan Dusan (1331–55). This territory would later be divided into the Federal Republic of Yugoslavia, Albania, and Greece.

In 1389 Ottoman Turks seized Serbia in the Battle of Kosovo, and by the late 1400s, Bosnia and Hercegovina came under Turkish control. In 1526, the Austria-Hungarian Empire controlled Croatia and Slovenia, many of whose people converted to Catholicism.

During the Austrian-Turkish War of 1593–1606, the Serbs rebelled in 1594 at Banat in Turkey. To retaliate, the Sultan burned St. Sava, a shrine holy to Moslems and Christians. The region remained under Austrian and Turkish authority for several centuries.

Bosnia

By the seventh century A.D. Serbs and Croats had settled lands now known as Bosnia and Hercegovina. In the fourteenth century, Bosnia (then a principality) linked with a southern duchy to become a province later called Hercegovina. Today Bosnia is a northern region while Hercegovina is in the south. To the north and west is Croatia, while the southern and eastern areas are bounded by the Federal Republic of Yugoslavia, the Federation of Serbia, and Montenegro. Bosnia maintains 20 miles of coastline on the Adriatic Sea, with Sarajevo as its capital. The people include Muslims, Serbs, and Croats.

In the sixteenth century Croatian, Serbian, Bulgarian, and Byzantine rulers fought over regional authority before Hungary took control. Under Ottoman influence some Serbs converted to Islam while many Christians fled in 1463 when Turks captured Bosnia. It wasn't until the seventeenth century that Austria, Russia, and the Turks fought for control of Bosnia and Hercegovina. Despite intense conflict the arts survived. The Pec art era (1557–1614) demonstrates both Italian and local influences.

Greece

For every false drop in her bawdy veins,
A Grecian's life hath sunk. (*Troilus and Cressida*, IV.i.70–71)

The glories of ancient Greece were reborn in Renaissance Europe as scholarly translations resurrected Aristotle and Plato from the dusty libraries of former cultural centers like Athens. Shakespeare's *Timon of Athens* and *A Midsummer Night's Dream* are set in Greece, while other works reference the great city of ancient learning in tragic and comic plots including *The Rape of Lucrece, Coriolanus, Julius Caesar, Antony and Cleopatra, King Henry VI—Part Three, Troilus and Cressida, The Taming of the Shrew, The Comedy of Errors, Cymbeline, Titus Andronicus, Pericles,* and *As You Like It.*

Greece fell under Ottoman control shortly after the fall of Constantinople in 1453. In 1456 Athens was seized. Soon after, the Turks pushed into Serbia, Bosnia, and Albania. Greece never regained the former glories of its Golden Age.

Sandys' Descriptions of Southeastern Europe

English traveler George Sandys recorded highlights of his journeys through much of Europe during the Elizabethan era. Here is an excerpt from his description of southeastern Europe:

> We sayled all along in the sight of Dalmatia, at this day Sclavonia, of the Sclavi, a people of Sarmatia. They dissent not from the Greeke Church in their Religion. Throughout the North part of the World their Language is understood and spoken, even from thence almost to the Confines of Tartarie. The men weare halfe-sleeved Gownes of Violet cloth, with Bonnets of the same. They nourish onely a locke of haire on the crowne of their heads: the rest all shaven. The women weare theirs not long; and dye them blacke for the most part. Their chiefe Citie is Ragusa (heretofore Epidaurus) a Commonwealth of it selfe, famous for Merchandize, and plentie of shipping. Many small Ilands belong thereunto, but little of the Continent. They pay Tribute to the Turke, fourteene thousand zecchins yearely . . . Whereby they purchase their peace; and a discharge of duties throughout the Ottoman Empire. . . .
> (Sandys 1905, 89)

Sandys describes the island of Corfu, 54 miles long, about 12 miles from the mainland, with groves of oranges, pomegranates, figs, and olives. He also mentions Saint Maura, formerly called Leucadia. *The Winter's Tale* is partially set in Sicily in a location that suggests similar isolation.

Southeastern Europe was the center of the Byzantine Empire, the root of Orthodox Christianity, and the battlefield of the Moslem Middle East and Latin West. Constantinople, "the second Rome," damaged during the Fourth Crusade in 1204, lost its former luster. Selim I fought Venice for Adriatic control before claiming Palestine and Egypt, declaring himself protector of the Islamic faith. Shakespeare mentions the city of Antioch in *Pericles* and Ephesus in *The Comedy of Errors*.

Scythia was an ancient region of Asia and southeastern Europe, home to nomadic peoples. In *King Henry VI—Part One,* the countess compares her plot to the Scythian Tomyris's acclaim resulting from Cyrus's death (II.iii.6). *King Lear* vows a preference for the "barbarous Scythian" (I.i.116) over his daughter Cordelia in a malicious comparison, and *Titus Andronicus* poses the question "Was never Scythia half so barbarous?" (I.i.131), underscoring the region's reputation for savagery.

SPAIN

> Ferdinand,
> My father, King of Spain, was reckon'd one
> The wisest prince that there had reign'd by many
> A year before. (*King Henry VIII*, II.iv.48–50)

Christians, Moslems, and Jews coexisted in Spain until Queen Isabel's religious fervor expelled the Jews and reclaimed Granada from the Moors. The Holy Office of the Inquisition operated as a tribunal to preserve pure bloodlines and protect the Christian faith in Castile, where many converted Jews (called "New Christians") were believed to live.

New World claims enhanced Spain's economic prosperity, which contributed to the development of a powerful stance in Europe and America during the reign of Charles V and Philip II. Tensions remained, however, from religious reform and Turkish conflicts.

England's ties with Spain included Mary Tudor's marriage to Philip II and his later courtship of Elizabeth following Mary's death. The most dramatic tie in Shakespeare's lifetime was the defeat of the Spanish Armada in 1588. Shakespeare chose a Spanish setting for his comedy *Love's Labour's Lost,* and he employed noble Spanish characters in *The Merchant of Venice* as demonstrated in Portia's arrogant suitor, the prince of Aragon. Another prince of Aragon (Don Pedro) and his evil brother Don John are featured in *Much Ado About Nothing.* Shakespeare may have had in mind Charles V and his illegitimate son Don John of Austria with legitimate heir Philip II in creating Spanish nobles for his plays.

Spanish Literature

Spanish literature is represented by writers like Mateo Aleman (1547–1614) whose work *Guzman de Alfarache* was published in 1599. Felix de Vega Carpio (1562–1635) wrote *El Mejor Alcalde el Rey,* which influenced French, English, and German writers. Gabriel Tellez, writing under the name of Tirso de Molina (1571–1648), was a follower of de Vega. His work, including *Burlador de Sevilla,* used cross-dressing conventions seen in works by Shakespeare like *Twelfth Night* and *The Merchant of Venice* when women don men's clothing for survival or success.

Perhaps the best-known Spanish author of this era is Miguel de Cervantes Saavedra (1547–1616), who came from a poor family and received a general education. As a soldier he was maimed at Lepanto in 1571 when the Christian Holy League defeated the Turks. Later Cervantes became a prisoner of Barbary pirates, was sold as a slave, and ransomed in 1580. His European travels fostered appreciation for Renaissance culture.

In Spain he worked as a tax collector but was jailed for improper accounts. He was in and out of prison on several occasions for debt. While imprisoned he wrote *Don Quixote,* a satire of popular Spanish chivalry tales. Part I was published in 1605 and Part II in 1615. A principal character, Sancho Panza, illustrates the practical and faithful servant, while Don Quixote represents an outmoded chivalrous relic lost in the modern world.

Cervantes' work influenced many writers including Ben Jonson, and like Shakespeare's work has stood the test of time.

Philip II

Philip II of Spain (1527–98) was the most powerful ruler in the late sixteenth century. His father Charles V (1500–58) was Holy Roman Emperor from 1519 to 1556, and king of Spain as Charles I (1516–56).

In addition to the Spanish throne, Philip inherited Luxembourg, Naples, Sicily, and the western coast of Africa as well as Spanish holdings in the Western hemisphere. He also ruled Sardinia, part of northern Italy, and the Netherlands. In 1580 he claimed Portugal in the name of his Portuguese mother; this united the Iberian Peninsula and tightened Spanish control of Oriental spices and New World precious metals. But English-Spanish relations were threatened by England's exploration of the Atlantic and Pacific coasts of the New World.

Seeking to restore Roman Catholicism in Europe while repelling Islam, in 1567 Philip ordered the Moriscos (Spanish Moors or Moslems) to stop speaking Arabic and to cease from practicing Islam. Several battles followed, leading to the Moors' expulsion from Spain in 1609.

Philip married Mary Tudor in 1554, but she died childless in 1558. He then wooed Elizabeth, who strung him along until the 1570s. Cautious and hard-working, Philip was detail-oriented and courteous, devoted to the arts, and zealous in religious duty. He lost many loved ones in a short span of time, including his parents, a sister, four wives, four sons, and a daughter, which seems to have added a melancholy element to his nature.

Philip III succeeded Philip II, ruling from 1598 to 1621. Philip IV ruled from 1621 to 1665. Shakespeare depicts the Hispanic protagonists of *Love's Labour's Lost* as bookish and celibate, and portrays the Spanish Don Adriano de Armado (perhaps a parody of the Spanish armada) as a melancholy and legalistic figure who concludes the play. Perhaps Shakespeare's depictions reflect popular images of Spain's ruling family.

The Armada

By 1588 the Spanish Armada, or navy, included 130 vessels, 20,000 soldiers, 10,000 sailors, and 2,000 guns, and was the largest fleet in the world. The English had only 190 ships that sat lower in the water and produced longer-range artillery.

Crippled by storms and a powder shortage, the Spanish Armada was defeated by the English in 1588. England's dominant role in world trade was strengthened by this victory as Spain's role was curtailed.

In the 1604 Treaty of London, England made peace with Spain, strengthening the economies of both nations through increased trade. But their accord heightened tensions among Dutch and English Protestants who feared Spanish intolerance.

PORTUGAL

What, not one hit? . . . From Lisbon, Barbary, and India. (The Merchant of Venice,
III.iii.267–269)

Portugal led European colonialism during the fifteenth and early sixteenth centuries. Gomes Eannes de Azurara (d. 1474) wrote *The Discovery and Conquest of Guinea,* which chronicles the voyages of Henry the Navigator and details western Africa. Historiographers Gaspar Correa (1490–1565), Joao de Barros (1496–1570), and Lopes de Castanheda (1500–59) wrote accounts of Portuguese ventures in the East.

Popular Renaissance writers included Luis Vas de Camoens (1524–80), a nobleman who received training in the classics, Italian, and the Bible. He lost an eye in military service, and between 1549 and 1553 he was imprisoned. He lived in India from 1553 until 1570 and died in 1580. His *Lusiads* (1572) is an epic work celebrating Vasco de Gama's 1497 voyage to India.

While Shakespeare does not use Portugal as a main setting, he references the country's geography in *As You Like It* and a trading venture to Lisbon in *The Merchant of Venice.* In 1607 Dutch traders forced the Portuguese from the Spice Islands, ending the Portuguese trade monopoly in this region. Drama like *The Island Princess,* performed in 1621, highlighted problems with Portuguese trade in the Moluccas. Dryden's *Amboyna* underscored similar issues.

FRANCE

> *. . . I love France so well that I will not part with a village of it.* (*King Henry V*,
> V.ii.173–174)

During the reign of Elizabeth, France remained an ally and a threat. Earlier English kings claimed sovereignty in both countries and England frequently considered France an English possession. Charles IX ruled France between 1550 and 1574, at one point courting Elizabeth as a political maneuver.

French Literature

The classical rebirth inspired French writers to produce drama like *Cleopatre* by Jodelle in 1552, while Robert Garnier (1535–1601) utilized biblical themes. Alexandre Hardy (ca. 1570–1631), actor turned playwright, emphasized nature in his work.

Frances's greatest literary age came in the seventeenth century, however, in writings by Pierre Corneille (1606–84) and Jean Racine (1639–99).

Francois Rabelais (c. 1483–1553), an early literary figure, bridged medieval and modern French literature. His study of medicine and his travel throughout France and Italy help shaped his views in *Pantagruel and Gargantua* (1532), an allegory that explores issues like education, politics, church, and law through satire, demonstrating insensitivity to women.

Shakespeare parodies Gargantua's speech in *As You Like It:*

> You must borrow me Gargantua's mouth
> first; 'tis a word too great for any mouth of this age's size.
>
> *(III.ii.225–27)*

Pierre de Ronsard (1524–85) was trained as a diplomat and traveled to England, Scotland, and the Low Countries during Mary Stuart's time. Deaf, he witnessed religious controversies involving the Huguenots and Catherine de Medici.

Michel de Montaigne

The son of a Bordeaux merchant, Michel Eyquem de Montaigne was born in 1533 and died in 1592. Educated in law, he became a magistrate in the superior court of the Bordeaux parlement.

Montaigne devoted a good portion of his life to scholarly pursuits and writing. By nature he was melancholy and a religious skeptic; he studied human nature from the philosopher to the savage.

Health forced him from public office, though he later served two terms as mayor of Bordeaux. He completed three books of essays exploring the human condition and urged the "middle way" in religion. His essay titled *Of Cannibals* may have helped shape Shakespeare's Caliban in *The Tempest,* though Montaigne offers a noble view of Native Americans:

It is a nation, would I answer Plato, that hath no kinde of traffike, no knowledge of Letters, no intelligence of numbers, no name of magistrate, nor of politike superioritie; no use of service, of riches or of povertie; no contracts, no successions, no parti-apparell but naturall, no manuring of lands, no use of wine, corne, or mettle. The very words that import lying, falshood, treason, dissimulations, covetousness, envie, detraction, and pardon, were never heard of amongst them. How dissonant would hee finde his imaginarie commonwealth from this perfection! . . .

Furthermore, they [the savages] live in a country of so exceeding pleasant and temperate situation, that as my testimonies have told me, it is verie rare to see a sicke body amongst them; and they have further assured me, they never saw any man there, either shaking with the palsie, toothlesse, with eies dropping, or crooked and stooping through age. They are seated alongst the sea-coast, encompassed toward the land with huge and steepie mountains, having betweene both, a hundred leagues or thereabout of open and champaine ground . . .

They spend the whole day in dancing . . .

I am . . . grieved, that prying so narrowly into their faults we are so blinded in ours. . . . (Montaigne 1933, 164, 166)

Montaigne met three Native Americans at Rouen in 1561–62, and he communicated with them through an interpreter, rendering information of the following kind:

. . . Three of that nation, ignorant how deare the knowledge of our corruptions will one day cost their repose, securitie, and happinesse, and how their ruine shall proceed from this commerce, which I imagine is already well advanced . . . were at Roane in the time of our late King Charles the ninth, who talked with them a great while . . . They had perceived, there were men amongst us full gorged with all sortes of commodities, and others which hunger-starved, and bare with need and povertie, begged at their gates. . . . (Montaigne 1933, 171)

International Affairs

Religious controversy stirred strife throughout northern Europe in the late sixteenth century. In 1562 the French government sought to suppress Huguenot unrest. The English adviser Dudley had advocated a militant Protestant foreign policy, and the dominant Catholic stance failed in France; the Treaty of Troyes followed in 1564. Hostilities concluded by 1570 when the English and French agreed not to meddle in Scottish affairs.

As Spain's influence spread, England and France reached a new level of mutual support and shared interests. In 1572 the two countries enacted the Treaty of Blois and Elizabeth appeared to consider marriage with prominent nobles, the duke of Anjou or his brother, the duke of Alencon. That year on St. Bartholomew's Day, August 24, a massacre of French Huguenots fed the growth of Protestantism, urged by zealous English Protestants like Secretary Walsingham. But in June 1573, Charles IX made peace with the Huguenots.

In 1574 Charles IX died and was succeeded by his brother, the Catholic duke of Anjou who would become Henry III. By 1576 religious war again swept France. Elizabeth sought to balance power in the regions controlled by France and Spain, and an uneasy peace reigned for several years. But embers of distrust continued to burn and by 1584–85 the region again had become volatile.

In December 1588 the Catholic League leader, the duke of Guise, was assassinated and in July 1589, Henry III likewise was murdered, paving the way for Henry of Navarre to take the French throne. Henry IV, who reigned from 1588 to 1610, took more interest in southern France, leaving the north open to exploitation and violence. England sent troops to Normandy and Brittany to secure those regions and ensure national security.

The Renaissance was manifested in France through architecture and the influence of several invasions of Italy by Charles VIII (1494), Louis XII (1500) and Francis I (1515–25). Baroque art flourished under Henry IV. Louis XIII reigned from 1610 to 1643 in a period that introduced the beginnings of Versailles as the French capital and the influence of Cardinal Richelieu (1585–1642). Under Louis XIV (1643–1715), the French dominated European culture for a time.

Like other English literary works, Shakespeare's drama suggests French influence, from phrases like "bon jour" to historical figures that include Joan of Arc; perhaps half of his plays reference France or French culture, including the history plays as a source of conflict, and others like *The Comedy of Errors, King Lear,* and *Hamlet.* France was never far from the consciousness of politically knowledgeable writers like Shakespeare.

GERMANY AND CENTRAL EUROPE

> *How like you the young German, the Duke of Saxony's nephew?* (The Merchant of
> Venice, I.ii.84–85)

The country now called "Germany" was in Shakespeare's time a cluster of lands called "the Germanies" that included the German states and other lands under the authority of the Holy Roman Empire.

Germany witnessed the rise of Protestants, many of which were Lutheran, named for the famous German reformer Martin Luther. Germany hosted much of the Thirty Years' War and the Peace of Westphalia in 1648.

None of Shakespeare's drama is set in Germany, but he does use German characters or references in works like *Othello* that lists Germans, Danes, and Hollanders as great drinkers, upper Germany as a close English neighbor in *King Henry VIII,* and a German boar to depict unthwarted lust in *Cymbeline.*

Humanism

A humanist, Nicholas of Cusa fostered connections between Germany and Italy. Rudolf Agricola (1444–85) was called the father of German humanism. As organist to Duke Ercole d'Este, Agricola immersed himself in study of the Greek and Latin classics. Upon his return to Germany he brought with him Italian ideas and culture. Johann Reuchlin (1455–1522) studied the classics, philosophy, and law, along with the Jewish Cabala. In 1506 he published a Christian Hebrew grammar.

Art

Michael Pacher (ca. 1435–98), woodcarver and painter, was one of the first German artists to demonstrate Italian influence in his work: the high altar in Saint Wolfgang Church near Salzburg and other Austrian and German churches. Veit Stoss (ca. 1445–1533) Nuremberg sculptor, blended Italian and Gothic techniques.

Other important figures emerged during this era, including Matthias Grunewald (ca. 1468–1528), primarily a religious artist, celebrated for his "Isehem Altarpiece" in 1515 at the Anthonite hospital near Colmar. His work accents pathos and expressive detail.

Another key figure was Albrecht Durer (1471–1528) who traveled to Italy in 1494 where he developed a taste for Italian Renaissance art which he used in printing. Many European publishers sought his woodcuts and engravings. Noteworthy examples are his *Melancholia* and *Four Horsemen of the Apocalypse*. His work illustrates interest in religious subjects and human struggles, as well as an appreciation of nature.

Lucas Cranach (1472–1553) and Hans Holbein the Younger (1497–1543) intertwined Italian, German, and Flemish techniques. Holbein lived in England from 1532 to 1543 and was the court painter for Henry VIII.

THE NETHERLANDS

Where stood Belgia, the Netherlands? (*The Comedy of Errors*, III.ii.138)

The Netherlands, also called the Lowlands, played a vital commercial role during the Tudor era. Queen Elizabeth borrowed from the Antwerp capital market to fund wars.

In December 1563 under the control of Spanish regent Margaret of Parma, the Netherlands placed an embargo on English cloth imports, hoping to stir dissention that would raise an outcry against Elizabeth. The goal was to topple her from the throne and replace her with a Roman Catholic ruler, or barring extreme action, at least promote more tolerant conditions toward English Catholics.

In 1564 the Protestant ruler of East Friesland offered the German port of Emden for English cloth exports through England's Merchant Adventurers

Company. The English agreed, which freed Elizabeth from financial and commercial dependence on the Netherlands.

In 1573 Don Luis de Requesens became Spanish governor of the Netherlands and he tried to develop a more conciliatory policy. But by 1576 the next governor, Don John of Austria, faced religious conflict led by Dutch leader William the Silent who sought religious toleration. In November an alliance formed between the Netherlands's northern and southern provinces, leading to the pacification of Ghent.

In August 1585 England signed the Treaty of Nonsuch with the Dutch who would come under English protection. Elizabeth sent 1,000 horses and 5,000 foot soldiers under Leicester. But Leicester unwittingly accepted the position of governor-general, formerly a Spanish title, which upset the English queen who did not want to offend Spain. English patriots defended the Netherlands, and Sir Philip Sidney was killed at the battle at Zutphen in August 1586.

Elizabeth's goal was to establish a decentralized Netherlands under loosely held Spanish authority. To a large degree she was successful.

In 1602 the Dutch East India Company was formed with trade centers in Desjima, Japan; Mokha, Yemen; Surat, Persia; and Batavia (or Jakarta), Indonesia. Chinese silk and spices like cinnamon and nutmeg became popular items of trade, referenced, for example, in Shakespeare's *Love's Labours Lost, King Henry V,* and *Pericles.*

SCOTLAND

"If that you will France win,
Then with Scotland first begin." (King Henry V, I.ii.167–168)

To the north of England, Scotland sometimes supported and sometimes threatened English interests. During the time of Elizabeth I, many French lived there and were considered potentially dangerous allies of Mary Stuart who sought Elizabeth's throne.

The Scots were viewed as uncivilized, nearly "as bad" as the Irish, and the English believed Scots could not be trusted. Protestants were called Presbyterians and followed the teachings of John Knox, though highlanders remained predominantly Catholic.

James IV

In 1503 James IV married Margaret Tudor, creating an alliance between Scotland and England. After 1509 James ruled without Parliament, depending instead on his council and the court. He was a firm leader, establishing more sheriffs and justices, especially in Scotland's western region. A patron of the arts, he built up the navy and in 1506 he created the College of Surgeons.

But by 1513 the English were at war with France and James led the Scottish army to meet the English at Flodden. The English overpowered the Scots and James was killed.

James V

Seventeen-month-old James V succeeded his father to the Scottish throne. Soon after, his mother Margaret married Archibald Douglas, sixth earl of Douglas, who kept James nearly a prisoner from 1525 to 1528.

James was popular with the commoners, sometimes dressing as a farmer, but the nobles thought him cruel when in 1537–40 he instituted the Act of Revocation, which demanded compensation from those who had encroached on royal lands.

Taking the title Lord of the Isles, he introduced the English torture of hanging, drawing, and quartering. Thinking to marry a French princess, he traveled to France in 1536, but instead wed Mary of Guise. As his authority dissipated, he died at age 31. His daughter Princess Mary succeeded him.

Mary Stuart, Queen of Scots

Mary Stuart was the daughter of Henry VIII's sister Margaret and James IV of Scotland. During Elizabeth's reign the Catholics proclaimed Mary first in line to the English throne.

Two obstacles stood in Mary's way. One was her alien status according to common law. The second factor was that Henry VIII's will put Margaret's descendents lower than those of his sister Mary. To bolster her claim to the English throne, Mary Stuart married Lord Darnley, and their son, James VI of Scotland, became the presumptive English heir.

In 1558 Mary wed the French heir and soon became the queen consort of France as well as queen of Scotland. England was concerned about a possible French-Scottish alliance based on Catholic support which might try to claim England for Mary. In 1559 a peace was concluded among England, Spain, and France, providing a temporary lull. That same year Scottish Protestants rebelled against Mary of Guise, Mary Stuart's mother. French forces came to stop the uprising, followed by the intervention of English troops to repel the French. The conflict was settled at the 1560 Treaty of Edinburgh in which Mary Stuart surrendered the English arms she had been displaying as well as her claim to the English throne while Elizabeth lived, but not to the succession.

In 1565 Mary wed Lord Darnley, who had killed her lover David Rizzio. In August, Mary's half-brother the earl of Moray led Scottish Protestant nobles against Mary in the Chaseabout Raid and the couple fled to England. Thereafter, Mary promised not to interfere with Scotland's Protestantism. In June 1566 their son James VI of Scotland was born, but the following year on February 9 the earl of Bothwell murdered Lord Darnley. When Mary wed Bothwell, her subjects revolted. She was defeated at Carberry Hill and imprisoned. The Protestant earl of Moray became regent to infant James.

Mary escaped from prison and fled to England where she was kept under watch for the next 19 years. Politically suspect, Mary was also Elizabeth's cousin, and Elizabeth attempted to treat her graciously. In 1586 documentation linked Mary Stuart to the Babington Plot and Parliament successfully urged Elizabeth to order Mary's execution, which was carried out the following year. Mary's son James VI of Scotland succeeded Elizabeth as James I of England in 1603.

One of Shakespeare's bloodiest tragedies, *Macbeth,* is set in Scotland, and histories like *King Henry V, King Henry VI—Part One, King Henry VI—Part Three,* and *King Richard III* allude to Scottish battles, threats, or themes.

IRELAND

Th' uncivil kerns of Ireland are in arms. (*King Henry VI—Second Part,* III.i.310)

In A.D. 1172 the Irish king invited English knights to help keep out invaders, and many English people remained there. The declaration of an Irish kingdom in 1541 introduced additional conflicts between the English and the Irish, and England began looking for ways to revive its weakening authority in that country.

England in Ireland

The English government based in Dublin and surrounding areas was called "the Pale." By 1641, the Anglo-English held one-third of the profitable land in Ireland's three southern provinces. During the sixteenth and seventeenth centuries the religious schism between Catholicism and Protestantism widened, and bitterness toward Ireland increased during the 1570s when support for English settlements hinted at political control.

England was concerned about the danger of an independent Ireland, as well as the possibility of England's enemies settling there.

In the 1570s Englishman Sir Thomas Smith, assisted by Walter Devereaux, earl of Essex, attempted to plant colonies in Ireland. Their men were forbidden to have Gaelic wives and a common council was established to help guide laws and taxes. An English legal system was introduced to judge disputes, although Ireland had a legal court system for such issues.

There had been a standing army in Ireland since 1534, but English soldiers were notorious for pillaging and insubordination. Some fled, starved and naked, to Gaelic Irish chieftains like Shane O'Neill or the earl of Tyrone, as had settlers to the Native Americans in North America.

Shakespeare's History Plays

Shakespeare's history plays connect Ireland with war: "For we will make for Ireland presently" (*King Richard II* I.iv.52), and "The Duke of Gloster, to whom the order of the siege is given, is altogether directed by an Irishman" (*King Henry V* III.i.66–67).

In *King Henry VI—Part Two* are speeches concerning the Duke of York's attempt to recoup the English crown:

> The Duke of York is newly come from Ireland,
> And with a puissant and a mighty power
> Of gallowglasses and stout kerns
> Is marching hitherward in proud array,
> And still proclaimeth, as he comes along,
> His arms are only to remove from thee
> The Duke of Somerset, whom he terms a traitor.
>
> *(IV.ix.24–30)*

And in the final act:

> From Ireland thus comes York to claim his right,
> And pluck the crown from feeble Henry's head.
> Ring bells, aloud, burn bonfires clear and bright
> To entertain great England's lawful king!
>
> *(V.i.1–4).*

After the 1579–83 revolt, a cross section of English society settled in Ireland. Magnates (called "undertakers") were given tracts of land called seigniories. Sir Walter Raleigh received land there. But territorial squabbles followed and some settlers returned to England as absentee landlords, leaving the land for the Irish to farm.

In 1599 the earl of Leicester led a force to Ireland to confront the Tyrone-led uprising. When Leicester made a treaty and returned to England unsummoned, Elizabeth refused to renew his patents or wine licenses, which destroyed his credit. Disgruntled, 30-something Essex teamed with the earls of Southampton, Bedford, and Rutland to stage a mild revolt, hoping to capture the support of the masses. Their plan failed and Essex was executed.

Some felt that Elizabeth sent her soldiers to Ireland inadequately funded. She cited the Dutch mercantilist efforts as a model of business-funded colonialism, expecting English merchants to supply the needs of Irish enterprises. Consequently, many blamed her when English soldiers went over to the Irish and unrest continued. In 1608–09 the Londonderry Plantation was established at Ulster by the City of London.

POLAND

> *. . . her rags and the tallow in them will burn a Poland winter.* (*The Comedy of Errors,*
> III.ii.98–99)

Shakespeare's references to Poland are few and vague, representing the cultural and geographical distance between the two countries. Sigismund III (1566–1632) succeeded Stephen Bathory who died in 1586 to reign as king of Poland from 1587 to 1632 and king of Sweden from 1592–1599. He was the son of John III of Sweden and Catherine, sister of Sigismund II of Poland. A Roman Catholic, he married Anne of Habsburg in 1592, strengthening ties with Europe.

In 1589 the Tartars invaded Poland but were defeated. The next year the Tartars planned another assault, but the English ambassador who was then at Constantinople made peace between the two countries.

Deposed by the Swedish Diet in 1599 for his anti-Protestant stand, Sigismund's efforts to hold remaining territories led him to war against his uncle and nephew, to whom he lost Livonia in 1629. He wanted to rule Russia and conquered Moscow temporarily in 1610 but was expelled in 1612 by Michael Romanov.

Sigismund III was tall and lean, with short, black hair and a thin, yellowish beard. The court's seat was in Crakow, and revenues to the crown included income from a few silver mines. The Poles were ignorant in navigation, but reportedly courteous and kindhearted to visitors.

Jan Kochanowski (1530–84), a writer, studied at the universities of Cracow, Padua, and Paris. He wrote lyrical poetry including *Threni, the Psalms,* and *A Summer Song of St. John's.* His writing exhibits the influence of Petrarch, Ariosto, Tasso, and Ronsard in themes of patriotism and criticism of Polish decadence.

Shakespeare alludes to Norway's assault of the Poles in *Hamlet* and to Poland's cold climate in *The Comedy of Errors.*

DENMARK

Something is rotten in the state of Denmark. (*Hamlet,* I.iv.89)

In 1397 the Union of Kalmar merged the three kingdoms of Denmark, Norway, and Sweden under Margaret (wife of King Haakon of Norway), yet each of the kingdoms remained autonomous. After her death in 1412 rebellion separated the three states.

Born in 1577 as the seventh of the ruling Oldenburg family, Christian IV ruled Denmark in the late sixteenth and early seventeenth centuries. By an English traveler's account, the king was about 15 years old, with a fair complexion, and was "big-set." He could speak Dutch, French, and Italian. Crime rates were relatively low, perhaps because manslaughter and rape convicts were beheaded and robbers were hung in chains to rot. Rather than kneel to the king, the customary greeting was to take hands as we do today. Christian's brother Ulricus was a student at Wittenberg, Germany, reminding us that in Shakespeare's play set in Denmark, Hamlet, too, had been a Wittenberg student. *Hamlet* and *Macbeth* refer to Norway, while *Othello* alludes to a Dane as one of a cluster of northern Europeans who could be outdrunk by the English.

SUMMARY

Europe was an exciting region during the Renaissance. As new boundaries were set, rulers and customs changed rapidly and frequently. Political treaties were made and broken as quickly as monarchs claimed or lost thrones. Seeds of modern society were sown and the lands we know as Europe today took shape or shifted boundaries under powerful individuals with will and authority.

Because communication was rapidly evolving with inventions like the printing press and expanding trade enterprises, residents of Europe's largest city were bombarded with news from the European continent. Births of monarchs, deaths of dynasties, and inventions of theories and products propelled Shakespeare's world into an ever-widening spiral of human dynamism.

Sweeping movements like the Renaissance and Reformation impacted most European societies. At the heart of each monarch and in the mind of each great thinker was a unique human being. William Shakespeare excelled in capturing the essence of such individuals in the many characters he brought to life in the pages of his drama, some based on actual European figures, with others created from his imagination or popular culture.

SOURCES

Artz, Frederick B. *Renaissance Humanism, 1300–1550*. Kent, Ohio: Kent State University Press, 1966.

Ashton, Robert. *Reformation and Revolution 1558–1660*. London: Paladin, 1985.

Bartlett, Kenneth R., and Margaret McGlynn, eds. *Humanism and the Northern Renaissance*. Toronto: Canadian Scholars, 2000.

De la Crois, Horst, and Richard G. Tansey. *Gardner's Art through the Ages*. 6th ed. rev. New York: Harcourt, 1975.

Derrick, John. *Image of Irland*. 1597.

Foxe, John. *Foxe's Christian Martyrs of the World*. Urhrichsville Ohio: Barbour.

Hughes, Charles, ed. *Shakespeare's Europe: Fynes Moryson (being unpublished chapters of Fynes Moryson's Itinerary) (1617) with an Introduction and an Account of Fynes Moryson's Career*. 2d ed., with new index. New York: Benjamin Blom, 1903.

Hyland, Peter. *An Introduction to Shakespeare: The Dramatist in His Context*. New York: St. Martin's, 1996.

Jensen, De Lamar. *Renaissance Europe: Age of Recovery and Reconciliation*. 2d ed. Lexington, Mass.: D. C. Heath, 1992.

"Michael Romanov." Columbia Electronic Encyclopedia. 6th ed., copyright 2000. Columbia University Press.

Montaigne, Michel de. *The Essayes of Montaigne*. John Florio's translation; introduction by J.I.M. Stewart. New York: Modern Library, 1933.

Purchas, Samuel B. D. *Hakluytus Posthumus or Purchas His Pilgrimes, Contayning a History of the World in Sea Voyages and Lande Travells by Englishmen and others*, Vol. VIII. Glasgow: James MacLehose and Sons; New York: Macmillan, 1905.

Rowse, A. L. *The Elizabethan Renaissance*. London: Macmillan, 1971.

"Rudolf II (Holy Roman Empire)." Microsoft Encarta Online Encyclopedia, 2001.

Ruggiero, Guido. "Marriage, love, sex, and Renaissance civic morality." In *Sexuality and Gender in Early Modern Europe*, ed. James Grantham Turner 10–30. Cambridge: Cambridge University Press, 1993.

Sandys, George. *A relation of a Journey begunne, Anno Dom. 1610. Written by Master George Sandys, and here contracted. Hakluytus Posthumus or Purchas His Pilgrimes. Contayning a History of the World in Sea Voyages and Lande Travells by Englishmen and Others,* Vol. VIII. Glasgow: University Press; New York: Macmillan, 1905.

"Serbia." Encarta.msn.com

Zophy, Jonathan W. *A Short History of Renaissance and Reformation Europe: Dances over Fire and Water.* Upper Saddle River, N.J.: Prentice Hall, 1996.

QUESTIONS

1. What factors limited England's knowledge of its European neighbors?
2. Why did Shakespeare and other writers base stories in distant lands?
3. What made travel difficult during this period of history?
4. In which of his plays does Shakespeare emphasize classical over Christian beliefs?

CRITICAL THINKING AND RESEARCH PROJECTS

1. How does Shakespeare explore the great chain of being in history plays dealing with government and its leaders?
2. Consider Shakespeare's use of art (sculpture, painting, architecture) in his sonnets. Write a paper analyzing his views of art generally, or of one art form in particular.
3. Shakespeare's critics complain about his lack of a university education. Compare a Shakespeare play to one on a similar European theme by a university-educated contemporary, that is, Shakespeare's *The Merchant of Venice* with Christopher Marlowe's *The Jew of Malta.* Explain how Shakespeare's writing is superior or inferior—or focus on how it is merely different.
4. Research a lesser-known European leader of this time and explore his or her contributions to Renaissance culture.
5. Detail specific references to a European region in Shakespeare's work and research possible reasons for or meanings of these references.

FOR FURTHER READING

Glete, Jan. *War and the State in Early Modern Europe.* London: Routledge, 2002.

McCullough, David Willis. *Chronicles of the Barbarians.* New York: Times Books, 1998.

Palmer, William. *The Problem of Ireland in Tudor Foreign Policy 1485–1603.* Woodbridge Suffolk; Rochester: Boydell, 1994.

Pettegree, Andrew. *Europe in the Sixteenth Century.* Oxford: Blackwell, 2002.

Roberts, J. M. *A History of Europe.* Oxford: Helicon, 1996.

Te Brake, Wayne. *Shaping History: Ordinary People in European Politics 1500–1700.* Berkeley: University of California Press, 1998.

Thackeray, Frank W., and John E. Findling. *Events That Changed the World in the Seventeenth Century.* Westport, Conn.: Greenwood, 1999.

Wheatcroft, Andrew. *The Habsburgs: Embodying Empire.* London, U.K.: Penguin, 1995.

WEB SITES

http://www.bartleby.com/65/ru/Rudolf2.html

http://lcweb2.loc.gov/egi-bin/query/r?frd/cstdy:@field(doc1D_yu0018)

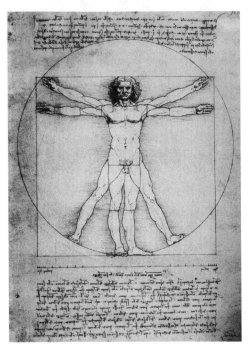

Leonardo da Vinci's "Vitruvian Man," 1492.

10

THE RENAISSANCE

Such noble scenes as draw the eye to flow, we now present.
(*King Henry VIII*, prologue 4–5)

The Renaissance began in Italy in the fourteenth century and swept through northern Europe during the 1400s and 1500s. The definitive hallmark was renewed interest in ancient Greek and Roman writers like Ovid, Aristotle,

Horace, and Seneca. While many scholars studied the works in Greek and Latin, a number of good translations made it possible for readers to enjoy classical works in their own languages.

When the Ottoman Turks gained control of Constantinople in 1453, scholars fled to Italy, taking copies of the ancient texts. Florence was one of the cities that hosted institutes for classical learning and revival. Libraries and academic centers opened their doors to renewed study of Latin and Greek, and sometimes Hebrew or Arabic.

A second feature of this era was the birth of Protestantism, which grew out of the sixteenth-century Reformation in northern Europe, leaving in its wake a profound effect on the religious, political, and social institutions of Europe and beyond. Out of the original Roman Catholic faith sprang branches of worship that evolved into denominations like Lutheranism, Calvinism, and Puritanism.

Globalization was a third characteristic of this period. As European regions solidified land holdings and tightened borders, nationalistic fervor intensified, developing an economy bolstered by foreign trade and colonization. Portugal and Spain led exploratory expeditions to Africa, Asia, and the New World. England and other European countries opened trade companies and sent their own representatives to distant territories.

How did these movements affect Shakespeare? From a pivotal location with the Globe Theater on the Thames River, Shakespeare enjoyed a close view of London society which reflected ideas and movements from abroad. The sonnet trend, for example, had begun with Petrarch in Italy two centuries before. Poets like Sidney, Donne, and Shakespeare adopted the convention and provided unique adaptations. Many of Shakespeare's plots reflect characteristics of both ancient and modern worlds.

Though it is difficult to trace every major movement of the Renaissance to a direct influence on Shakespeare's society, we can discern many effects by examining key ideas that governed philosophy, science, and religion in European culture.

THE GREAT CHAIN OF BEING

> . . . a king may go a progress through the guts of a beggar. (Hamlet, IV.iii.30–31)

Shakespeare's writing manifests the theory of interlocking spheres of hierarchy that defined life as it was understood in his time. The philosophy of existence was characterized by Greek and medieval teachings, derived from Aristotle and based on visual observation. Accordingly the earth was at the center of the universe, surrounded by orbiting planets.

The second century Hellenistic astronomer Ptolemy refined this view to suggest that planets revolved in epicycles in their rotation around earth, a view reflected in Shakespeare's King John:

> Now, now, you stars that move in your right spheres. . . .

> (V.vii.74)

The defining hierarchy placed God at the head of creation, followed by angels, humanity (with monarch as head), animals, plants, and minerals. Human families and human bodies were viewed as microcosms of the universe, each with a head and relevant parts working together efficiently to benefit the whole.

An outgrowth of this philosophy was the divine right of kings as absolute monarchs instituted by the will of God, a view that derived mainly from the Tudors. In 1609 James I took this concept a step further in a speech before Parliament:

> Kings are justly called Gods, for that they exercise a manner or resemblance of Divine power upon earth: For if you will consider the Attributes to God, you shall see how they agree in the person of a King. God hath power to create, or destroy, make, or unmake at his pleasure, to give life or send death, to judge all, to be judged nor accomptable [sic] to none: To raise low things and to make high things low at his pleasure, and to God are both soul and body due. And the like power have Kings. (http://www.wwnorton.com/college/history/ralph/workbook/ralprs20.htm)

The chain of being poised humans between angels and beasts, unifying spirit with matter which was composed of four elements: two earthbound—earth (cold and dry) and water (cold and moist)—and two heaven-directed—air (hot and moist) and fire (hot and dry). Human nature was shaped in corresponding fashion by the four representative humors: melancholy, sanguine, phlegmatic, and choleric.

The chain of being united theology and politics in manifestation of God's will, with the ruler as God's instrument of that will.

HUMANISM

. . . he furnish'd me
From mine own library
with volumes that
I prize above my dukedom. (*The Tempest,* I.ii.166–168)

Humanism is the revival of classical learning, including literature, philosophy, and the sciences. Medieval humanism formed the basis of Renaissance studies when Latin classics provided a liberal education that included grammar and rhetoric.

The classical tradition goes back as far as the Sophists of the fifth century B.C., with a focus on public speaking and oratory. This tradition continued through the Middle Ages. Texts like Martianus Capella's summary of the *Seven Liberal Arts* and Cassiodorus's *Institutes* (including logic, arithmetic, geometry, astronomy, music, grammar, and rhetoric) helped to further this tradition during the Renaissance. Literature centered on man and this world as opposed to the medieval focus on God and the other world.

Northern Italy initiated the development of middle-class capitalistic values, allowing leisure for the arts and an appreciation for the ancients. Classical studies became more widespread due to refugee immigration of Byzantine scholars after the fall of Constantinople to the Turks. Men like More, Erasmus, and Copernicus helped pave the way for movements in religion, philosophy, and science.

Christian and Classical Learning

Science cooperated with occult practices like numerology and the cabala while astronomy linked with astrology to move Europe from medievalism to modernism. Classical teachings by Cato, Cicero, Livy, and Virgil were taught along with new findings and theories in science and faith.

As the influence of earlier great thinkers like Thomas Aquinas began to diminish, fifteenth- and sixteenth-century minds questioned secularism and rulers' rights, exemplified in the writing of Sir Thomas More (1478–1535), an English statesman who was beheaded for his faith, and Desiderius Erasmus (1466?–1536), a Dutch scholar and traveler who brought a humanistic perspective to Christian ethics.

New World discoveries helped to consolidate European identity. Christian humanists renewed an emphasis on theology over philosophy. They strove to mesh classical and Christian studies, in some cases by introducing the Hebrew language in grammar school. Puritans sifted classical works for parallels to Christian beliefs, sometimes quoting Plato, Aristotle, and others from the pulpit or in their writings.

Higher Education

While university training was not a common expectation, higher education began to flourish. Universities multiplied, with 11 new campuses in Germany during the fifteenth century; Wittenberg was the most famous of these. In Spain, 16 universities were founded during the early 1600s, including the University of Granada. Many of Shakespeare's plays depict tutoring scenes or use language of learning, including "books" or "bookish," "library," "college," "scholar," "student," "school," "schoolmaster" or "schoolboys," "teach," "inkhorn," "education," "read" or "reads," and so on.

As in England, Europe's well-born sons received a university degree and some went on to become professional writers, though it was difficult to earn a living in the arts. The concept of "Renaissance man" evolved, demonstrated in the successful attainment of many skills rather than one specialty. For example, the leading French Renaissance scholar Guillaume Bude (1467–1540) was a lawyer, classicist, and teacher who founded the College de France in 1530. Jacques Lefevre d'Etaples (1450–1536) was influenced by Pico della Mirandola's interest in mysticism, the occult, and Cabalism; his work influenced humanists seeking to create a reform movement within the Catholic Church.

In Florence, Cosimo de' Medici, wealthy banker and political figure, founded Academia in 1457, appointing Marsilio Ficino as head of an institution

where scholars met to share their studies. Ficino translated Plato and conducted seminars on Platonic ideas; he also wrote *The Platonic Theology*.

Pico della Mirandola studied at Bologna, Padua, and Florence. Later he
learned Hebrew and Arabic. In 1486 he wrote *On the Dignity of Man,* suggesting that all philosophers see a part of the truth. He died at age 31.

Humanist Reformers

Humanists sought to educate society using newly printed works and translations of earlier Latin and Greek works, making knowledge available to the general public.

One such humanist was the duchess of Alençon and queen of Navarre,
Marguerite d'Angouleme (1492–1549), sister of Francis I. She helped to make
the universities at Bourges and Navarre humanist centers. She knew Latin,
Spanish, and Greek and studied the Scriptures in their original form. A Christian
humanist, she wrote poems like *Le Miroir de l'ame pecheresse* (The mirror and
the sinful soul). Her work *The Heptameron,* 70 tales based on Boccaccio's
Decameron, combines religious and bawdy perspectives.

Spain was a central site for the merging of several humanist developments,
including Arab studies and Jewish mysticism. Greek refugees flocked to the
Iberian peninsula and its universities. Spanish humanists studied at the Italian
universities during the Renaissance, returning home with new ideas. Antonio
de Nebrija (1444–1522) wrote a treatise against the vulgarities of Latin and
books on Spanish geography and history, including *The Decades,* leading to his
appointment as the royal historian. He was especially interested in the Bible
and biblical criticism. A humanist reformer named Juan Luis Vives (1492–1540)
wrote *De institutione feminae Christianae* (On the education of a Christian
woman), which advocated female education.

Humanist Scholars

Rudolf Agricola (1444–85), the father of German humanism, studied at Erfurt,
Louvain, and Cologne before furthering his studies in Italy. Returning to
Germany in 1479, he spent his last six years promoting the northern Renaissance
in culture and religion. Johann Reuchlin (1455–1522) was admired throughout
Europe. He studied at Orleans, Paris, Basel, and Rome, intrigued by the Jewish
Cabala.

Englishmen John Whethamsted and Thomas Linacre studied in Italy, with
Linacre receiving a medical degree in 1496 at Padua and publishing work on
the Greek physicians and translations of Galen (Shakespeare mentions Galen in
King Henry IV—Part Two). Linacre became court tutor under Henry VII and
Henry VIII. John Colet (1466–1519) explored scholastic philosophy and
rhetoric before traveling to Italy to study at the Florentine Academy. With a desire to make the apostle Paul's words realistic and meaningful, he founded Saint
Paul's School in London, which emphasized that truth must be discovered individually and personally.

Sir Thomas More (1478–1535) was born in London and educated in the law, becoming a speaker in the House of Commons by 1523 and Lord Chancellor of England from 1529 to 1532. He resigned when Henry VIII divorced Catherine of Aragon. When More refused to acknowledge the king as head of the English church, Henry charged him with treason and had him beheaded. More's best-known work *Utopia,* where charity, reason, cooperation, and virtue ruled, was published in 1516 and describes the potential for ideality on an imaginary island.

> If evil opinions cannot be quite rooted out, and if you cannot correct habitual attitudes as you wish, you must not therefore abandon the commonwealth. Don't give up the ship in a storm because you cannot control the winds. And do not force unheard-of advice upon people, when you know that their minds are different from yours. You must strive to guide policy indirectly, so that you can make the best of things, and what you cannot turn to good, you can at lest make less bad. For it is impossible to do all things well unless all men are good, and this I do not expect to see for a long time. *(Jensen 1992, 382)*

William Shakespeare contributed to a play entitled *Sir Thomas More* that was produced in 1603–04.

The Baroque Era

The term "baroque" may come from the Portuguese "barroco" meaning "an irregularly shaped pearl." Sometimes used disparagingly, baroque generally refers to post-Renaissance architecture which some regard as decadent—unstructured, overadorned, and grotesque, perhaps the Catholic response to Protestantism. However, baroque style also includes spacious and dynamic, sensual and ecstatic elements. Baroque expansionism reflected the wars between city-states that were replaced by wars between countries and continents.

The Baroque is the age of theatre, when art becomes opulent. Fashions were more ornate and less functional. Art included work by El Greco (Domeniko Thetokopoulos, 1547–1614), Inigo Jones (1573–1652), Rembrandt Van Rijn (1606–69), and Peter Paul Rubens (1577–1640).

THE EUROPEAN RENAISSANCE

> *. . . other men . . . Put forth their sons to seek preferment out:*
> *Some to the wars, to try their fortune there;*
> *Some to discover islands far away;*
> *Some to the studious universities. (Two Gentlemen of Verona, I.iii.6–10)*

The period 1485 to 1625 has been called the Renaissance, the Age of Exploration, the Age of Discovery, and the Reformation. Others date the Renaissance between the Black Death (1348–51) and the Thirty Years' War (1618–48). This period marks Europe's transition from the medieval to the modern world through a series of cultural outgrowths.

Moving man to the center of the universe and displacing God outward, Renaissance thinkers introduced humanist philosophy based on the medieval rediscovery of classical philosophy, art, and values. The early modern period is characterized by interest in human capabilities. The Renaissance drew people into smaller, more localized communities from the feudal estates of the Middle Ages. In a prospering economy, ideals of beauty, love, and power became practical goals for the middle class as well as the elite.

New World discoveries and trade with distant regions introduced new cultural perspectives. Printing contributed to the spread of learning, with increasing use of paper over parchment. Study of the classics and Scripture inspired artists to create meaning and beauty in unique patterns, often by combining the two themes. Humanists attempted to harmonize nature with humans and humans with God.

Cultural expansion and geographical exploration were propellants of new ideas, as European nations competed for Eastern trade and Western colonization. Nationalism swept the continent, bringing with it a growing sense of selfhood and "otherness" which led to intolerant attitudes and violent means of controlling "difference," whether in religious views or racial hues.

Class Structure

With the rise of a society built on commercial enterprise, capitalism created a merchant class that linked rich and poor. In Italy a family's bloodline rather than its wealth remained the true measure of nobility. Distinctions between classes blurred as wealthy merchants competed with noble landowners for power.

In his work *On Nobility,* Florentine humanist Poggio Bracciolini argued for the existence of two noble types—the right and the wrong, the good and the bad—with landed gentry comprising the first group and rich business owners, the second. Fashion and dress reflected class systems. Italian styles were exquisite, with excessive cosmetics.

Clergy composed a third group. Though they did not pay taxes and could not be prosecuted in civil courts, the clergy wielded great influence. Sometimes clerical authority was used to ill purpose, as when Dominican friar Girolamo Savonarola railed against the Florentine Jews in the 1490s, his invective spilling over into political turmoil that led to his execution.

Another social class included craftsmen and artisans. Guilds for each group offered protection and sometimes advancement. Then as now the lower classes included those without jobs or property.

Music

> . . . I know she taketh most delight
> In music, instruments, and poetry. (*The Taming of the Shrew,* I.i.92–93)

Music reflects or perhaps even forms the values of a society, and music of the Renaissance is admired for its contribution to culture. Several key figures composed or performed music that society enjoyed. It is likely Shakespeare and his contemporaries were familiar with the names of many composers, or more likely, with their compositions.

Thomas Tallio (1505–85), an organist, published vocal music. He wrote choral music in the ornate Latin style and he developed the English anthem. His last and best-known work is *The Lamentations of Jeremiah*.

Giovanni de Palestrina (1525?–94) was a choirboy as early as 1537 and an organist by 1544. He married Lucrezia Gori in 1547 and they had three children. In 1551 Palestrina was appointed maestro di cappella of the Cappella Giulia in Rome. By 1554 he was writing masses and madrigals. His conservative style emphasized balance.

Orlande de Lassus (1532–94) served Gonzaga of Mantua, whom he accompanied to Sicily and Milan. In 1553 he joined the archbishop of Florence's household, and by 1556 he was a singer. De Lassus traveled widely and was influential, and the pope made him the Knight of the Golden Spur in 1574. De Lassus wrote more than 2,000 works of all genres, including masses, psalms, hymns, and secular music in Italian, French, and German.

William Byrd (1542/3?–1623) was the greatest English composer of the age. Though Catholic, he provided music for the Chapel Royal as well as for the Church of England liturgy. His work includes anthems, psalms, and consort songs, and blending music for groups of instruments, especially viols.

Shakespeare's writing uses song to accent celebrations and rituals. For example, *A Midsummer Night's Dream* concludes with a song and dance by Oberon commemorating the marriage of three couples. In *The Merchant of Venice* background music plays during Bassanio's reflection on the correct choice of casket. Even the tragic *Antony and Cleopatra* includes a bacchanal-type celebratory song. Music was an important part of Elizabethan stage drama.

Politics

What, rate, rebuke, and roughly send to prison
Th' immediate heir of England! (*King Henry IV—Part Two*, V.ii.70–71)

Like art, politics and religion played key roles in the European Renaissance. Religious dissension boiled over, leading to schisms, and later, reform. Political intrigue operated at city, state, and empire levels as old boundaries were changed for new, and allegiances were parlayed and replaced.

Shakespeare's histories illustrate political theories like Machiavelli's, and he alludes to other modes of leadership in works like *The Tempest* and *King Lear*. As a court dramatist, Shakespeare undoubtedly was familiar with political treatises of the day. While he wisely kept his personal views to himself, in this section we look at possible influences.

Niccolo Machiavelli   In his work *The Prince* (ca. 1513), Niccolo Machiavelli expounds a secular approach to rule in a departure from the chain of
being concept. Machiavelli felt the social order could be constructed by the
will of a politician, a leader who would make firm, forthright decisions.
Somewhat Calvinist in his view of humanity, Machiavelli saw people as essen-
tially evil and in need of control. His concept of a leader was as a ruthless individual willing to use any means, but especially cunning and strength, to get
results. Machiavelli wrote this work as a guide plan for Giuliano de' Medici,
advocating the use of deceit and even murder to achieve princely ends and
maintain order. His perspective sometimes is misunderstood to encourage cruelty, when it was intended as a pragmatic approach to controlling unruly
masses or immoral opportunists.

Machiavelli's ideas appeared in dramatic form in plays like Christopher
Marlowe's *The Jew of Malta* which includes a Prologue reference:

> To some, perhaps, my name is odious,
> But such as love me guard me from their tongues,
> And let them know that I am Machiavel, . . .
> I count religion but a childish toy
> And hold there is no sin but ignorance.

> *(Prologue. 5–9, 14–15)*

Shakespeare likewise makes use of the name in *The Merry Wives of
Windsor* and *King Henry VI—Parts One and Three*. His villains—many drawn
from English history—hint at the dark aspects of Machiavellian leadership, as
seen in this speech by Gloster:

> I can add colors to the chameleon,
> Change shapes with Proteus for advantages,
> And set the murtherous Machevil to school.
> Can I do this, and cannot get a crown?

> *(King Henry VI—Part Three, III.ii.191–194)*

Machiavelli also wrote *The Art of War* and a volume on Florentine history.
Violence and force, like the manipulation of religious authority and the mirror
of public theatre, became tools of power in Renaissance Europe. Machiavelli's
works emphasize the glories of virtuous rule, even though he believed that
questionable means sometimes are necessary to achieve success.

Literature

Words, words, words. (Hamlet, II.ii.192)

Renaissance writers mined classical works like Aristotle's *Poetics* and Horace's
Techniques of Poetry for literary tutelage. While dramatists continued to observe the Aristotelian unities, some experimented with new forms.

Giovanni Boccaccio (1313–75) lived in Florence and Naples. An excellent Greek student, he was Dante's first professor. He also had an affair with Maria, the illegitimate daughter of King Robert of Naples. Boccaccio's work displays a contrast between the sensual and the spiritual sides of love in the tradition of Plato. His was the first work in the vernacular utilizing a simple prose style with occasional crudity. His *Decameron* offers a hundred tales told during ten days at a villa outside Florence during the 1348 plague. Many writers from a variety of cultures emulated his style, including Shakespeare in *A Midsummer Night's Dream* and *Much Ado About Nothing* where courtly folk pursue love and playfully banter.

Ludovico Ariosto (1474–1553) came from a noble family. After studying law at the University of Ferrara he enjoyed life at the court of Este while writing comedies and satires. His *Orlando Furioso,* a romantic epic, emphasizes the distinction between idealism and realism. His work displays a courteous attitude toward women, yet likewise depicts the female warrior—the type of female found in Shakespeare's Portia in *The Merchant of Venice* and the Egyptian queen in *Antony and Cleopatra.* Ariosto's writing blends grace and coarseness in a style that came to be known as "volupta."

Torquato Tasso (1544–95) was born at Sorrento and received a quality education in the classics. He joined Padua's Academy of the Ethereals and spent a good part of his life moving from one place to the next. Tasso's writing demonstrates religious and poetic inspiration as depicted in his pastoral drama *Aminta* (1573), a form that rapidly spread throughout Western Europe. Tasso distinguishes the man of thought from the man of action, a contrast explored by Shakespeare in *Hamlet.* His epic *Jerusalem Delivered* combines images of war and love, the supernatural and the natural. Tasso also ponders the influence of the Turks. At the end of his life he was sent to the hospital of St. Anne for the poor and lunatic.

The Fugger Newsletters, 1568–1604   During the Renaissance, prose writing also impacted culture. It would be decades before newspapers or periodicals came into vogue, but commercially established families found it necessary to keep in contact via frequent letters, some of which eventually were shared with the public. One of the best examples of such correspondence is evidenced in the Fugger letters, or newsletters, during the second half of the sixteenth century.

The Fugger family built a banking fortune during the late 1500s and early 1600s. They lent money to European heads of state, including the Habsburgs who ruled central Europe, the Netherlands, Spain, and Italy.

Count Philip Edward Fugger (1546–1618) created a newsletter that included topical news items from his hometown of Augsburg, in which he posted current event stories from employees of the branch offices. Much of the material was later copied, and in 1655 Emperor Ferdinand III bought the family's library, which included the newsletters.

Such letters provided detailed information about daily life. In England, Philip Henslowe's diary, which recorded his business transactions as well as personal events, offered similar information. Readers can learn about the costs of drama production and the business machinations of an energetic theater manager.

Self-portrait, Sofonisba Anguissola, painting the Madonna, 1556.

Art

For I will [raise] her statue in pure gold. (*Romeo and Juliet*, V.iii.299)

A plethora of art forms sprang to life during the Renaissance. Many period works help us relive great events of history and literature captured in the skill of renowned painters and sculptors.

Everyday times and people are represented by English artists like Nicholas Hilliard. Similar themes appear in paintings by Low Country artists like John de Critz the Elder. A variety of forms proliferated, including portrait and landscape painting, architecture, painted wall hangings, engravings, and family art works depicting genealogies and coats of arms.

Philosophers viewed the universe as a series of interlocking hierarchies. Images of chains and ladders may be seen in works like Perugia's 1579 *Rhetorica christiana* and Boethius's *De musica* and *Consolation of Philosophy*. In Neoplatonic thought, humans climbing celestial ladders exchange physical for spiritual senses, evidenced in works like Albrecht Durer's *Melancolia I* (1514), displaying a fusion of biblical and platonic ideals.

Architecture flourished as family residences and public buildings were adorned with sculptured doors, cabinets, baptisteries, and panels. Funerary art also emerged.

Patronage was the primary source of income for artists. The pope provided a livelihood for many aspiring geniuses, as did rulers throughout Europe. Noble families hired painters, sculptors, and architects to create monuments attesting to family status, holdings, or connections.

Renaissance art highlighted religious and classical subjects, guided by techniques of proportion and balance. Intrigued by the human body and its relation to the cosmos, painters and sculptors arranged subjects in natural positions to depict humans as overseers of nature. Perspective, dimension, and light with shadow formed new applications. The merging of two lines of vision to form an acute angle utilized plane geometry to align hard science with creative ingenuity. Unity within an organized cosmos came to be increasingly valued following the seismic conflicts within Christianity and discoveries by European adventurers.

Lorenzo Ghiberti of Florence spent nearly a quarter of a century designing and building the bronze north doors of the Florence baptistery, followed by another 30 years on the east doors. The first set of 28 panels portrayed New Testament scenes, while the second set illustrated Old Testament motifs. His panels came to be known as the "Gates of Paradise" (Jensen 1992, 164).

Michelangelo Buonarroti (1475–1564), sculptor, architect, and painter, worked in Florence and Rome. Influenced by Plato, Michelangelo was a true "universal man," multitalented and moral. His work evidences character and mood, as seen in marble statues based on religious themes, like his *Pieta* and *David*. His painting of the Sistine Chapel ceiling (over 6,300 square feet) is a monumental testament to the genius and fortitude of Michelangelo's talent.

Sandro Botticelli (1444–1510), painter and student of Fra Filippo Lippi, sought artistic inspiration in classical and religious sources. His paintings project sensual beauty and grace. Botticelli's *Birth of Venus* is interpreted as an allegory depicting astrological or mythological meaning. The figure of Venus, like others of classical origin, enjoyed huge popularity in art and literature during the Renaissance. Shakespeare's *Venus and Adonis* is an adaptation of this theme in his poetry.

Leonardo da Vinci (1452–1519), painter and sculptor, trained in Florence and studied under Verrocchio. Many of Da Vinci's works remained unfinished; most experiment with light and shadow. Two of his greatest works, *The Last Supper* and the *Mona Lisa,* depict mastery of facial expression and physical movement (Jensen 1992, 177). Leonardo's notebooks contain detailed information about his drawings and interests, including engineering and human anatomy. His philosophy of art was that inspiration is guided by perspective to reflect nature.

Raffaello Sanzio or "Raphael" (1483–1520) was the son of a court painter who studied under Pietro Perugino and later, Leonardo da Vinci. Pope Julius II invited Raphael and other celebrated artists to the papal court. Raphael's *School of Athens* depicts Plato and Aristotle amid other philosophers. Many of his works feature simple madonnas.

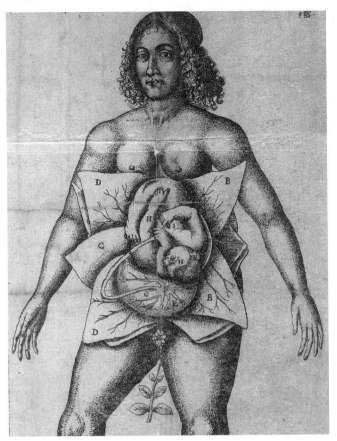

Anatomical drawing of a woman and unborn child in the uterus, from "The Midwives Book," 1671.

Other talented artists deserve attention that this space cannot provide. The following figures provide additional glimpses of Renaissance talent. Tiziano Vecellio or "Titian" (1477–1576) experimented with mannerism and the baroque. His famous patrons included the Holy Roman Emperor Charles V. Hans Holbein came from Basel to England to paint portraits of Henry VIII and members of his court. Leone Battista Alberti, a fifteenth-century architect, drew up plans for Rome's St. Peter's Cathedral. Alberti's treatise on architecture was translated into several languages and was especially valued for his teaching of perspective that merged principles of math and art.

Science

Does not our lives consist of the four elements? (Twelfth Night, II.iii.9–10)

Interest in science increased as new discoveries and developments spurred experimentation in a wide range of studies.

Theories included dualism and polarity, motion and rest, and the Creator's design versus human design. The four elements, building blocks of the cosmos, were thought to shape human behavior. In Shakespeare's day it was understood the earth was round:

The acts commenced on this ball of earth.

(King Henry IV–Part Two, Induction. 1. 5)

Platonic theory alludes to earth's "four spheres":

1. A fluid level of which we know little.
2. The hollow level where good spirits dwell.
3. Within this was a sphere of air, called the middle region, which was cold and perhaps evil, filled with stars and darkness, with two parts.
   a. One was the pure air above the clouds called the "emphyrean" region, home of gryphons and eagles.
   b. In lower air, below the clouds, was the air for humans to breathe.
4. The lowest region was the earth's center, called hollow earth, which was cold and home to bad spirits.

The notion of an Aristotelian universe with earth at its center, orbited by the planets, remained popular well into the fifteenth century. Although men like Nicholas of Cusa theorized that the earth rotated around the sun, it was not until Nicolaus Copernicus (1473–1543) set out to refine rather than to challenge Aristotle's beliefs that fundamental adjustments gained widespread acceptance. Copernicus's *De revolutionibus orbium* was written in 1530 but remained unpublished until his death in 1543.

Aristotle's "clock work" theory of a Supreme Being who wound the universe like a clock and set it in motion gained popularity. Perhaps ten of Shakespeare's plays refer to clocks or time, as do many of the sonnets. References to "mechanical" in *Julius Caesar* and "whirlagig" in *Twelfth Night* suggest natural processes under human control.

Galileo Galilei   Galileo (1564–1642) was an Italian scientist and philosopher who applied mathematical principles to the study of astronomy and physics. Born in Pisa, his father was a musician for a noble family. In 1581 Galileo entered the University of Pisa where he studied the pendulum and Aristotelian physics, and later proved that objects fall at the same rate of speed in a vacuum, no matter what their weight. He went on to write *De Motu* (On motion) and in 1592 became professor of mathematics at Pisa. Galileo studied mechanics and shipbuilding, and he patented a pump modeled on European prototypes.

Galileo never married, but a relationship with Marina Gamba resulted in two daughters who entered the convent and a son who joined Galileo when he took a position with the Medici family in Florence in 1610. Galileo's most famous invention was a telescope that magnified an object 20 times, replacing weaker scopes that magnified only three times. His discoveries, including views of the moon, four satellites of Jupiter, and sunspots, supported the Copernican theory that the earth revolves around the sun, not vice versa. Because of these untraditional assertions, Galileo faced the Inquisition and was placed under house arrest until his death.

Nicolaus Copernicus   Nicolaus Copernicus (1473–1543) entered the University of Krakow in 1491 before studying medicine at Padua. In 1500 he became chair of the Mathematics Department at Rome, and in 1507 he began to teach that the earth circled the sun, refuting the belief that the sun circled the earth. His studies unlocked the simple premise of a spherical universe:

> First, we must remark that the universe is spherical in form, partly because this form being a perfect whole requiring no joints, is the most *complete of* all, partly because it makes the most capacious form, which is best suited to contain and preserve everything; or again because all the constituent parts of the universe, that is the sun, moon and the planets appear in this form; or because everything strives to attain this form, as appears in the case of drops of water and other fluid bodies if they attempt to define themselves. . . . (http://www.fordham.edu/halsall/mod/1543copernicus2.html)

Copernicus's studies supported earlier theories to instigate further exploration of the universe.

Nostradamus   Michel de Nostradame (Nostradamus) (1503–66), French astrologer and physician, attended the University of Montpellier from 1522 until 1525 when plague closed the medical school. His efforts to fight plague were surprisingly successful and he was offered a teaching position when the university reopened.

Restricted by an academic routine, Nostradamus accepted an offer to study with Joseph Scaliger, a highly regarded European scholar in Agen. A later plague outbreak killed Nostradamus's wife and two children and a conflict with Scaliger damaged his reputation. Like Leonardo, Nostradamus was charged with heresy.

In 1538 he began traveling throughout France and Italy, practicing medicine and making prophecies. In 1547 he settled in Salon and married again. By 1550 Nostradamus had begun publishing almanacs, and in 1554, *Presages*. Between 1554 and 1565 he wrote *Centuries*, collections of 100 quatrains of prophetic verse.

His prophecies have been interpreted to mean different things. Many people today hold to the teachings of Nostradamus, believing his prophecies will prove true in today's world.

Johannes Kepler   Johannes Kepler (1571–1630) was a German astronomer and philosopher. Studying theology and classics at the University of Tubingen, he is best known for confirming the Copernican system of planetary motion.

Figure II-1. **The Sultan Mehmet II.** Attributed to Gentile Bellini.
© National Gallery Collection; by kind permission of the Trustees
of the National Gallery, London/CORBIS.

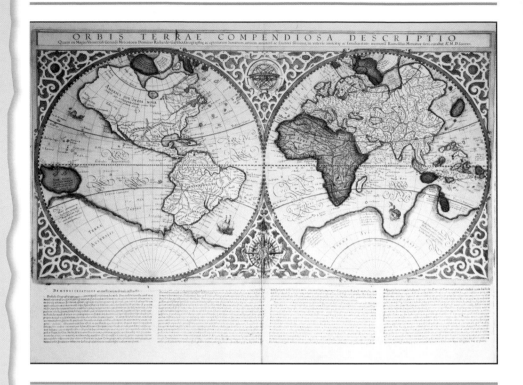

Figure II-2. **World Map from Mercator Atlas Showing Terra Australia, 1595.** Royal Geographical Society, London/Bridgeman Art Library, London. © SuperStock, Inc.

Figure II-3. **Air.** One of the four paintings showing the four elements ordered in 1607 by Cardinal Federico Borromeo of Milan. Canvas, 46 x 67 cm. Louvre, Paris, France. Art Resource, New York.

Figure II-4. **Title page of the first edition of the King James Bible, London, 1611.** The Granger Collection.

Copernicus believed that the planets move around the sun and that the earth spins from west to east on a north-south axis at the rate of one rotation per day. Kepler added three principles to the Copernican system:

1. The planets orbit the sun in elliptical paths.
2. The closer to the sun the planets are, the more rapidly they move.
3. The ratio of the cube of a planet's mean distance is the same for all planets.

In 1596 Kepler published *Cosmographic Mystery.* He was chair of the Department of Astronomy and Mathematics at the University of Graz from 1594 to 1600, where he assisted the Danish scientist Tyco Brahe in his observatory near Prague. When Brahe died in 1601, Kepler succeeded him as court mathematician and astronomer to Rudolf II. In 1609 Kepler published his *Astronomia Nova,* followed in 1619 by *Harmonice Mundi.* His work influenced later scientists, including the English Sir Isaac Newton.

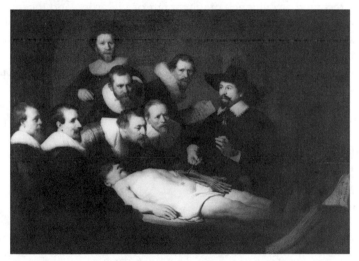

The Anatomy Lesson. Rembrandt, Dutch, 1606–1669. The Anatomy Lesson of Dr. Tulip, 1632. Oil on canvas, 169.5 × 216.5 cm. The Hague, Mauritshuis.

ALTERNATIVE LIFESTYLES

Cesario, come—
For so you shall be while you are a man;
But when in other habits you are seen,
Orsino's mistress, and his fancy's queen. (*Twelfth Night,* V.i.385–388)

While promiscuity and deviance have always claimed their share of attention in Western culture, the Renaissance provided a fertile environment for exploration of and experimentation with alternative lifestyles and sexuality.

Sex remains a topic of interest in any time period, and the Renaissance was no exception. Period writings in literature, pamphlets, and records outline new ways of viewing love and relationships. Shifting cultural boundaries began to relax medieval notions of sexual purity, evidenced, for example, in some couples cohabiting before taking church vows. Renaissance drama capitalized on sexual punning and immoral behavior, acknowledging while not exactly endorsing extramarital relations. Shakespeare's *Measure for Measure,* set in Vienna, contrasts the hypocrisy of a self-righteous ruler who abandoned his fiancée with the sincere love of a jailed man for his pregnant girlfriend.

European society generally used biblical standards as moral boundaries, yet unconventional relationships were evident in many cultures.

Homosexuality and Cross-Dressing

The term "homosexual" was not used during the Renaissance. Instead, same-sex relations were labeled as "sodomy," including buggery and tribade activity. Prostitution and sodomy sometimes were viewed interchangeably. Such acts could be presented as evidence of witchcraft or wizardry, and those caught in the act (or in some cases merely accused) could be put to death. Teens might receive a beating or a few weeks in jail, but older partners were treated more harshly, some burned at the stake.

A few European cities regulated sexual commerce while others forbade it. Laws more stringently outlawed cross-dressing. Homoerotic desire, though technically illegal, was tacitly evidenced, like female prostitution, at all levels of society. Cross-dressing, a popular convention found in the drama of Shakespeare and others, was imported from Italian comedy. Some critics believe dramatists used this convention as a vehicle to display homoerotic behavior.

Literary Allusions

Before the Reformation, sodomy was an ecclesiastical offense pertaining mostly to clergy who were forced to practice celibacy. In fact, the term may refer to acts like masturbation and extramarital activity in general rather than to homosexuality specifically. Deviation from married heterosexual relations was associated with witchcraft in the public mind. In 1533, Parliament passed An Act for the Punishment of the Vice of buggery:

> Forasmuch as there is not yet sufficient and condign punishment appointed and limited by the due course of the laws of this realm for the detestable and abominable vice of buggery committed with mankind or beast. . . . (http://www.sbu.ac.uk/stafflag/buggeryact.html)

Sodomy was considered a felony for which the penalty was death without benefit of clergy and forfeiture of the felon's property. Mary I repealed this statute with many others from her father's reign, but in 1563 Parliament revived the 1533 statute.

Renaissance literature offers limited insights into same-sex unions. Critics have found scant evidence of lesbian relationships based on prosecution records, with a few in France, Germany, Switzerland, and Italy. Current research suggests the possibility of homosexual attraction in same-sex environments such as convents, educational institutions, or the military. Verses hint in a veiled way at such encounters, as suggested, for example, in Pontus de Tyard's 1573 elegy *A Lady Enamoured of Another Lady.*

John Donne's poem *Sapho to Philaenis* details the Greek poet's attraction to another woman. Other writers present more questioning or critical views, such as Ben Jonson's *Epigram on the Court Pucell* which seems to denigrate lesbian attraction. Generally, female attractions grew out of similar backgrounds and tastes beginning with a solid friendship and progressing to strong affections largely devoid of sexual contact.

James I maintained a bevy of attractive young courtiers such as James Hay, Robert Carr, and George Villiers, and his interests were well recognized at court and abroad. Homosexual behavior seems to have been condemned publicly and practiced marginally without arousing much official concern.

NOBLE WOMEN

Dear queen . . . Give me that hand of yours to kiss. (*The Winter's Tale*, V.iii.45–46)

As in England, women's roles in Europe were limited. Most women married and bore children, some of which survived childhood. Occasionally women took jobs in the public sector but these positions were low status and poorly paid. They included nursing in orphanages and hospitals, midwifery, and marketing domestic goods. Girls who did not marry entered the convent or were cared for by family members. Sumptuary laws controlled the degree to which fashion could be copied by all but aristocrats, as dress reflected class culture.

Aided by social position inherited by birth or marriage, a number of women mastered classical learning and took an active interest in the arts. Isabella d'Este, daughter of the duke of Ferrara, was celebrated for her beauty, mind, and taste. Contemporaries called her the "the first lady of the world." Receiving a valuable education, she took an active role in drawing talented artisans to the Mantua court where she also established a great library. About two thousand of her letters still exist, including one from the husband of her sister Beatrice, who demonstrated a similar personality:

> I cannot explain a thousandth part of the things that the Duchess of Milan and my wife do, and of the pleasure they take in horse-riding at full gallop, coming up behind their ladies-in-waiting and making them fall off. Now they are in Milan, and as it was raining yesterday, they went with four or five ladies on a shopping expedition on foot about the city, with those rough cloth hoods on their heads to keep them dry. As it is not the fashion to go about with these here, it seems that some

women were pleased to pass remarks, and my wife got angry and began to shower abuse on them, so that it seemed they would come to blows. They came home all spattered and torn, which was a beautiful sight. I believe that when your Ladyship is here, they will go about with greater spirit, because they will have you with them, and you are very high tempered so that if anyone dares to abuse them, your Ladyship will defend them with your knife. (Jensen 1992, 74)

Isabella monitored local political events and succeeded in having her eldest son rule as duke of Mantua, with her second son as cardinal.

Other spirited women include Caterina Sforza who led the defense of Forli against Cesare Borgia in 1499. When he eventually won, she went to Rome as a prisoner but was called "the Amazon of Forli" by the pope. She also wrote a book of medical and cosmetic advice and recipes.

Margaret of Parma, illegitimate sister of Philip II, ruled the Netherlands for nine years and postponed an uprising there. Louise of Savoy, whose son Francis became king of France, helped to negotiate peace between France and Spain in 1529 in what became known as the Paix des Dames, or Women's Peace, which was concluded with the help of Margaret of Austria, aunt of Charles V.

Lucrezia Borgia's father used her as a pawn in marrying her to three Italian warlords to build alliances. In 1483 at age 13 she married Giovanni Sforza. The next year her father annulled the marriage and wed her to Alfonso of Aragon, illegitimate son of the late king of Naples. The two fell in love, but her husband was killed two years later, probably from political intrigue. Her third marriage was to Alfonso d'Este, younger brother of Isabella and Beatrice, who ruled Ferrara from 1505 to 1534. She bore him seven children and died in childbirth at age 39.

Catherine de Medici brought refinements to the French court. Though blamed for the St. Bartholomew massacre, she faced Protestant Huguenots and helped promote stability. Louise Labe, sixteenth-century artist, poet, and musician, served in the army at age 16 with her father and later formed a salon of poets and artists.

SUMMARY

Renaissance Europe became a center of grandeur and creativity, inspiring talented individuals to share their genius with the culture that nurtured them. This was a unique period in Western civilization when revival of the classics combined with contemporary humanism to create a new social order that fostered cultural growth and individualistic expression.

SOURCES

Artz, Frederick B. *Renaissance Humanism, 1300–155*. Kent, Ohio: Kent State University Press, 1966.

Bartlett, Kenneth R., and Margaret McGlynn, eds. *Humanism and the Northern Renaissance*. Toronto: Canadian Scholars, 2000.

Barzun, Jacques. *From Dawn to Decadence: 1500 to the Present.* New York: HarperCollins, 2001.

"Counter-Reformation." Encyclopedia.com (Electric Library).

De la Crois, Horst, and Richard G. Tansey. *Gardner's Art through the Ages.* 6th ed. rev. New York: Harcourt, 1975.

Jensen, De Lamar. *Renaissance Europe: Age of Recovery and Reconciliation.* 2d ed. Lexington, Mass.: D. C. Heath, 1992.

"Johannes, Kepler." Microsoft Encarta Online Encyclopedia. 2001.

Rowse, A. L. *The Elizabethan Renaissance.* London: Macmillan, 1971.

Ruggiero, Guido. "Marriage, Love, Sex, and Renaissance Civic Morality." In *Sexuality and Gender in Early Modern Europe,* ed. James Grantham Turner, 10–30. Cambridge: Cambridge University Press, 1993.

Zophy, Jonathan W. *A Short History of Renaissance and Reformation Europe: Dances over Fire and Water.* Upper Saddle River, N.J.: Prentice Hall, 1996.

QUESTIONS

1. How did scientific beliefs influence writers like Shakespeare and his contemporaries?
2. What themes do literature and art share?
3. What are some popular classical and Biblical themes of Renaissance art?
4. How did noble European women become popular with the public?

CRITICAL THINKING AND RESEARCH PROJECTS

1. Examine the development of a well-known theme in literature or art by several artists, comparing their treatment of the same subject.
2. Analyze a literary work to explain its political or scientific influence.
3. Compare Shakespeare's view of the universe as expressed in his writing to popular theories by Kepler or Copernicus.
4. Analyze Shakespeare's treatment of a classic story—does he seem to respect or denigrate the classics?

FOR FURTHER READING

Erikson, Peter, and Clark Hulse. *Early Modern Visual Culture: Representation, Race, and Empire in Renaissance England.* Philadelphia: University of Pennsylvania Press, 2000.

Fox, Alistair. *The English Renaissance: Identity and Representation in Elizabethan England.* Oxford; Malden, Mass.: Blackwell, 1992.

Hadfield, Andrew. *The English Renaissance 1500–1620.* Oxford; Malden, Mass: Blackwell, 2001.

Haynes, Maria S. *The Italian Renaissance and Its Influence on Western Civilization.* Lanham, Md.: University Press of America, 1991.

Rowse, A. L. *The Elizabethan Renaissance: The Cultural Achievement.* Chicago: Ivan R. Dee, 2000.

Stephens, James. *Francis Bacon and the Style of Science.* Chicago: University of Chicago Press, 1975.

Yates, Frances A. *Ideas and Ideals in the North European Renaissance.* College Essays, Vol. III. London: Routledge, 1984.

WEB SITES

http://www.wwnorton.com/college/history/ralph/workbook/ralprs20.htm

http://www.fordham.edu/halsall/mod/1543copernicus2.html

http://www.sbu.ac.uk/stafflag/buggeryact.html

Internet Encyclopedia of Philosophy: Renaissance.
http://www.utm.edu/research/iep/r/renaiss/htm

Virtual Renaissance: Chronology of Art and Science.
http://www.twingroves.district96.k12.il.us/Renaissance/GeneralFiles/C_ArtScience.html

The Feast of Sadeh. Firdawsi (active 975–1010), "Shah-nameh" (Book of Kings): Feast of Sadeh. From a manuscript dedicated to Shah Tahmasp (1524–1576). Attributable to Sultan Muhammad. Colors: ink, silver and gold on paper. Painting: Gr. H 9-½ in (27.4 cm), Gr. W 9-1/16 in (23 cm). Iranian. Paintings. Tabriz. Safavid Period, ca. 1520–22. The Metropolitan Museum of Art, Gift of Arthur A. Houghton, Jr., 1970. (1970.301.2) Photograph © 1992 The Metropolitan Museum of Art.

11

EASTERN EMPIRES

Why, she defies me,
Like Turk to Christian.
(*As You Like It,* IV.iii.32–33)

Under Elizabeth's rule, England embraced global significance and claimed territories the world over. Guided by capable navigators like Sir Walter Raleigh and cartographers like Richard Hakluyt, the English charted numerous lands and waters.

221

European explorers, African mysteries, and Asian attractions planted exploratory interests in England's fecund minds. Like other dramatists, William Shakespeare took advantage of contemporary events published in broad sheets (an early newspaper) that appeared in London streets. Along with letters of merchants and nobles, government reports and proclamations kept England in touch with global developments. Authors framed stories, settings, and characters in dramatic plots, enticing patrons with late-breaking events from four hemispheres—east, west, north, south.

Acting troupes like the Lord Chamberlain's Men learned firsthand of faraway events from seafarers' recollections and stories told in Bankside alehouses and taverns. The newest plays drew people of every class from all parts of London as well as visitors from the Continent. Playgoers included nobles, merchants, English yeomen and European statesmen, apprentices, prostitutes, and even prisoners. Turks, Jews, and Africans paraded across playhouse and makeshift stages to entertain London audiences with universal themes and diverse perspectives.

English travelers returned with accounts of far-reaching empires, whetting popular taste for exotic images that laced period drama. Settings like windswept Asian steppes and dry Middle Eastern deserts captured audiences' imaginations in plays like *Pericles* and *Antony and Cleopatra*.

RUSSIA

> *This will last out a night in Russia.* (*Measure for Measure,* II.i.134)

In an era of expansion, the English monarchy clarified national identity by establishing relationships with other countries and defining England by contrast as much as by comparison. Tudor and Jacobean travelogues provide readers today with information about English impressions of faraway countries.

Russia, huge and distant, seemed a barbaric place to many Elizabethans, as suggested in this description by visitor George Abbot:

> The people of this countrie are rude, and unlearned, very superstitious, a kinde of Christians: but rather following the Greeke church. Their buildings is most of wood, even in their chiefe city of Musco: insomuch, that the Tartars wholy in the Northeast of them, breaking oft into their countries, even unto the very Musco: doe set fire on their Cities, which by reason of their woodden buildings are quickly destroyed . . . This Empire is at this day, one of the greatest dominions in the world: both for compass of grounde, and for multitude of men: saving that it lieth far North, and so yeeldeth not pleasure or good trafique, with many other of the best nations. (Abbot 1970, 9)

Some Russian peoples moved westward, rejecting Tartar rule and invading Lithuania. As in Poland, serfdom controlled peasants' lives.

Threatened by Polish expansion in the late 1500s, Moscow was taken by Sigismund III in 1610 and his son Ladislaus was elected czar. But in 1612 Romanov expelled the Poles and was elected the new czar.

Michael Romanov (1596–1645) forged a peace between Poland and Sweden and was succeeded by his son Alexis. During his rule Westernization came to Russia from England and Germany, impacting manufacturing and culture. Though Russia was perceived as a united body of people, it actually consisted of several people groups, including the Tartars, often mentioned in Elizabethan drama as a fearsome and war-like race.

The Tartars

> *. . . From stubborn Turks, and Tartars never train'd*
> *To offices of tender courtesy.* (*The Merchant of Venice,* IV.i.32–33)

Abbot traveled throughout Europe and Asia in the late 1500s and his accounts enhanced Elizabethan understanding of Eastern cultures. The Tartars of northern Asia formerly were called Scythians and remained under Russian rule; both terms are referenced in Shakespeare's plays as allusions to a barbaric race.

The princes or rulers of this region were called Crim Tartars. Giles Fletcher (1549?–1611), ambassador and member of Parliament, describes the Tartars' physical characteristics in his 1591 account:

> For person and complexion they have broade and flatte visages, of a tanned colour into yellowe and blacke, fierce and cruell lookes, thinnhaired upon the upper lippe, and pitte of the chinne, light and nimblee bodied, with short legges, as if they were made naturally for horsemen: whereto they practise themselves from their childhoode, seldome going afoot about anie businesse. Their speech is verie sudden and loude, speaking as it were out of a deepe hollowe throate. When they sing you would thinke a kowe lowed, or some great bandogge howled. Their greatest exercise is shooting, wherein they traine up their children from their verie infancie, not suffering them to eate till they have shot neere the marke within a certaine scantling. They are the very same that sometimes were called Scythae Nomades, or the Scythian shepheards, by the Greekes and Latines. Some thinke that the Turks took their beginning from the nation of the Crim Tartars. (Fletcher in Hadfield 2001, 133)

Like Abbot's, Fletcher's description highlights the uncivilized nature of the Tartars, or Scythians, a view shared by writers like Shakespeare who employ references to "Scythia" and its people as images of savagery. For example, in Shakespeare's most violent play, *Titus Andronicus,* his leading villains include Tamora, queen of the Goths, and her two grown sons. Vicious deceivers themselves, the sons (soon to become rapists and murderers) criticize Rome's cruelty (in slaying their rebel brother) as worse than that of Scythia:

CHIRON: Was never Scythia half so barbarous.
DEMETRIUS: Oppose not Scythia to ambitious Rome . . . (I.i.131–132)

Fletcher also provides observations of the Russians, the other dominant people group:

> The private behaviour and qualitie of the Russe people, may partly be understood by that which hath beene sayd concerning the publique state and usage of the Countrey. As touching the naturall habite of their bodies, they are for the most part of a large size, and of very fleshly bodies: accounting it a grace to be somewhat grosse and burley, and therefore they nourish and spread their beards, to have them long and broad. But for the most part they are very unwieldy and unactive with-all. Which may be thought to come partly of the climate, and the numbnesse which they get by the cold in winter, and partly of their diet that standeth most of rootes, onions, garlike, cabbage, and such like things that breede grosse humors, which they use to eate alone, and with their other meates.
>
> . . . The woman goeth in a red or blewe gowne, when she maketh the best shewe, and with some warme Shube of furre under it in the winter time. But in the sommer, nothing but her two shirts (for so they call them) one over the other, whether they be within doores, or with-out. On their heads, they weare caps of some coloured stuffe, many of velvet, or of cloth of gold: But for the most part kerchiefs. Without ear-ings of silver or some other mettall, and her crosse about her necke, you shall see no Russe woman, be she wife, or maide. (Fletcher in Hadfield 2001, 135, 138)

Narratives like these led to increased understanding as well as discriminatory stereotypes and fostered trade between Russia and England, as well as to the founding of the Muscovy Company.

AFRICA

> *I would they were in Afric both together.*
> (*Cymbeline*, I.i.167)

To the south and slightly east of England, the continent of Africa posed chal-lenges and intrigue. Divided into several nations and dominated by the Turkish Ottoman Empire, Africa represented an uncivilized frontier that offered an array of treasure. Shakespeare's plays reference Barbary horses, known for swiftness, especially in the history plays and tragedies like Othello. African blacks had been brought to Europe in displays of Africa's resources. They often represent

Map of Africa. Giovanni del Vecci (1536–1615), "Map of Africa." From the Sala del Mappsmondo. Fresco, 1574. Palazzo Farnese, Caprarola (Viterbo), Italy. © Scala/Art Resource, NY.

marginal images or token symbols. For example, Juliet's beauty shines like the jewel in an Ethiop's ear (*Romeo and Juliet* I.v.46). *The Winter's Tale* mentions "an Ethiopian's tooth" as a fit comparison to "fann'd snow" in describing a milky-white hand (IV.iv.364), almost as though to parallel the much-prized elephants' tusks of ivory. In the same play, Libya is a source of "success." Though Turkish control discouraged western settlement, Europeans ventured to the continent to stake claims, taking natives for slaves and goods for trade.

Several history plays reference Africa or its nations, including a Barbary horse in *King Richard II,* and in *King Henry IV—Part Two,* Pistol exclaims, "I speak of Africa and golden joys" with gold perhaps alluding to commercial treasure. (King Henry IV—Part Two, V.iii.100)

Travelogues provide insight into African culture, primarily *The History and Description of Africa and of the Notable Things Therein Contained,* written by a converted Moor by the name of John Leo (1495/6–1552), known as Africanus. John Pory, a translator associated with Richard Hakluyt, translated the work into English in 1600. It is possible the work influenced Shakespeare at the time he wrote *Othello.*

Africanus's Account

A North African Arab, John Leo or Africanus was captured in the Mediterranean Sea and presented as a "gift" to Pope Leo X (Hadfield 2001, 139). Africanus claims "Africa" was an Arabic term meaning "to divide," since the continent is divided from Europe by the Mediterranean Sea and from Asia by the Nile River. Another legend purports that "Africa" comes from "Ifricus," the king of Arabia, allegedly the first African inhabitant.

Africanus's account highlights four African nations: Barbary, Numidia, Libya, and the land of Negroes. Here is his description of Barbary:

> Barbaria taketh beginning from the hill called Meies, which is the extreme part of all the mountaines of Atlas, being distant from Alexandria almost three hundred miles. It is bounded on the North side with the Mediterranean Sea, ". . . stretching thence to mount-Meies aforesaid, and from mount-Meies extending it selfe to the streites of Gibraltar . . ." (John Leo His First Booke of the description of Africa, and of the memorable things contained therein. Done into English in the year 1600, by John Pory. And now edited with an Introduction and Notes, by Dr. Robert Brown. In three volumes, Vol. I. New York: Burt Franklin, Publisher, n.d.)

Numidia extended a hundred miles west of Egypt along Africa's northern coast and was known for producing dates. Libya, comprising a desert, began east at the Nile and pushed west to the ocean coast. The fourth area, called the land of Negroes, began at Gaoga and extended west to Gualata. The land of the Negroes included the Niger River and stretched toward the Indian sea, bounded on the north by the Red Sea in a region called Ethiopia. This country was ruled by Prete Gianni and was inhabited mostly by Christians, with a community of Moslems.

In South Africa, called the "zona torrida," people were "exceedingly black" and called Negroes. Treasures included gold and elephant teeth. Although Christianity reached parts of the Congo, many people had reverted to pagan faiths by Shakespeare's time.

It was believed by some that Africans descended from Palestinians, while others alluded to a Sabean line derived from Arabs. Another theory held that African people were linked to Noah's son Ham. It is evident that Arabian people migrated into northern Africa over several centuries' time. Here is an excerpt from Africanus's description:

> . . . the greater part of Arabians which inhabit Numidia, are very wittie and conceited in penning of verses; wherein each man will decipher his love, his hunting, his combates, and other his woorthie actes: and this is done for the most part in ryme, after the Italians manner . . . The Arabians which dwell betweene mount Atlas and the Mediterran sea are far wealthier then these which we now speake of, both for costlines of apparel, for good horse-meate, and for the stateliness and beautie of their

tents ... They are somewhat more vile and barbarous then those which inhabite the deserts, and yet they are not altogether destitute of liberalitie: ... so soone as the king of Portugall began to beare rule over Azafi and Azamor, there began also among them strife and civill warre. Wherefore being assailed by the king of Portugall on the one side, and by the king of Fez on the other, and being oppressed also with the extreme famine and scarcitie of that yeere, they were bought unto such miserie, that they freely offered themselves as slaves unto the Portugals, submitting themselves to any man, that was willing to releeve their intolerable hunger: and by this meanes scarce one of them was left in all Duccala ...

Those Arabians which inhabite in Barbarie or upon the coast of the Mediterran sea, are greatly addicted unto the studie of good artes and sciences: and those things which concerne their law and religion are esteemed by them in the first place ... Their Churches they frequent verie diligently, to the ende they may repeat certaine prescript and formal prayers; most superstitiously perswading themselves that the same day wherein they make their praiers, it is not lawfull for them to wash certaine of their members, when as at other times they will wash their whole bodies. .... (Africanus in Hadfield 2001, 148)

... Also, the Moores and Arabians inhabiting Libya are somewhat civill of behaviour, being plaine dealers, voide of dissimulation, favourable to strangers, and lovers of simplicite. Those which we before named white, or tawney Moores, are stedfast in friendship: as likewise they indifferently and favourably esteeme of other nations. ...

Moreover they maintain most learned professours of liberall artes, and such men are most devout in their religion, now therefore let us consider, whether the vices of the Africans do surpasse their vertues & good parts. Those which we named the inhabitants of the cities of Barbarie are somewhat needie and covetous, being also very proud and high-minded, and woonderfully addicted unto wrath. ...

Abounding exceedingly with choler, they speake always with an angrie and lowd voice.

All the Numidians being most ignorant of naturall, domesticall, & commonwealth-matters, are principally addicted unto treason, trecherie, murther, theft, and robberie. This nation, because it is most slavish, will right gladly accept of any service among the Barbarians, be it never so vile or contemptible. ...

Likewise the inhabitants of Libya live a brutish kinde of life; who neglecting all kindes of good artes and sciences, doe wholly apply their mindes unto theft and violence. ...

The Negros likewise leade a beastly kinde of life, being utterly destitute of the use of reason, of dexteritie of wit, and of all artes ... except their conversation perhaps be somewhat more tolerable, who dwell in the principall townes and cities: for it is like that they are somewhat more addicted to civilitie. .... (Africanus in Hadfield, 144–151)

With few additional sources of information, Elizabethans based their impressions of Africa on accounts such as this one. Evidently some African regions were on the tour route. In *The Taming of the Shrew,* for example, an elderly man named "Pedant" proposes traveling to Tripoli "if God lend me life" (IV.ii.76).

Egypt

> . . . *Welcome from Egypt, sir.* (*Antony and Cleopatra,* II.ii.171)

Renowned for knowledge of astronomy and mathematics, Egypt was sought by rulers like Alexander the Great who built the city of Alexandria, and the Macedonian Ptolemy I, who ruled Egypt from 305 to 285 B.C. Kings succeeding Ptolemy I were called "Ptolemy" from 323 to 30 B.C. Egypt later fell subject to Rome until the Roman Empire disintegrated, and in Shakespeare's time, Egypt came under Turkish rule.

George Sandys (1578–1644) graduated from Oxford University and traveled through parts of Europe and the Middle East. His account called *A Relation of a Journey Begun Anno Dom. 1610. Foure Bookes Contayning a description of the Turkish Empire, of Aegypt, of the Holy Land, of the Remote Parts of Italy, and Ilands Adjoyning* appeared in 1615, from which this excerpt is taken:

> . . . Of all the Heathen, they were the first that taught the immortalitie of the soule, & the transmigration thereof into another body, either of man or beast, clean or uncleane, as it had behaved it selfe in the former . . . The Aegyptians first invented Arithmeticke, Musicke, and Geometry; and by reason of the perpetuall serenitie of the aire, found out the course of the Sunne and the starres, their constellations, risings, aspects, and influences. . . . (Sandys in Hadfield 2001, 159–160)

Egypt continued to lure travelers through ensuing centuries and was thought to be the homeland of the Gypsy people, from which their name derives.

Shakespeare revived the tale of *Antony and Cleopatra* from this ancient land to re-create the timeless tale of sexual and political conquest. Other plays make reference to Egypt as well, usually with allusions to the Old Testament plagues directed by Noah against the Pharaoh. *Sonnet 123* highlights the theme of constancy despite the potential changes of time and Shakespeare uses the pyramids as a landmark of the past:

> No! Time, thou shalt not boast that I do change:
> Thy pyramids built up with newer might
> To me are nothing novel, nothing strange;
> They are but dressings of a former sight.

> *(II.1–4)*

Barbary

The King, sir, hath wager'd with him six Barbary horses. . . . (Hamlet, V.ii.147)

The region known as Barbary sometimes was called Mauritania and is now identified as a country on Africa's northwest coast. Like Africa, Barbary was divided into four kingdoms. Maroco (Morocco) contained seven provinces—Hea, Sus, Guzula, Maroco proper, Duccala, Hazcora, and Tedles. The second kingdom was Fez and included Azgara, Elabat, Errif, Garet, and Elcauz. The third area was Telensin, with three areas—the mountains, Tenez, and Algezer. The fourth region was Tunis, which included Bugia, Constantina, Tripolis, and Ezzaba (part of Numidia). Barbary stretched from the western coast of Egypt to the Atlantic Ocean and included areas known as Algeria, Tunisia, Tripoli, and sometimes Morocco. Linked to acts of piracy through the nineteenth century, this region is mentioned in Shakespeare's plays to connote savagery.

In Shakespeare's plays, "Barbary" often refers to horses valued for their speed. References occur in *Othello, The Merchant of Venice, As You Like It,* and some of the history plays. Allusions to the area include Tunis in *The Tempest,* Tripoli in *The Merchant of Venice* and *The Taming of the Shrew,* (which also mentions the ancient city of Carthage) and Mauritania in *Othello.*

Hannibal initiated the second Carthaginian War, took part of Spain from the Romans, and then went over the Pyrenee mountain range that extends 260 miles between Biscayne Bay and the Mediterranean Sea, separating France and Spain. From there Hannibal traveled over the Alps to Italy where he stayed 15 years, until, incited by Scipio's attempt to capture Carthage, he returned to Africa and was defeated.

Mauritania Tingitana, the route followed by Saracens migrating to Spain, lies along the Mediterranean Sea. Its principal inhabitants are the Mauri people. It was here and in Tunis that Charles V fought the Moors.

> The Arabians, as they have sundrie mansions and places of aboad, so doe they live after a divers and sundry manner. Those which inhabite betweene Numidia and Libya leade a most miserable and distressed life, differing much in this regard from those Africans, whom wee affirmed to dwell in Libya. Howbeit they are farre more valiant than the said Africans; and use commonly to exchange camels in the lande of Negros: they have likewise great store of horses, which in Europe they cal horses of Barbarie. They take woonderfull delight in hunting and pursuing of deere, of wilde asses, of ostriches, and such like. . . .
> (Africanus in Hadfield 2001, 143–144)

Regarding the women:

> . . . Their women (according to the guise of that countrie) goe very gorgeously attired: they weare linnen gownes died black, with exceeding

wide sleeves, over which sometimes they cast a mantle of the same colour or of blew, . . . If any man chance to meete with them, they presently hide their faces, passing by him with silence, except it be some of their allies or kinsfolks . . . When they goe to the warres each man carries hs wife with him, to the end that she may cheere up her good man, and give him encouragement. . . . (Africanus in Hadfield 2001, 145)

Africanus writes that the Barbarian Arabs were devoted to the study of science and letters as well as to law and religion. They also enjoyed renown for mathematics, philosophy, and astrology, and were known for keeping their word and capable of great jealousy. Perhaps his descriptions reflect loyalties to his master, the Pope.

ARABIA

Here's the smell of the blood still.
All the perfumes of Arabia will not sweeten this little hand. (Macbeth, V.i.50–51)

Arabia as the Elizabethans knew it was divided into three parts. The northern region was called Arabia Deserta, and like its name, was a desert. The large southern portion was called Arabia Felix, with balms like myrrh and fruits, spices, and gems. The middle section, Arabia Petra, was accented by rocks and stones. Arabia was bounded by Palestine on the north, the Gulf of Persia on the east, Egypt on the west, and the Indian Ocean on the south.

Islam

It was here that Mohammad (also spelled "Mahomet") (570?–632) was born and founded the religion of Islam, leaving for his followers a written text of precepts and stories called the Koran, or "alcoran." Shakespeare alludes to the Turks' and Moors' Moslem beliefs in several plays as western countries experienced gradual exposure to Middle eastern culture.

Another term Elizabethans associated with Moslems was "saracen," which referred not only to Moslems during the time of the Crusades but also to a pre-Islamic tribe of people who wandered the Syrian-Arabian deserts. "Saracen" (or "Sarazen") refers to this people's descent from the Biblical Sara. Although biologically they descend from the Egyptian handmaid of Sara whose name was Hagar, they prefer to think of themselves as Sara's offspring since Hagar bore Ishmael to Abraham upon Sarah's urging. When Sara later bore her own child, she sent Hagar with her son Ishmael into the wilderness. Arabians are also called Ishmaelites.

During the Renaissance many battles were fought with the Turks who claimed European lands. Turks were viewed as Europe's primary enemy, and they provide a threatening backdrop to plays like *Othello*.

Islamic Culture

Islamic art flowered before and during this time in reflecting images used to decorate, illustrate, or represent the Koran. Moslems sought to praise God rather than define deity through art. Their beliefs prevent the depiction of living souls, so popular themes include nature motifs like trees, flowers, and rosettes, and geometric figures such as triangles and pentagons.

Mathematical designs combine with artistic style to suggest beauty through precision and freedom. Ottoman and Moghul art reflect emblematic human figures using clay, brick, or plaster in colors of blue or crimson, especially in central Asia and Iran. Art forms included mosaics, carpets, and jewelry. Architectural structure is represented in the seventeenth-century Taj Mahal, the Red Palace, and the Alhambra, an Islamic legacy.

Moslems believed that music affirmed man's worldly existence. Many compositions were drawn from Greek philosophical sources and ancient Iranian melodies. Cyclical form and melodic chant were two dominant features.

PERSIA (MODERN-DAY IRAN)

> *. . . I am bound to Persia, and want guilders for my voyage.*
> (*Comedy of Errors*, IV.i.3–4)

Renowned for great riches and past empires, Persia lay west of India, with Assyria and what used to be called Media (now part of Iran) on the north, Syria and Palestine on the west, and the "maine ocean" due south. Persia's kings are named in many great works, including the biblical books of Daniel and Esther. Rulers like Cyrus, Darius, and Xerxes ruled the Persian Empire until Alexander the Great conquered Persia in the fourth century B.C.

The Persians were admired as great warriors who battled the Scythians, Egyptians, and Greeks. With Persia's help the Jews were delivered from Babylon and aided in rebuilding the second Temple at Jerusalem. During the sixteenth century Persian soldiers on horseback repelled the warlike Turks. Like other Middle Eastern nations, Persia followed the Islamic faith and was governed in Tudor times by the Shah or Sophie.

PALESTINE

> *I know a lady in Venice would have walk'd*
> *barefoot to Palestine for a touch of his nether lip.*
> (*Othello*, IV.iii.38–39)

The Holy Land, or Palestine, continued to intrigue Europe long after the Crusades. Pilgrims, clerics, and travelers flocked to the centuries-old Judeo-Christian holy sites of Solomon's Temple and Jesus' ministry. George Sandys included information about Palestine in his travel writing:

> [Palestine] is for the most part now inhabited by Moores, and Arabians: those possessing the vallies, and these the mountaines. Turkes there be few: but many Greeks, with other Christians, of all sects and nations, such as impute to the place an adherent holinesse. Here be also some Jewes, yet inherit they no part of the land, but in their owne country do live as aliens; a people scattered throughout the whole world, and hated by those amongst whom they live; yet suffered, as a necessary mischiefe: subject to all wrongs and contumelies, which they support with an invincible patience. . . . (Sandys in Hadfield 2001, 160)

Sandys takes particular note of the Jews living in Palestine:

> . . . They bury in the fields by themselves, having onely a stone set upright on their graves: which once a yeere they frequent, burning of incense, and tearing of their garments, for certaine dayes they fast and mourne for the dead, yet even for such as have been executed for offences . . . Of late they have bene blest with another Hester, who by her favour with the Sultan, prevented their intended massacre, & turned his fury upon their accusers. (Sandys in Hadfield 2001, 164–165)

In 1632 William Lithgow included commentary on Jerusalem in his travel notes:

> Anno 1612. upon Palme-Sunday in the morning, wee entred into Jerusalem, and at the Gate wee were particularly searched, to the effect wee carried in no Furniture of Armes, nor Powder with us, and the poore Armenians (notwithstanding they are slaves to Turkes,) behoved to render their weapons to the Keepers, such is the feare they have of Christians. (Lithgow 1928, 179–80)

Religious differences abounded in the Holy City:

> Where being arrived, they forthwith brought me to a Roome, and there the Guardian washed my right foote with water, and his Viccar my left: and done, they kissed my feete, so did also all the twelve Friers that stood by: But when they knew afterward that I was no Popish Catholicke, it sore repented them of their Labour. I found here ten Frankes newly come the nearest way from Venice hither, sixe of them were Germanes, noble Gentlemen, and they also good Protestants, who were wonderfull glad to heare me tell the Guardian flatly in his face, I was no Romance Catholicke, nor never thought to be. . . .
> (Lithgow 1928, 180)

Lithgow and fellow pilgrims viewed sites that draw today's travelers to Jerusalem:

> Monday earely, we Pilgrimes went foorth to view the monuments within the Citty, being accompanied with the Padre Viccario, and a French Predicatore: the places of any note wee saw were these: first they shewed us the place where Christ appeared to Mary Magdalen, who sayd: Touch me not, for I am not yet ascended to my Father, John 20.15. and this place by them is supposed to be the Center of middle part of the World. Next, where Saint James the first Bishop of the Primitive Church was beheaded: then the House of Saint Thomas, but that is doubtful (say they) because it is not yet confirmed by the Papall Authority . . . The Holy Grave is covered with a little Chappell, standing within a round Quiere, in the west ende of the Church: It hath two low and narrow entries: As we entred the first doore, three after three, and our shoes cast off, for these two roomes are wondrous little, the Guardiano fell downe, ingenochiato, and kissed a stone, whereupon (he sayd) the Angell stood, when Mary Magdalen came to the Sepulchre, to know if Christ was risen, on the third day as he promised: And within the entry of the second doore, we saw the place where Christ our Messias was buried, and prostrating our selves in great humility, every man according to his Religion, offered up his prayers to God.
>
> The Sepulchre it selfe, is eight foote and a halfe in length, and advanced about three foote in height from the ground, and three foote five inches broad, being covered with a faire Marble stone of white colour. . . . (Lithgow in Hadfield 2001, 180–181)

Beyond Christian allusions to Palestine or Jerusalem, the region also represented the Western quest to stave off Eastern control of the holy shrines.

THE OTTOMAN EMPIRE

> *What? think you we are Turks or infidels?*
> (*King Richard III*, III.v.41)

The Ottomans, or Turkish Empire, existed from 1299 to 1919 and included southwestern Asia, northeastern Africa, and southeastern Europe, with its capital at Constantinople after 1453. Regions under Turkish control included the Balkans (Macedonia, Serbia, and Bulgaria) and Turkey. The dynasty commenced with the rule of Osman I (also spelled "Othman") (1259–1326).

Turks, often called "Saracens" or "infidels," were admired for courage and strength but feared for their threat to Christendom. From the fifteenth through the seventeenth centuries, Turkish warriors advanced into European states to expand holdings and extend Islam. Literature of this period includes frequent references to Turkish customs. At least a dozen of Shakespeare's plays reference "Turks" or "Turkish," along with additional allusions to regions under Turkish control. Several Westerners recorded accounts of the Turkish court during visits there, including Fynes Moryson, whose observations were published in 1617:

> Amurath the sonne of Selime succeeded Emperor in the yeare 1574 . . . when I began my journey towards Turkey. He was said to have lived with his Sultana (or Empresse) 32 yeares, and to have had no Concubine for the first 20 yeares, but the people murmuring, that contrary to the Custome of his Ancestors, he suffered the succession of his Empire to depend upon one sonne, thereupon to have taken some concubines. (Moryson 1601, 3–7)

This emperor was "white and ruddy, with a cheerful countenance and corpulent." Apparently good-natured, he hated cruelty, yet successfully warred against Persia, Africa, and Hungary. He lived 51 years to 1595. His son ordered the body carried to the grave by eunuchs clothed in black with white turbans. That same evening his 19 brothers paid homage, after which the new emperor ordered mute servants to strangle them, following tradition, to avoid infighting over the dynasty.

The emperor greatly respected his mother and granted her a good amount of authority. Persia even sent a woman ambassador to the Turkish court to negotiate with the Sultana and her women, so great was her influence.

The new heir ordered his father's three concubines with child to be left with eunuchs who would strangle any male children. He sent away his father's dumb men, dwarves, and sodmietical boys. To choose a consort for the evening, the emperor would pass by his harem and give a handkerchief to his chosen partner; she would be perfumed and richly dressed for the rendezvous. When harem women reached the age of 25, they were given in marriage to high-ranking officers.

Many travelers' accounts provide insight to Turkish borders and society:

> The Turkish Empire in our tyme is more vast and ample then ever it was formerly containing most large provinces. In Africk it beginnes from the straight of Gibralter and so contains Mauritania, Barbaria, Egipt, and all the Coasts of the Mediterranean sea . . . From Egipt it contaynes in Asia the three Provinces of Arabia, all Palestina, Syria, Mesopotamia, the many and large Provinces of Natolia or Asia the lesser, and both the Provinces of Armenia to the very confines of Persia (in these tymes much more straightned then in former ages) . . . In Europe it contains all Greece and the innumerable Ilands of the Mediterranean sea, some few excepted, (as Malta fortified by an order of Christian knights, Sicilye and Sardinia subject to the king of Spaine, and Corsica subject to the Citty of Genoa, . . . Also it contaynes Thracia, Bulgaria, Valachia, almost all Hungary, Albania, Slavonia, part of Dalmatia and other large Provinces to the Confines of the Germane Emperor, and king of Poland. (Moryson in Hadfield 2001, 167)

... For the private Family each man may have as many Wives as he is able to feede so he take a letter of permission from the Cady, and some of them keepe their wives in diverse Cittyes to avoyd the strife of women; yet if they live both in one house with him, they seldome disagree, being not preferred one above another. The Turkes use not to take a dowrye but as they buy captive women, (whome they may sell againe or keepe for Concubines or for any other service); so they also buy Free women to be their wives ... Divorce is permitted for perverse manners, for barrennes or like faults allowed by the Cady. (Moryson in Hadfield 2001, 172)

As Shakespeare mentions in *Othello,* The Turks were at war with the Venetians, pirating vessels that weighed as much as 700 tons.

Richard Knolles included contributions from more than 30 writers in *The Generall Historie of the Turkes* to provide readers with a detailed description of Turkish history:

The glorious Empire of the Turkes, the present terrour of the world, hath amongst other things nothing in it more wonderfull or strange, than the poore beginning of itselfe, so small and obscure, as that it is not well known unto themselves, or agreed upon even among the best writers of their histories, from whence this barbarous nation that now so triumpheth over the best part of the world, first crept out or tooke their beginning. Some (after the manner of most nations) derive them from the Trojans, let thereunto by the affinity of the words "Turci" and "Teucri," supporting (but with what probabilitie I know not) the word "Turci" or "Turks ... (Knolles 1603, p. 1)

Knowles suggests other sources for the Turks, including Persia and Tartaria, as well as the tribes of Dan and Napthali from the people of Israel.

Thomas Dallam includes an account of his transporting an organ to the Turkish emperor's court:

... The Grand Sinyor satt still, behouldinge the presente which was befor him, and I stood daslinge my eyes with loukinge upon his people that stood behinde him, the which was four hundrethe persons in number. Tow hundrethe of them weare his princepall padgis, the youngest of them 16 yeares of age, som 20, and som 30. They weare apparled in ritche clothe of goulde made in gowns to the mydlegge; upon theire heades litle caps of clothe of goulde, and som clothe of Tissue; great peecis of silke abowte theire wastes instead of girdls; upon their leges Cordivan buskins, reede. Theire heads wear all shaven, savinge that behinde Their ears did hange a locke of hare like a squirel's taile; theire beardes shaven, all savinge their uper lips. Those 200 weare all verrie proper men, and Christians borne.

The thirde hundrethe weare Dum men, that could nether heare nor speake, and theye weare likwyse in gouns of riche Clothe of gould and Cordivan buskins; bute theire Caps weare of violett velvett, the croune of them made like a lether bottell, the brims devided into five picked (peaked) cornereres. Som of them had haukes in theire fistes.

The fourthe hundrethe weare all dwarffs, bige-bodied men, but verrie low of stature. Everie Dwarfe did weare a simmeterrie (scimitar) by his side, and they weare also apareled in gowns of Clothe of gould.
(Dallam 1893, 69–70)

Shakespeare and other writers used Turkish references for many reasons. The threat of Turkish invasion provides a dramatic foil for English histories and tragedies. References to Turkish décor highlighted the oriental or exotic theme of a work, while behaving like a Turk drew fiery criticism. Clearly, Turks fascinated Shakespeare and his peers.

AUSTRALIA

> As I told thee before, I am subject to a tyrant,
> A sorcerer, that by his cunning hath
> Cheated me of the island. (*The Tempest*, III.ii.42–44)

Although Arab seafarers visited Australian shores probably before A.D. 1500, Australia did not become well known to Europeans until the late 1600s. Yet allusions, mythological or otherwise, to a southern territory are documented in European writings as "Terra Australis," indicating a globe-shaped continent.

During the sixteenth century Spain expanded exploration from South America to the South Pacific Ocean where the Solomon Isles were discovered by Alvaro de Mendana de Neira in 1567. Additional voyages unsuccessfully sought gold in surrounding waters. In the seventeenth century the Dutch pushed south from the Cape of Good Hope to Indonesia and from there explored lands further south. In 1606 Willem Jansz passed through the Torres Strait between Australia and New Guinea; this passage was named for the Spaniard who claimed it later that year.

In 1616 Dutchman Dirk Hartog's ship was blown off course from its destination of Batavia (now called Jakarta), and he landed on the western Australian coast. He recorded his visit on a pewter plate left behind. Subsequent voyagers explored New Zealand and Tasmania, although the English did not arrive until late the following century.

Shakespeare alludes to the undiscovered potential of the area in *As You Like It:* "One inch of delay more is a South-sea of discovery" (III.ii.196–197).

CHINA AND CATHAY

> . . . they are not China dishes, but very good dishes.
> (*Measure for Measure*, II.i.94)

The Far East presented a lure that few Europeans could resist. Although England had traded with China for centuries before the time of Shakespeare, it was

Map of China by Abraham Ortelius, 1592.

during the Renaissance that cultural exchanges became more frequent, result-ing in increased mercantile opportunities and social impact.

George Abbot describes some of the practical travel concerns presenting obstacles to these exchanges:

> The English have laboured to their great expences, to finde out the way by the North Seas of Tartaria, to goe into Cathaio [Cathay], and China. But by reason by the frozen Seas, they have not yet prevailed. Although it is now reported that the Flemmings have discovered that passage: which is like to be to the great benefite of the Northerne partes of Christendome.
>
> . . . beyond Tartaria, on the North-east part of Asia, lyeth a great country called Cathaie, or Cathaia: the boundes whereof extend themselves on the North, and East, to the uttermost seas: and on the South, to China. The people are not much learned, but more civill then the Tartars, and have good and ordinary trafique with the countries adjoyning. (Abbot 1970, B1)

Many rulers surrounding Cathay paid tribute to the Great Cham (or Cane) of Cathaie, also called the chief governor, who was

> . . . esteemed for multitude of people, and largenesse of Dominion, to be one of the great Princes of the world: but his name is the less famous: for that he lieth so far distant from the best nations: and the passage unto his country is so dangerous, either for the perils of the seas, or for the long space by lande: his chiefe imperiall city is called Cambalu.

On the South-side of Cathaie, and East-parte of Asia: next to the sea lyeth China. The people whereof, Osorius described by the name of Sine: and called their country 'Sinarum regio.' This is a fruitfull country, and yeeldeth great store of rich commodities, as almost any country in the world. The people of China are learned almost in all Arts, very skilfull workemen in curious fine works of all sorts: so that no country yeeldeth more precious marcahndize then the workmanship of them.

Their soldiers are "very politque and crafty," as described by Petrus Matheus, historiographer to the King of Spain for the Eastern Indies:

...they have had from very auntient time ... two things, which we hold to bee the miracles of Christendome, and but lately invented. The one is the use of guns for their warres, and the other is printing: which they use not as we do; but downward directly: and so their lines at the top, to begin againe. (Abbot 1970, B2)

Chinese accounts were more complete than those of the West. China was deemed the richest and most populous nation in the world, with 300 million people by 1700. India, China, and Japan were considered the most industrious nations of this time. Earlier caravans established trading relations with the Far East, but new navigational systems on the seas sought to maintain or increase trade for tea, porcelain, and silk.

In 1550 the Mongols seized Peking and their control of Tibet and Turkestan was recognized in the resulting treaty of 1570. During the 1580s and 1590s the Chinese experienced problems with pirates on its eastern coast. In the 1590s the Ming dynasty sent forces to rescue Korea from Japanese invasion. One of the key artists of this period was Tung Chi-Chang (Dong Qichang) who lived between 1555 and 1637.

In 1582 Matteo Ricci, an Italian Jesuit, came to Macao. With strong scientific and mathematical expertise, he was the first foreigner allowed to live permanently in Peking. Other Jesuits became mapmakers and astronomers for the emperor. The relationship between East and West often was mutually respectful.

Shakespeare references China in plays such as *Much Ado About Nothing* when Benedick lists several difficult tasks he'd rather do than engage in wordplay with Beatrice: "I will ... fetch you a hair off the great Cham's beard" (II.i.268–269).

JAPAN

Lo in the orient when the gracious light
Lifts up his burning head, each under eye
Doth homage to his new-appearing sight. (Sonnet, 7, 1–3)

羽柴關白豊臣秀吉公

Portrait of Toyotomi Hideyoshi (of Japan), 1599.

A group of four main and several smaller isles off Asia's eastern coast and northeast of Korea comprise the land called Japan. Marco Polo acquainted Westerners with Japan's location and characteristics in his book *Travels* in the early thirteenth century.

In the sixteenth century the archipelago known today as Japan was called "Japana" covering about 142,706 square miles. Its name meant "Land of the Rising Sun." In Shakespeare's writing, references to the eastern sunrise may allude to countries like Japan and China.

Travelogues of Shakespeare's day described Japan's people as similar to those of China. It was believed Japan was very rich, with commodities like silk and pearls for which Western countries could trade. Visited by Jesuit priests centuries earlier, the country held pockets of Christian converts.

Several rulers strove to unite the diverse regions of the Japanese isles, among them Oda Nobunaga who succeeded in linking major eastern and western cities for trade during the sixteenth century. In 1573 he deposed the Shogun but was killed before he could take control. General Toyotomi Hideyoshi succeeded him and continued the unification of Japan during the 1580s and 1590s while trying to invade Korea. The general was succeeded by Tokugawa Iexasu in 1600.

In 1543 the Portuguese arrived to trade, bringing goods from China, Europe, and Asia and introducing the use of tobacco. In 1549 Francis Xavier revitalized Roman Catholicism in Japan, and many thousands were converted. But in 1614 the missionaries were expelled and converts faced punishment.

Shakespeare's plays and sonnets reference the Orient as a source of treasure like pearls, likening young girls to this image: "Bright orient pearl, alack, too timely shaded" (*The Passionate Pilgrim* X.3). Similar images occur in *Antony and Cleopatra* and *Venus and Adonis,* among others.

EAST ASIA

> . . . I will fetch you a toothpicker now from the furthest inch of Asia.
> (*Much Ado About Nothing,* II.i.266–267)

In Elizabethan England a taste for luxuries developed in response to Portuguese and Spanish goods brought from the East. As the demand for cotton, silk, medicines, perfume, and pearls increased, implemented in part by the Portuguese trade monopoly that followed the possession of Goa in 1511, the Dutch also initiated trade with the Asian isles.

Late in the sixteenth century, England also sought to trade with the Far East, despite China's law forbidding the entry of aliens. Elizabeth sent a letter to the Chinese emperor seeking permission to send two merchants, whose ship unfortunately sank before reaching China. Samuel Purchas relied on Spanish Jesuits' reports for information about Chinese society until the 1620s when more English travelers began to write accounts of their experiences in the Far East.

Shakespeare does not distinguish between Asia and East Asia in his references. He alludes to "Asia" generally in history plays like *Antony and Cleopatra* to report a military advance: "Labienus (This is stiff news) hath with his Parthian force/Extended Asia" (I:ii.99–101), and in *The Comedy of Errors:* "Five summers have I spent in farthest Greece/Roaming clean through the bounds of Asia" (I.i.132–133). East Asia often implies exotic riches like pearls or beckoning challenges.

Molucca Islands

Comprising four islands formerly known as the Spice Islands, the Moluccans produced 90 percent of the world's cloves supply. The islands contain 33,315 square miles in area and are part of Indonesia's island group. English, Dutch, Portuguese, and Spanish explorers fought over the region, leaving a legacy of violence. The capital city Amboina is frequently mentioned in Elizabethan travel literature that includes descriptions of savagery and nudity.

With a mixed religious heritage, Hindu rajas and Muslim sultans ruled the people until Portuguese explorers seized control. In the seventeenth century a Dutchman pioneered seed migration there. A popular tragi-comedy staged in England in 1621, *The Island Princess,* is set in the Moluccas.

Moluccan spices were valued in trade, evidenced in this seventeenth-century observation by the Spanish Argensola, here translated into English. Argensola comments on the commercial avarice generated by the island spices which lured merchants from western lands:

> All over the Moluccos there grows a sort of reddish sticks, which burn in the Fire, raise a Flame, and are like a burning Cole, without wasting: They look to be of a Stony Nature, moulder away betwixt the Fingers, and are easily broken by the Teeth. . . . Nature was profuse with those People; especially as to the Cloves, which I distinguish from the Long-Peper Pliny perhaps spoke of, when he nam'd the Garyophillum. But since the Profit of that so highly valu'd Product, was to occasion such bloody Wars, such incredible Voiages, from all Parts of the World, that the real Dangers, are even beyond human Beliefe; it may well be controverted, whether it were most for the publick Tranquility, that this Spice should be known, or ever conceal'd: for its Plenty and Virtue, which awaken'd the Avarice of the remotest Nations, has glutted those Seas with the Wracks of Ships, and Fleets, and call'd thither Armies of Rebels, making their passage through Streights before unknown, in the Sight of Mountains cover'd with blew Ice and Snow, as never reach'd by the Suns bright Beams; and yet they venture at all, not out of any Zeal of promoting Religion, or Civility, but only to load with that Spice, which has occasion'd Disobedience and Superstition. This is the precious Commodity, which gives Power and Wealth to those Kings and causes their Wars. A Wonder of Nature, which plainly shows it has created nothing so harmless, but what is abus'd by human Malice. This is the true Fruit of Discord, rather than the fabulous Apple of the three Goddesses, since for it there has been, and still is, more Fighting than for the Mines of Gold. . . . (Argensola 1708, 40)

In 1607 Dutch traders forced the Portuguese out of trade with the Spice Islands when Dutchmen halved pepper prices. Most English traders left by 1621. Shakespeare references spices like cloves and nutmegs in plays like *Love's Labour's Lost* and ginger in *Measure for Measure*. Spices are mentioned in *Pericles, The Winter's Tale,* and *Coriolanus,* while pepper-gingerbread refers to a gentle manner in *King Henry IV—Part One.*

INDIA

In faith, he is a worthy gentleman, . . . as bountiful as mines of India.
(*King Henry IV—Part One,* III.i.163, 166–167)

The Mughal Dynasty I (1526–56) was founded by Babur, who brought artillery to the country. This period ushered in the second classical age of North India; Delhi became the imperial capitol with the backdrop of a Turkish-Iranian cultural influence.

The Second Mughal Dynasty (1556–1627) saw a period of consolidation under the leadership of Akbar who welded the provinces into a strong, united empire. During this period England's East India Company, begun in 1600, established a political presence in the East.

For Elizabethans and Europeans, India meant either East India or the West Indies. Travelers made the difficult land or sea journey to East India to trade for spices and other goods sought by European consumers. George Abbot describes its geographical limits:

> On the South-side of China, toward the Molucco Islands, and the Indian Sea, lyeth the great country of India: extending it selfe from the Southeast parte of the continent, by the space of many thousand miles westward unto the river Indus, which is the greatest river in all that country, except Ganges: one of the greatest rivers in the world, which lieth in the East part of the same Indies. This is that same country, so famous in ancient time for the great riches thereof, for the multitude of people, . . . for the passage thither of Alexander the great through all the length of Asia: for his adventuring to goe into the South Ocean with so mightie a Navie, which few or none had ever attempted before him . . . The riches hereof hath bene very great with abundance of golde: . . . The commoditie of spice is exceeding great . . . The Portingales [Portuguese] were the first, which by their long navigations beyond the Equinoxiall, and the farthermost parte of Africa, have of late years discovered these countries . . . As heretofore the king of Portingale: so now the king of Spaine, who is reputed owner of them . . . the King of Spaine hath there a vice-roy . . . they doe every yeare, send home great store of rich commodities into Spaine. (Abbot 1970, 18–19)

Abbot went on to point out the lack of a central religion, though some knowledge of Islam was evident. At Cranganor, Protestant-like Christians were found by the Portuguese "from the time of Thomas the Apostle: by whome it is recorded by the auntient Ecclesiastical history, part of India was converted" (Abbot 1970, 20).

English merchants founded the East India Trade Company to send envoys to India, which remained a vast resource controlled by the Spanish. Well into the 1600s, Peter Mundy (ca. 1596–1667) traveled extensively through the Orient and kept a diary of his experiences from which this excerpt depicting a ruler's cruelty is drawn:

> This Governour, Abdulla Ckaun, is said to bee [have been] the death of above 200000 persons, a Cruell natured and Covetuous Tirant, and

therefore more fitter to bee always imployed againste Theeves and Rebells then to reside in a peaceable Governement. Beinge sent by Jehangueere against Sultan Ckorum [Khurram], when hee was out in rebellion, hee revolted from the father to the Sonne. On a tyme his brother shewed him a poore woman almost dead, and a little childe cryeinge and pulling att the mothers Dugg for milke. Hee tooke his Launce and runn them both through, sayeing hee would remedie them both. Annother time there was a great buildinge filled with poore Captived Weomen and Children, when word was brought him that they would quickly perish with hunger and cold if they were not releived. Hee cawsed the said building to bee sett on Fire and soe burnt them all upp together. (Mundy in Hadfield 2001, 233)

"The Indies" referred to East India and the West Indies (America) following discoveries by explorers like Columbus, Magellan, Drake, and Raleigh.

Shakespeare's romances make frequent mention of India's mysteries and treasures. *The Merchant of Venice* alludes to "the beauteous scarf/Veiling an Indian beauty" (III.ii.98–99) while "my metal of India" is found in *Twelfth Night* (II.v.14). In *Love's Labour's Lost* Biron compares universal admiration of Rosaline to Eastern worship:

> Who sees the heavenly Rosaline,
> That (like a rude and savage man of Inde),
> At the first op'ning of the gorgeous east,
> Bows not his vassal head; and, strooken blind,
> Kisses the base ground with obedient breast?

> *(IV.iii.217–221)*

A Midsummer Night's Dream centers on a fairy couple's argument over an Indian boy desired by both. Histories like *King Henry VIII* and tragedies like *Troilus and Cressida* mention India's riches as embodied in desirable women like Anne Boleyn and Cressida. India presented gems and wealth sought by western adventurers.

SUMMARY

Elizabethan travelers shared exciting descriptions about expansive travels to and trade with distant realms. English warfare, exploration, and colonization traveled the furthest limits of the known and unknown world. This was a time of speculation and conquest for England and other European nations. William Shakespeare and his contemporaries captured the exotic flavor of contact with Eastern civilization in their period literature to present it live before audiences thirsting with curiosity about the worlds opening before them and presented in dramatic form.

Excerpt from First Charter to the East India Company, December 31, 1600

Elizabeth, by the grace of God [&c.]. Whereas our most dear and loving cousin, George, Earl of Cumberland, and our well-beloved subjects, Sir John Harte, of London, knight, Sir John Spencer, of London, knight, Sir Edward Michelborne, knight, William Cavendish, esquire, Paul Banninge, Robert Lee, Leonard Hollydaye, John Watts, John Moore, Edward Holmeden, Robert Hampson, Thomas Smithe, and Thomas Campbell, citizens and aldermen of London, [and 204 others] have of our certain knowledge been petitioners unto us for our royal assent and license to be granted unto them, that they, at their own adventures, costs and charges, as well as for the honour of this our realm of England as for the increase of our navigation and advancement of trade of merchandise within our said realm and the dominions of the same, might adventure and set forth one or more voyages, with convenient number of ships and pinnances, by way of traffic and merchandise to the East Indies, in the countries and parts of Asia and Africa, and to as many of the islands, ports, cities, towns and places thereabouts, as where trade and traffic of merchandise may by all likelihood be . . . had; divers of which countries and many of the islands, cities and ports thereof, have long since been discovered by others of our subjects, albeit not frequented in trade of merchandise:

[2] Know ye therefore that we, greatly tendering the honour of our nation, the wealth of our people, and the encouragement of them and others of our loving subjects in their good enterprises, for the increase of our navigation and the advancement of lawful traffic to the benefit of our commonwealth, have . . . granted . . . unto our said loving subjects . . . that they from henceforth be one body corporate and politic, in deed and in name, by the name of the Governor and Company of Merchants of London trading into the East Indies. . . .

(http://www.constitution.org/sech/sech_088.htm)

SOURCES

Abbot, George. *A Briefe Description of the Whole World*. Amsterdam: Theatrum Orbis Terrarum Ltd., 1599; New York: De Capo, 1970.

Africanus, Leo. *The History and Description of Africa and of the Notable Things Therein Contained. Done into English in the Year 1600 by John Pory*. Ed. with introduction and notes by Dr. Robert Brown. In three volumes, Vol. 1. New York: Burt Franklin, n.d.

Andrews, K. R., N. P. Canny, and P. E. H. Hair, eds. *The Westward Enterprise: English Activities in Ireland, the Atlantic, and America 1480–1650*. Liverpool, UK: University Press, 1978.

Argensola, Bartholomew Leonardo de, Chaplain to the Empress, and Rector of Villahermosa. *The Discovery and Conquest of the Molucco and Pilippine*

Islands, containing their history, ancient and modern, natural and political: their description, product, relgion, government, laws, languages, customs, manners, habits, shape, and inclinations of the natives. With an account of many other adjacent islands, and several remarkable voyages through the streights of Magellan, and in other parts. Written in Spanish, now translated into English, and illustrated with a map and several cuts. London: n.p. 1708.

"Australia." Microsoft Encarta Online Encyclopedia. 2001. http://encarta.msn.com

Dallam, Thomas. Diary. *Early Voyages and Travels in the Levant, 1599–1600.* J. Theodore Bent, ed. London: Hakluyt Society, 1893.

Hadfield, Andrew, ed. *Amazons, Savages and Machiavels: Travel and Colonial Writing in English, 1550–1630, An Anthology.* Oxford: Oxford University Press, 2001.

Hughes, Charles, ed. *Shakespeare's Europe—Fynes Moryson, Being Unpublished Chapters of Fynes Moryson's Itinerary (1617).* With an introduction and an account of Fynes Moryson's career. London: Sherratt and Hughes, 1903.

Knolles, Richard. *The Generall Historie of the Turkes from the first beginning of that Nation to the rising of the Otooman Familie, with all the notable expeditions of the Christian princes against them. Together with the Lives and Conquests of the Ottoman Kings and Emperours, faithfyllie collected out of the best histories both auntient and moderne and digested into one continual Historie until this present yeare 1603.* London: Printed by A. Islip, 1603.

Lithgow, William. *Rare Adventures and Painefull Peregrinations,* ed. B. I. Lawrence. London: Jonathan Cape, 1928.

Leo, John. *The History and Description of Africa.* Done into English in the year 1600, by John Pory. And now with an introduction and notes by Dr. Robert Brown. In three volumes. Vol. I. New York: Burt Franklin, Publisher, n.d.

Moryson, Fynes. *Itinerary.* 1601.

Mundy, Peter. "The Travels of Peter Mundy in Asia (1628–34), Observations of India." In Hadfield, *Amazons, Savages and Machiavels,* 225–234.

Rowse, A. L. *The Elizabethans and America.* New York: Harper, 1959.

The World of Islam—Islamic Art. World Wide Pictures, Ltd. Films for the Humanities, Princeton, N.J., 1988.

Wright, Louis B., and Elaine W. Foule, eds. *English Colonization of North America.* New York: St. Martin's, 1968.

QUESTIONS

1. Why were Asian countries often referenced in terms of gold, jewels, and brilliance?
2. How did Africa come to be associated with darkness and barbarianism?

CRITICAL THINKING AND RESEARCH PROJECTS

1. Check the records of an English navigator's voyage to the East. Explain who the passengers would be, which supplies were needed, and what stops were made, as well as the purpose for such a voyage.
2. Analyze a ruler of any of the countries described in this chapter.

3. What impressions about Eastern lands did Shakespeare create in his plays and sonnets?

4. Prepare a time line that parallels the life of Shakespeare (or another Elizabethan) with exploratory voyages to African, European, and Asian continents. Speculate on how these voyages might impact the life of an Elizabethan.

5. Research diplomatic relations between England and one of the Middle Eastern or African countries. Show how that relationship is reflected in Shakespeare's writing.

FOR FURTHER READING

D'Amico, *The Moor in English Renaissance*. Tampa: University of Southern Florida Press; Gainesville: Florida University Presses, 1991.

Disney, Anthony, ed. *Historiography of Europeans in Africa and Asia 1450–1800*. Aldershot, UK: Variorum, Ashgate, 1995.

Fairbank, John King, and Merle Goldman. *China: A New History*. Cambridge, Mass.: Harvard University Press, 1992, 1998.

Farmer, Edward L., Gavin R. G. Hambley, Byron K. Marshall, David S. Kopf, and Romeyn Taylor. et al. *Comparative History of Civilizations in Asia*. Boulder, Colo.: Westview, 1986.

Gilles, John. *Shakespeare and the Geography of Difference*. Cambridge: Cambridge University Press, 1994.

Jones, Eldred D. *Othello's Countrymen: The African in English Renaissance Drama*. London: Oxford University Press, 1965.

Keay, John. *India: A History*. New York: Grove, 2000.

Kinross, Lord. *The Ottoman Centuries: The Rise and Fall of the Turkish Empire*. New York: Morrow Quill, 1977.

Loomba, Ania, and Martin Orkin. *Post-colonial Shakespeares*. London; New York: Routledge, 1998.

MacDonald, Joyce Green, ed. *Race, Ethnicity, and Power in the Renaissance*. Madison, N.J.: Fairleigh Dickinson University Press; London and Cranbury, N.J.: Associated University Press, c. 1997.

Mahmud, S. F. *A Short History of Islam*. Oxford: Oxford University Press, 1988.

Rodney, Walter. *A History of the Upper Guinea Coast 1545–1800*. Oxford: Clarendon, 1970.

Said, Edward. *Orientalism*. London: Routledge, 1978.

Subrahmanyam, Sanjay. *The Portuguese Empire in Asia 1500–1700: A Political and Economic History*. New York: Longman, 1993.

Winius, George D. *Studies on Portuguese Asia 1495–1689*. Burlington, USA: Variorum, 2001.

Sir Walter Raleigh portrait by Nicholas Hillard (1522?–1618).

12

WESTERN WORLDS

From the east to western Inde,
No jewel is like Rosalind.
(*As You Like It,* III.ii.88–89)

In the wake of Portuguese, Spanish, and Dutch exploration of the Western hemisphere, expansion became more of a necessity than a luxury for Tudor England. Portuguese navigators already had voyaged to India, Africa, and the

New World to claim regional resources. Spain, France, and the Netherlands quickly followed suit, leaving Elizabeth with little recourse but to launch her own expeditions into the competitive seas of the global domain.

Competent and illustrious men who probably frequented London's entertainment district chartered mercantile enterprises. Walter Raleigh, John Smith, and Francis Drake would have been comfortable at local alehouses or theaters when they weren't enacting their own personal dramas. William Shakespeare undoubtedly enjoyed firsthand opportunities to discuss the many ventures being planned or taking place.

News of current events in the West Indies circulated vigorously on England's side of the Atlantic. John Hawkins's slave trade, the display of Native Americans on European soil, the failure of the Roanoke colony—these and other stories drew the excitement and speculation of London and the European community. Writings by Shakespeare and his contemporaries demonstrate lively interest in global enterprises and foreign lands.

Shakespeare uses the term "world" numerous times in each drama, indicating his awareness of exploration and settlement in both hemispheres. With more than a dozen references to the New World in plays like *The Comedy of Errors, King Henry VIII, The Merchant of Venice, Twelfth Night,* and *The Merry Wives of Windsor,* his writing displays Shakespeare's keen interest in the global arena.

"Horrenda & inaudita tempestas," illustration by Theodor de Bry, 1594.

THE AMERICAS

When they will not give a doit to relieve a lame beggar, they will lay
out ten to see a dead Indian. (The Tempest, II.ii.31–33)

The idea that habitable lands lay west of England across the vast Atlantic Ocean originated from Plato, fourth-century B.C. Greek philosopher. Yet there is no evidence to suggest that Europeans visited the Western hemisphere before the time of Christ.

During the fifteenth century, Christopher Columbus discovered Haiti, followed by his exploration of Cuba and then the mainland he called Hispaniola.

The colonization and trade that followed sometimes served one-sided interests. Spanish explorers found tribal peoples "very gentle, and very tender, and of an easie complexion, and which can sustaine no travel, and doe die very soone of any disease whatsoever" (de Las Casas in Hadfield 2001, 251). Taking advantage of the natives' simplicity, Spaniards exchanged knives and glasses for gold and other resources, forcing the people into servitude. Jesuits who witnessed these exchanges wrote disparaging reports:

> The Indies were discovered the yeere 1492. and inhabited by the Spanish the yeere next after ensuing . . . Upon these Lambes so meeke, so qualified and endued of their Maker and Creator, as hath bin said, entred the Spanish incontinent as they knew them, as, Wolves, as Lions, and as Tigres most cruell . . . [they] kill them, martyr them, afflict them, torment them, and destroy them by strange sorts of cruelties never neither seene, nor read, nor heard of the like . . . so far forth that of above three Millions of soules that were in the Ile of Hispaniola, and that we have seene, there are not now two hundred natives of the Countrey. The Ile of Cuba, the which is in length as farre as from Valladolid until Rome, is at this day as it were all waste. Saint Johns Ile, and that of Jamayca, both of them very great, very fertill, and very faire, are desolate . . . in one of the Provinces of New Spaine, a certaine Spaniard went one day with his Dogges on hunting of Venison, or else Conies, and not finding game, hee minded his Dogges that they should bee hungrie, and tooke a little sweet Babie which hee bereaved the mother of and cutting off from him the armes and the legges, chopped them in small *gobgets,* giving to every Dogge his Liverie or part thereof, by and by after these morsels thus dispatched, he cast also the rest of the bodie or the carkasse to all the kenell together. . . . (de Las Casas in Hadfield 2001, 251–252, 255)

Richard Eden's translation of Peter Martyr D'Anghera's 1555 account, *The Decades of the Newe World, or West India,* show the other side of native culture:

> . . . you must passé over the mountaynes inhabited of the cruell Canybales a fierce kynde of men, devourers of mans flesshe, lyving withowte lawes, wanderinge, and withowte empire. . . . (Eden in Hadfield 2001, 241)

Shipwreck, survival, and subjugation of the natives are all thematic elements of *The Tempest*. Compare these accounts of Ariel and Caliban, the contrasting island spirits who both are made to serve Prospero the invader:

> I prithee,
> Remember I have done thee worthy service,
> Told thee no lies, made thee no mistakings, serv'd
> Without or grudge or grumblings. Thou did promise
> To bate me a full year.

> *(I.ii.247–249)*

Like Indians forced to mine metals for the Spaniards, Ariel pleads for release from captivity after serving Prospero for a year as promised, and Prospero ultimately keeps that promise. Caliban, perhaps a scrambling of "cannibal," is a different story. Treated as a debased and deformed subspecies, Caliban is kept as Prospero's prisoner and slave:

> This island's mine by Sycorax my mother,
> Which thou tak'st from me. When thou cam'st first,
> Thou strok'st me and made much of me, wouldst give me
> Water with berries in't, and teach me how
> To name the bigger light, and how the less,
> That burn by day and night; and then I lov'd thee
> And show'd thee all the qualities o' th' isle,
> The fresh springs, brine-pits, barren place and fertile.
> Curs'd be I that did so! All the charms
> Of Sycorax, toads, beetles, bats, light on you!
> For I am all the subjects that you have,
> Which first was mine own king; and here you sty me
> In this hard rock, whiles you do keep from me
> The rest o' th' island.

> *(I.ii.331–343)*

Prospero defends his "right" to enslave Caliban from the latter's attempt to violate Miranda. We can only speculate whether Shakespeare was depicting settlement of the West Indies, and if so, what kind of comment the play makes. Despite Caliban's debased nature, Shakespeare seems to infuse a sympathetic tone in describing Prospero's usage.

As explorers established colonies, New World crops like corn and tobacco were sent back to England and other countries in lieu of gold and silver sought by European crowns. Here is an excerpt from Thomas Hariot's account of Virginia and a crop that would later earn millions of dollars and become perhaps the most disputed commodity in history:

> There is an herbe which is sowed a part by itselfe & is called by the inhabitants Uppo 'woc: In the West Indies it hath divers names, according to the severall places & countries where it groweth and is

used: The Spaniardes generally call it Tobacco. The leaves thereof being dried and brought into powder: they use to take the gume or smoke thereof by sucking it through pipes made of claie into their stomacke and heade; *from* whence it purgeth superfluous fleame & other grosse humors, openeth all the pores & passages of the body: by which meanes the use thereof, not only preserveth the body from obstructions; but also if any be, so that they have not beene of too long continuance, in short time breaketh them: whereby their bodies are notably preserved in health, & know not many grievous diseases wherewithall wee in England are oftentimes afflicted.

This Uppo ʾwoc is of so precious estimation amongst them, that they thinke their gods are marvelously delighted therwith: Whereupon sometime they make hallowed fires & cast some of the pouder therein for a sacrifice: being in a storme upon the waters, to pacifie their gods, they cast some up into the aire and into the water: . . . also after an escape of danger, they cast some into the aire likewise: but all done with strange gestures, stamping, somtime dauncing, clapping of hands, holding up of hands, & staring up into the heavens, uttering therewithal and chattering strange words & noises. . . . (Hariot in Hadfield 2001, 268–69)

Conversely, King James warned of the problems associated with tobacco use. See excerpt from *Counter-Blaste to Tobacco* at the end of this chapter.

Magellan's Circumnavigation

In 1519 Ferdinand Magellan (Fernao Magalhaes) voyaged across the Atlantic Ocean for the Far East, in part to stake a claim in the Spice Island trade, challenging the Portuguese monopoly. His ship reached the coast of Brazil after two months and then sailed along the coast toward Patagonia, where he named the straits for himself. A mutiny destroyed two ships, but the rest continued the quest in August 1520, and the following March they arrived at the island of Guam.

A few weeks later they were in the Philippines, where Magellan died and another ship was lost. The remaining crew traded at Borneo and the Moluccas, and the two ships separated—the *Trinidad* planned to cross the Pacific while the smaller *Victoria* continued across the Indian Ocean, rounded Africa, and headed up the Atlantic coast to Europe, with 13 of the original 280 crew members arriving in Seville in 1522. The *Trinidad* never returned.

Other Spanish seamen sailed to the New World and beyond for wealth, fame, or missions on voyages that promoted ongoing discoveries and conquest.

Mexico and South America

. . . he hath an argosy bound to Tripolis, another to the Indies;
I understand moreover upon the Rialto,
he hath a third at Mexico. . . . (The Merchant of Venice, I.iii.18–20)

In Elizabethan times the lands known today as Mexico and Central America were considered part of the Americas generally, or simply "Mexico." The region was explored by Spanish missionaries and then colonized by Spanish explorers. England learned much from their written records.

A Spaniard Dominican, Diego de Duran, was brought up among Indians in Texcoco, which was then the Mexican center for culture and learning. In his *Historia de las Indias de la Nueva Espana,* he describes the natives as sensitive and affectionate. Duran appreciated the beauty of their poetry and their harmonious social life.

Bernal Diaz (1492–1581) was the last survivor of the conquest of Mexico. He died on his estates in Guatemala, leaving a detailed account of historical events. Other Spanish claims in the New World were established by well-known adventurers.

In 1519 Hernando Cortés left Cuba with 66 men and 16 horses, and fought his way to the capital Aztec city of Tenochtitlan in the Mexican highlands. It wasn't until 1521 that his navy was strong enough to overcome the Aztecs. Afterward he explored other territories including the area near Panama which he claimed for Spain.

In 1530 Francisco Pizarro and his family began a final assault on the Peruvian Incas in the Andes Mountains following disastrous earlier attempts. Through deceit and manipulation, Pizarro took control of the capital Cuzco in November 1533.

A decade or so later, Jimenez de Quesada conquered northwest South America (the land known as Colombia today). By 1545 Bolivia's rich silver veins, called the Potosí mines, increased European interest in the region. Other South American lands including Orinocco and Chile remained free for a time. By mid-century, strong units of European government were thriving in North and South America. As a result, the Council of the Indies was created to serve as administrative council and court of appeals.

The Spanish king established a viceroy system to govern the South American colonies, which were divided into two areas. New Spain included Mexico, Central America, and the Caribbean islands, with the viceroy in Mexico City. The southern area was called Peru, and included all of the western lands of South America and the government seat at Lima.

The Portuguese were eager to find a trade route to the East. On one such expedition they discovered Peru and Brazil, and more South American discoveries soon followed.

Brazil

Brazil remained under Portuguese control whose primary focus was directed at Southeast Asia for trade. Threatened by Spanish and French invaders in 1530, the Portuguese sent Martin Afonso de Souza to set up bases in Rio de Janeiro and Pernumbuco. By the 1500s Indian and African slaves were harvesting products like cotton, cacao, wood, and sugar to enrich stakeholders.

Lisbon in Portugal and Spain's Seville became entry points for goods like indigo, vanilla, and silver from the East and West Indies. New staples such as potatoes, corn, coffee, and tobacco made their way into European society through these portals.

From the western coast of South America many Portuguese and Spanish explorers pushed further west in an effort to find the East Indies and "Terra Australis." Though Australia was not "discovered" until late in the sixteenth century and remained unoccupied by Europeans for another 200 years, other important lands were located including the Spice Islands (also called the Moluccas) and other island groups. Many of Shakespeare's plays and poems refer to the "Orient" or oriental jewels, while *As You Like It* alludes to such adventures in Rosalind's comparing an inch of delay in Celia's story to "a South-sea of discovery" (III.ii.196–97).

ENGLISH COLONIES

Our king has all the Indies in his arms. (*King Henry VIII*, IV.i.45)

Witnessing the success of Iberian adventurers, Elizabeth backed several English enterprises in a quest for a share of the New World. Exploratory voyages had commenced under earlier Tudor rule and she was eager to stake a claim to the territories and wealth that were nourishing Spain and Portugal.

English Explorers

John Cabot received letters patent from Henry VII enabling him to sail to Newfoundland in the summer of 1497, but he was lost at sea during a second voyage. In 1536 Richard Hore guided a voyage to Newfoundland in two ships containing 30 passengers. One ship foundered at sea while the second became entrapped in Newfoundland's ice and the travelers began to cannibalize each other. Eventually a French ship rescued the survivors.

By 1522 Ferdinand Magellan had circled the globe, Cortes had conquered Mexico, and Pizarro was taking charge of Peru. Martin Frobisher made three voyages to search for a Northwest passage to the Spice islands in 1576–78. Reaching Baffin Island, Frobisher brought back an Inuit (similar to an Eskimo) and fool's gold. It wasn't until 1580 that Englishman Francis Drake completed a voyage around the world.

Sir Humphrey Gilbert suggested colonizing the Americas to support trade expeditions en route to the Far East, and in 1578 he was given letters patent to start colonies on the North American coast. His fleet reached Newfoundland in 1583 and a colony was planned for Norumbega, north of the Hudson River on the Atlantic seaboard. But Gilbert drowned near the Azores on the return home.

Sir George Peckham reported their efforts:

> On Munday being the fift of August, the Generall caused his tent to be set upon the side of an hill, in the viewe of all the Fleete of English men and strangers, which were in number betweene thirtie and fourtie sayle: then being accompanied with all his Captaines, Masters, Gentlemen and other souldiers, he caused all the Masters, and principall Officers of the ships, aswell Englishmen as Spanyards, Portugales, and of other nations, to repayre unto his tent: And then and there, in the presence of them all, he did cause his Commission under the great Seale of England to bee openly and solemnely read unto them, whereby were granted unto him, his heires, and assignes, by the Queenes most excellent Majestie, many great and large royalties, liberties, and priviledges. The effect whereof being signified unto the strangers by an Interpreter, hee tooke possession of the sayde land in the right of the Crowne of England by digging of a Turffe and receiving the same with an Hasell wand, delivered unto him, after the maner of the law and custome of England.
>
> Then he signified unto the company both strangers and others, that from thenceforth, they were to live in that land, as the Territories appertayning to the Crowne of England, and to be governed by such Lawes as by good advise should be set downe, . . . (Peckham in Hadfield 2001, 257)

Sir Walter Raleigh took the lead in colonizing the Americas for England, and he headed to Guiana while his cousin Sir Richard Grenville established a colony on Roanoke Island. John White and Thomas Harriot voyaged to Roanoke to study natural life and wrote *A Briefe and True Report of the New Found Land of Virginia*. When the colony disbanded in 1586, artist John White agreed to lead a new group and returned to England for supplies. When he came back in 1590, he found the colony deserted. It is likely that native warriors under Chief Powhatan massacred the settlers or that the settlers defected to Indian settlements.

In 1576 an Englishman named John Oxenham, with the help of the New World Cimaroon people, nearly seized control of the isthmus of Panama, a narrow land way connecting the North and South American continents. The Spanish had been using the isthmus to ship South American goods to Spain. Oxenham was unsuccessful and the isthmus remained a point of contention between English and Spanish at least until 1595, when an expedition to that area killed Sir Francis Drake and John Hawkins.

South American riches and Peruvian mines were enthusiastically promoted to potential English settlers. But desire for speedy profit became problematic when settlers pursued quick riches rather than long-term stability.

English exploration advanced into all regions of the globe by the late 1500s. In 1570 an expedition reached the Arctic Circle in search of a northern passage to the Moluccas and to China, but ice and cold forced the group's return. When explorers searched for a route to the South Pole, they found the climate too difficult and gave up.

Sir Francis Drake, English explorer (16th century).

Sir Francis Drake

On December 13, 1577, Francis Drake began his circumnavigation of the globe from Plymouth, England, in the Golden Hind. Drake hoped to follow Magellan's historic voyage, and passing through the Strait of Magellan along the Chilean coast toward California, he arrived in Ternate in the East Indies on November 3, 1579. Trading for spices in the Molucca Islands, Drake negotiated an agreement with the king of Ternate to permit English ventures on the islands in exchange for weapons and protection, thus providing England with a stake in Eastern trade. Drake then crossed the Indian Ocean, rounded Africa, and returned to England.

Drake's quest for adventure, wealth, and fame was a success. His men encountered lightly guarded Spanish vessels loaded with New World gold which they successfully won in a series of raids, further enriching their voyage.

Though Ferdinand Magellan had sailed to the New World 50 years before, he died soon after. Drake arrived in England in the fall of 1580, bringing hundreds of thousands of pounds worth of profit. He was rewarded with commercial success and the queen's knighting aboard ship. Drake later visited Florida in 1586.

Sir Walter Raleigh

Sir Walter Raleigh (also spelled "Ralegh"), (1552–1618), was an English courtier, navigator, and writer. After attending Oxford University, he fought

French Huguenots and became a favorite of Queen Elizabeth, who rewarded him with riches and titles.

Raleigh accompanied his brother Sir Humphrey Gilbert on two expeditions to the New World before Sir Humphrey was lost at sea in 1583. Sir Walter received his own patent to explore the lands claimed for English dominion in a letter patent dated March 25, 1589.

Raleigh tried unsuccessfully to start a South American settlement at Guiana in the Orinoco basin near the Amazon because of the belief that gold pervaded the area. In 1596 he published *The Discovery of the Large Rich and Beautiful Empire of Guiana*. Shakespeare alludes to the expedition in Falstaff's metaphoric praise of Mistress Page, especially in view of her financial substance, with plans for Mistress Ford:

> She bears the purse too;
> she is a region in Guiana, all gold and bounty. I will
> be cheaters to them both, and they shall be
> exchequers to me. they shall be my East and West
> Indies, and I will trade to them both.
>
> *(The Merry Wives of Windsor, I.iii.68–72)*

Raleigh helped start the Roanoke Island colony off the North Carolina coast, which lasted just a few years. He later was given a tract of 40,000 acres in Ireland where he introduced potatoes and tobacco.

Following an affair with Elizabeth Throgmorton, one of the queen's maids of honor, he was thrown into the Tower of London. He later married Elizabeth and enjoyed a successful marriage.

In a 1617 voyage to the Americas, Raleigh clashed with the Spanish and his oldest son Walter was killed in battle. Raleigh failed to find the legendary gold and other precious metals sought by the English. James I stripped Raleigh of his honors, as he was accused of conspiracy, and sent him back to the Tower where he spent 13 years altogether. King James I executed him in 1618, primarily to satisfy Spain.

Jamestown and New England

In the early 1600s James negotiated a treaty with Spain that ended hostilities between their nations and facilitated peaceful New World colonialism. In 1606 the Virginia Company began organizing trade and settlement in American coastal lands. Jamestown, the first settlement, was located on the banks of the James River in what is now Virginia. The chief crop, tobacco, enhanced colony profits.

As New England exploration increased, settlements were established by the Massachusetts Bay Company in Plymouth in 1620 and Boston shortly after. Early dissidents in these colonies later settled in Connecticut.

Religious principles and political incentives interested many colonists more than commercial success, though even these noble goals were hampered by conflicts with the Native Americans and the geography.

During Elizabeth's reign, England's government and private investors like Robert Dudley and Sir Edward Dyer began to sponsor voyages of discovery. Scientists and navigators collaborated with merchants to form enterprises for marketing goods from the West Indies.

Elizabeth had already sent expeditions to Persia, the Indian Ocean, and Russia. Richard Hakluyt the Younger made a career of collecting sea captains' narratives, especially those who had navigated voyages of discovery to the Americas. By the 1580s Hakluyt was writing "letter upon letter, pamphlet after pamphlet, book after book" urging England to pursue western planting.

The first permanent English colony in North America was established in 1585. Sir Walter Raleigh's cousin Grenville and crew settled on Roanoke Isle in Pamlico Sound where the first "American," Virginia Dare, was born on August 18. But due to limited supplies and miscommunication, the colony foundered after only a year.

Many English people bought shares in the Virginia Company or relocated to the colonies. One group received charters to explore northern and southern Virginia while another tried to start a colony in Maine in 1607. The Maine colony failed within a year and Puritans did not settle in northern New England until the 1620s and 1630s.

The second group of Virginia Company explorers established a settlement called Fort James that would later be known as Jamestown. During its first decade the mortality rate fluctuated between 4 and 30 percent. Difficult weather conditions and a desire for quick wealth interfered with the colony's operation. A supply ship wrecked on Somers Isle (now called Bermuda) when Sir Thomas Gates and Sir George Summers sailed to the New World to reinforce the dying colony. Letters between these men provide information about the conditions they found. Some of this information became accessible to writers like Shakespeare whose drama incorporated meaningful allusions. For example, in a letter dated July 15, 1610, William Strachey, shareholder and secretary of the Virginia Company, described Jamestown and the Bermuda shipwreck in tropical descriptions later found in Shakespeare's play *The Tempest*. Earlier references to New World riches can be found in *Othello* and *The Merchant of Venice*.

When a new governor, Lord De La Warre, arrived in 1610, he found 60 starving settlers who almost gave up to return to England. After 1624 when the colony moved inland, conditions improved due to fresh water sources and higher ground.

After 1612 tobacco became a principal crop, but it wasn't enough to support the colony. In 1616 the Virginia Company offered 50 acres of land with nominal rent to immigrants subscribing £12 10s of stock to the settlement. Two years later each dependent also received 50 acres. Many indentured bondservants sold their services for three to seven years to buy passage to the new land. Between 1618 and 1621 the Virginia Company brought 3,750 people to the colony, free and bondservants, including vagrant children and two hundred women.

Because of precarious conditions it was due to gifts of food and training provided by local tribesmen that the colony survived. Pocahontas is the most famous Native American who developed a bond with the Jamestown colony and perhaps helped to preserve it.

A Native American chief carrying a bow and wearing the warpaint and clothing appropriate for a feast or hunt, by John White.

NATIVE AMERICANS

> *(For, certes, these are people of the island,)*
> *Who though they are of monstrous shape, yet note*
> *Their manners are more gentle, kind, than of*
> *Our human generation you shall find*
> *Many, nay, almost any.* (*The Tempest*, III.iii.30–34)

European visitors often took extreme views of Native Americans. Some accounts recall Montaigne's "noble savage," depicting physical beauty and moral goodness. Others viewed Native Americans as savages, deserving of capture and slavery. Such views allowed colonists to manipulate and control New World peoples. Spanish Jesuits described their encounters with various tribes, including the Caribbean Arawaks and the Aztecs of Mexico.

Columbus brought several Native Americans to Spain on his return voyage; six survived and were baptized. Cartier took two Native Americans to France. In the 1570s while searching for a northwest passage to the Indies, Martin Frobisher captured an Inuit at Baffin Island whom he took to England where the Indian died. In 1616, a group of Jamestown settlers and Native American representatives that included Pocahontas visited England.

Queen Isabel of Spain forbade the sale of Native Americans and ordered the governor to protect and Christianize South American natives. However, when she died in 1504, Spanish settlers mistreated the natives. Native American laws were instituted in 1512 and 1542—the Laws of Burgos and the New Laws of Burgos, though African slaves were imported to replace native labor.

Portuguese, Spanish, and English writers provided numerous manuscripts describing New World encounters, including Jean de Lery's *History of a Voyage to the Land of Brazil,* published in Geneva, that described the Huguenot pastor's observations in 1557. Thomas Morton, who wrote *The New English Canaan,* was a fur trader who shared his favorite pastimes of hunting and trapping with the Native Americans. Morton found them friendlier than Europeans. Many English settlers escaped poverty, starvation, and hard work by fleeing to Native American society. At least 40 or 50 are known to have married Native American women; some took Native American names and even dressed as tribal members.

Thomas Hariot, a scientist sent on a 1585 expedition by Sir Walter Raleigh, wrote a lengthy description in 1588 of Native Americans, from which this excerpt is taken:

> . . . They weare the haire of their heades long and bynde opp the ende of the same in a knot under their eares. They then cutt the top of their heades from the forehead to the nape of the necke in manner of a cokscombe, . . . They either pownes, or paynt their forehead, cheeks, chynne, bodye, armes, and leggs, yet in another sorte then the inhabitantz of Florida . . . They weare a chaine about their necks of pearles or beades of copper, wich they muche esteeme, and ther of wear they also braselets ohn their armes. . . . (Hariot in Hadfield 2001, 273–74)

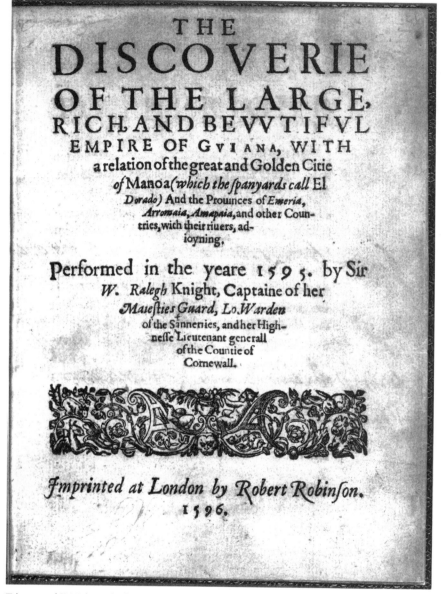

THE
DISCOVERIE
OF THE LARGE,
RICH AND BEVVTIFVL
EMPIRE OF GVIANA, WITH
a relation of the great and Golden Citie
of Manoa (*which the spanyards call* El
Dorado) And the Prouinces of *Emeria*,
Arromaia, *Amapaia*, and other Coun-
tries, with their riuers, ad-
ioyning.

Performed in the yeare 1595. by Sir
W. *Ralegh* Knight, Captaine of her
Maiesties Guard, *Lo.Warden*
of the Stanneries, and her High-
nesse Lieutenant generall
of the Countie of
Cornewall.

Imprinted at London by Robert Robinson.
1596.

Title page of Sir Walter Raleigh's *Discoverie of the Large, Rich, and Beautiful Empire of Guiana*

Sir Walter Raleigh explored the South American region of Guiana and
wrote a report to reassure Queen Elizabeth of the validity of his efforts:

> The Empyre of Guiana is directly east from Peru towards the sea, and . . .
> it hath more abundance of Golde then any part of Peru, and as many
> or moe great Cities then ever Peru had when it flourished most . . . I
> have beene assured by such of the Spanyardes as have seene Manoa the

imperial Citie of Guiana, which the Spaniards cal El Dorado, that for the greatnes, for the riches, and for the excellent seate, it farre exceedeth any of the world, at least of so much of the world as is knowen to the Spanish nations. . . . (Raleigh in Hadfield 2001, 280)

Raleigh also addressed the myth of the Amazon women:

The nations of these women are on the south side of the river in the Provinces of Topago, and their chiefest strengths, and retracts are in the Ilands scituate on the south side of the entrance, some 60, leagues within the mouth of the saide river. The memories of the like women are verie ancient as well in Africa as in Asia . . . But they which are not far from Guiana do accompanie with men but once in a yeare, and for the time of one moneth, which I gather by their relation to be in Aprill. And that time all Kings of the borders assemble, and Queenes of the Amazones, and after the Queenes have chosen, the rest cast lots for their *Valentines.* This one moneth, they feast, dance, & drinke of their wines in abundance, and the Moone being done, they all depart to their owne Provinces. If they conceive, and be delivered of a sonne, they returne him to the father, if of a daughter they nourish it, and retaine it, and as many as have daughters send unto the begetters a Present, all being desirous to increase their owne sex and kind, but that they cut of the right dug of the brest I do not find to be true . . . They are said to be very cruell and bloodthirsty, especially to such as offer to invade their territories. . . . (Raleigh in Hadfield 2001, 282–83)

Shakespeare's plays on several occasions mention Amazons as depicting fierce warriors.

Pocahontas

Intrigued by Native Americans, British writers noted their fierce beauty and savage warfare to capture the imaginations of English investors and immigrants. In the early seventeenth century, Native American princess Pocahontas came to England as an ambassador of her people, inspiring many with a cultured manner and gracious appearance, adding another dimension to English perceptions of Native Americans. Born in the 1590s in Virginia, Pocahontas (which means "little mischief") came to visit the Jamestown settlement in 1607 and there met John Smith. Petite, with olive skin and large, sparkling eyes, she is described in one of Smith's narratives as the "non-pareil" of her people.

When Smith was captured and threatened with stoning by Powhatan's tribe members, Pocahontas threw herself on him to save his life which led to Smith's adoption by the tribe. Her support helped to forge bonds between the two races, and she brought food to the starving colony on several occasions.

Injured by a gunpowder accident, Smith returned to England and Pocahontas was told he had died. When tensions escalated between whites and Native Americans, she was lured to a ship and taken hostage, though treated kindly. Living with the Reverend Alexander Whittaker and his wife in Jamestown, she adopted English dress and manners, attended bible class, accepted Christian baptism, and took the English name of "Rebecca." John Rolfe, a young settler of 28 who had lost wife and son, was impressed with Pocahontas along with the potential for bringing Christianity to the Native Americans and peace to the region. With the governor's permission they married in 1614 and within a year had a son whom they named Thomas.

In the spring of 1616 around the time of Shakespeare's death, the young family voyaged to England as part of a delegation that included several tribal members in an effort to inspire renewed interest in New World settlement. Lord Delaware, appointed by Queen Anne, became Pocahontas's sponsor and she made a delightful impression at court. Sir Walter Raleigh took her to see the earl of Northumberland in the Tower of London. Playwright Ben Jonson talked with her five minutes, then stared at her for 45. John Smith visited her at a London inn. See John Smith's account of their meeting at chapter's end. Shocked to find him alive, Pocahontas turned away for several hours before speaking. Finally she greeted him as "Father," a term of great respect. When he assured her of no need to do so, she spiritedly replied she would, and be "forever and ever your countryman."

In March 1617 she fell ill, probably with tuberculosis or smallpox, and her husband felt that returning to America was her only hope of recovery. On board the ship she began to hemorrhage from the lungs. She was removed and told her husband, "All must die. It is enough that the child lives. Hold me." She died in Gravesend and was buried in an English church that was dedicated to her. Son Thomas returned to Virginia in 1635 at age 20 and received lands from both his Native American grandfather and English father, founding family lines that remain to this day. John Smith never married and died in London in 1631. The early mingling of English and American cultures benefited both peoples, but at a cost.

NEW WORLD WRITING

> *Here is a letter, lady,*
> *The paper as the body of my friend,*
> *And every word in it a gaping wound*
> *Issuing life-blood.* (*The Merchant of Venice*, III.ii.263–266)

New World travelers kept written records of their adventures, some of which were circulated as propaganda to attract investors. Writings by Richard Eden, John Frampton, Thomas Nicholas, and Richard Hakluyt provide insightful glimpses of New World natives and the case for colonization.

A New World historian influenced by Columbus was Peter Martyr d'Anghiera (1457–1526), who wrote *De orbe novo* ("The new world," a term he coined), which was published serially between 1511 and 1530. Bartolome de Las Casas wrote *Historia de las Indias* (History of the Indies) about 1552 based on personal observation and the documents of navigators like Columbus.

Richard Hakluyt collected records and narratives from voyagers who had sailed around Western Europe and New World lands. His 1584 *Discourse of Western Planting* provided a rationale for settling uncharted regions that lay across the Atlantic Ocean.

John White created maps and watercolors of American botanicals that included 21 illustrations of Native Americans. Belgian printer Theodor De Bry published a survey entitled *America* which included Hariot's summary and 23 illustrations based on John White's drawings of the Algonkian Indians.

Favorable reports began trickling back to England, such as Edward Grimston's 1604 *The Naturall and Morall Historie of the East and West Indies,* based on observations of Spanish Jesuit Jose de Acosta. French lawyer Marc Lescarbot collaborated with Samuel de Champlain to publish their account of New World exploration. In 1609 Pierre Erondelle translated his observations as propaganda for the Virginia Company. Following the reawakening of classical interests in the Renaissance, the simple lifestyle of the Native Americans offered an attractive alternative as an inducement for settling lands in the Western hemisphere.

Several of Shakespeare's plays reference the exploration and mapping of new Western worlds, as illustrated in this speech of Maria in *Twelfth Night:*

> He does smile his face into more lines than is in the new map,
> with the augmentation of the Indies . . .
>
> *(III.ii.78–80)*

It is likely Shakespeare alludes to the 1599 edition of Gerardus Mercator's map in Richard Hakluyt's published voyages.

Trade

The free trade debate of 1604 contributed to the expansion of England's overseas trade. Asian spices were purchased from Lisbon, silver from central and eastern Europe and America, and luxury imports such as wine, silks, sugar, and tobacco from the East and West Indies.

Gold lured many investors. In 1608 frantic digging was reported in Jamestown. Pamphlets and sermons emphasized the rewarding opportunities that awaited English settlers in the new lands.

America and Elizabethan Literature

Ben Jonson and Marston's *Eastward Ho!* and Marlowe's *Tamburlaine* include references to the quest for gold. Shakespeare's *Timon of Athens* reflects the theme as well. Figures associated with London's drama and literary circles were closely affiliated with New World colonization, including William Strachey, who wrote a sonnet for Ben Jonson's *Sejanus* in which Shakespeare acted,

John Pory, Christopher Davison, and George Sandys. Strachey allegedly came to Blackfriars two or three times a week where he could have encountered Shakespeare.

William Strachey (1572–1621?) voyaged to Virginia in 1609 after being shipwrecked in Bermuda. Later he became secretary of Jamestown and wrote about his experiences which were published as *The Historie of Travell into Virginia Britania* (1612):

> It is straunge to see how their bodies alter with their dyett even as the deare and wylde beasts, they seeme fatt and leane, strong and weake, Powhatan and some others that are provident roast their fish and flesh upon hurdells and reserve of the same until the scarse tymes, Commonly their Fish and Flesh they boyle, either very tenderly, or broyle yt long on hurdells over the fire, or ells (after the Spanish Fashion) putting yt on a spit, they turne first the one side, then the other till yt be as dry as their Jerkyn-beef, in the West Indies, and so they may keepe yt a moneth or more, without putryfying. The broath of Fish or Flesh they sup up as ordinarily, as they eate the meate . . .
>
> If a great Commaunder arrive at the habitation of a Weroaunce, they spredd a Matt (as the Turks doe a carpett) for him to sitt upon, upon another right opposite they sitt themselves, then doe they all with a tunable voice of showting bid him welcome: after this doe 2.or more of their chief men make severall orations testifying their love, which they doe with such vehemency and so great earnestness of passion, that they sweat till they droppe, and are so out of breath, that they can scarse speake, in so much as a Straunger would take them to be exceeding angry or stark mad: after this verbal Entertaynement, they cause such victually as they have or can provide to be brought forthe with which they feast him fully and freely. . . . (Strachey in Hadfield 2001, 298, 300)

In Shakespeare's time the world began to shrink as new discoveries brought to light foreign lands and strange people. From "America" to the South Seas, and from cannibals to Anthropophagians, Shakespeare's drama offers tantalizing references that provide insight into England's quest for commercial trade and cultural expansion. Shakespeare's work evidences little-known regions like "Iceland" in *King Henry V,* with "cannibally" in *Coriolanus* and "cannibals" in *King Henry IV—Part Two. The Comedy of Errors* includes "America—the Indies" in a list of diverse regions used as a metaphorical feminine description. Shakespeare's work captured English impressions of the regions that today are occupied by those who study his writing.

SUMMARY

The character of England's monarchy and its representatives was tested and reflected in the settlements that sprang up overseas. Colonies flourished and failed, trade waxed and waned, and dignitaries exchanged visits in efforts to promote peace and make a profit.

Though commerce was a primary motivator of early travel, a quest for adventure and religious freedom also served as an impetus to fostering Britain's distinctive presence in the global community.

From travel accounts to literary drama, records of globalization help to reenact the exploration and settlement of lands well known to readers today. It is exciting to see these early adventures through the eyes of a master playwright like Shakespeare who brought such events to life on the English stage and on the pages of his drama.

Excerpt from Charter to the Virginian Colonies, April 10, 1606

James, by the grace of God [&c.]. Whereas our loving and well-disposed subjects Sir Thomas Gates and Sir George Somers, knightes; Richard Hackluit, clarke, prebendarie of Westminister; and Edward Maria Winghfeilde [sic], Thomas Hannam and Raleighe Gilberde, Esquiers, William Parker and George Popham, Gentlemen, and divers others of our loving subjects, have been humble suitors unto us that wee would vouchsafe unto them our license to make habitacion, plantacion, and to deduce a colonie of sondrie of our people into that parte of America commonly called Virginia, and other parts and territories in America, either appartaining to us or which are not now actually possessed by anie Christian prince or people, scituate, lying and being all along the sea coastes, between fower and thirtie degrees of northerly latitude from the equinoctiall line and five-and-fortie degrees of the same latitude, and in the mainend between the same fower-and-thirtie and five-and-fourtie degrees, and the islands thereunto adjacente or within one hundred miles of the coast thereof; and to that ende, and for the more speedy accomplishement of theire saide intended plantacion and habitacion there, are desirous to devide themselves into two severall colonies and companies, the one consisting of certaine knights, gentlemen, marchanntes and other adventurers of our cittie of London, and elsewhere which are and from time to time shall be joined unto them, which doe desire to beginn theire plantacions [&c.] in some fit and conveniente place, . . . all alongest the coaste of Virginia . . .

[2] Wee, greately commending and graciously accepting of theire desires for the furtherance of soe noble a worke, which may, by the providence of Almightie God, hereafter tende to the glorie of his divine Majestie in propagating of Christian religion to suche people as yet live in darknesse and miserable ignorance of the true knowledge and worshippe of God, and may in tyme bring the infidels and salvages living in those parts to humane civility and to a setlled and quiet governmente, doe, by theise our lettres patents, graciously accepte of and agree to theire humble and well-intended desires . . . and they shall and may beginne theire

saide firste plantacion [&c.] at anie place upon the saide coaste of Virginia or America where they shall thincke fitt . . . and that they shall have all the landes, woods, soile, groundes, havens, ports, rivers, mines, mineralls, marshes, waters, fishinges, commodities, and hereditamentes whatsoever, from the said first seat of their plantation. . . .

[4] And wee doe also ordaine . . . that eache of the saide colonies shall have a counsell, which shall governe and order all matters and causes . . . within the same severall colonies, according to such lawes, ordinannces and instructions or shalbe in that behalfe, given and signed with our hand or signe manuell, and pass under the privie seale of our realme of Englande: each of which counsells shall consist of thirteene persons, and to be ordained, made and removed from time to time according as shalbe directed and comprised in the same instructions; . . . (http://www.eaglering.com/foundations/virginia.html)

Excerpt from Richard Hakluyt's Discourse of Western Planting *(1584)*

1. That this westerne discoverie will be greately for the inlargement of the gospell of Christe whereunto the Princes of the refourmed relligion are chefely bounde amongst whome her Majestie is principall.

2. That all other englishe Trades are growen beggerly or daungerous, especially in all the kinge of Spaine his Domynions, where our men are dryven to flinge their Bibles and prayer Bokes into the sea, and to forsweare and renownce their religion and conscience and consequently theyr obedience to her Majestie.

3. That this westerne voyedge will yelde unto us all the commodities of Europe, Affrica, and Asia, as far as wee were wonte to travell, and supply the wantes of all our decayed trades.

4. That this enterprise will be for the manifolde imploymente of numbers of idle men, and for bredinge of many sufficient, and for utterance of the greate quantitie of the commodities of our Realme.

5. That this voyage will be a great bridle to the Indies of the kinge of Spaine and a means that wee may arreste at our pleasure for the space of tenne weekes or three monethes every yere, one or twoo hundred saile of his subjects shippes at the fysshinge in Newfounde Lande. . . .

11. That the Spaniardes have executed most outragious and more then Turkishe cruelties in all the west Indies, whereby they are every where there, become moste odious unto them, whoe woulde joyne with us or any other moste willingly to shake of their moste intollerable yoke, and have begonne to doo it already in dyverse places where they were Lordes heretofore.

18. That the Queene of Englande title to all the west Indies, or at the leaste to as moche as is from Florida to the Circle articke, is more lawfull and righte then the Spaniaredes or any other Christian princes. . . .
(http://www.auburn.edu/~lakwean/hist7530/doc1584_hakluyt.html)

Excerpt from John Smith's The Generall Historie of Virginia, New-England, and the Summer Isles *(1624)*

REGARDING POCAHONTAS

To the most high and virtuous Princess, Queen Anne of Great Britain.
Most admired Queen,

The love I bear my God, my King and Country, hath so oft emboldened me in the worst of extreme dangers, that now honesty doth
constrain me presume thus far beyond myself, to present your Majesty
this short discourse: if ingratitude be a deadly poison to all honest
virtues, I must be guilty of that crime if I should omit any meanes to be
thankful.

So it is, that some ten years ago being in Virginia, and taken prisoner
by the power of Powhatan their chief King, I received from this great
Salvage exceeding great courtesy, especially from his sone Nantaquaus,
the most manliest, comeliest, boldest spirit, I ever saw in a Salvage, and
his sister Pocahontas, the Kings most deare and well-beloved daughter,
being but a child of twelve or thirteen yeeres of age, whose compassionate pitiful heart, of my desperate estate, gave me much cause to respect
her: I being the first Christian this proud King and his grim attendants
ever saw: and thus enthralled in their barbarous power, I cannot say I felt
the least occasion of want that was in the power of those my mortal foes
to prevent, notwithstanding al their threats. After some six weeks fatting
amongst those Salvage courtiers, at the minute of my execution, she haz-
arded the beating out of her own brains to save mine; and not only that,
but so prevailed with her father, that I was safely conducted to
Jamestown: where I found about eight and thirtie miserable poor and
sick creatures, to keepe possession of all those large territories of
Virginia; such was the weakness of this poor Common-wealth, as had
the salvages not fed us, we directly had starved. And this reliefe, most
gracious Queen, was commonly brought us by this Lady Pocahontas.

Notwithstanding all these passages when inconstant Fortune turned
our peace to warre, this tender Virgin would still not spare to dare to visit
us, and by her our jars have been oft appeased, and our wants still supplied; were it the policy of her father thus to employ her, or the ordinance
of God thus to make her his instrument, or her extraordinary affection to
our nation, I know not; but of this I am sure; when her father with the ut-
most of the policie and power, sought to surprise me, having but eighteen
with me, the dark night could not affright her from coming through the
irksome woods, and with watered eies gave me intelligence, with her best
advice to escape his fury; which had he knowne, he had surely slaine her.
Jamestown with her wild traine she as freely frequented, as her fathers
habitation; and during the time of two or three yeeres, she next under
God, was still the instrument to preserve this colony from death, famine
and utter confusion . . . (http://members.aol.com/mayflo1620/pocahontas.html)

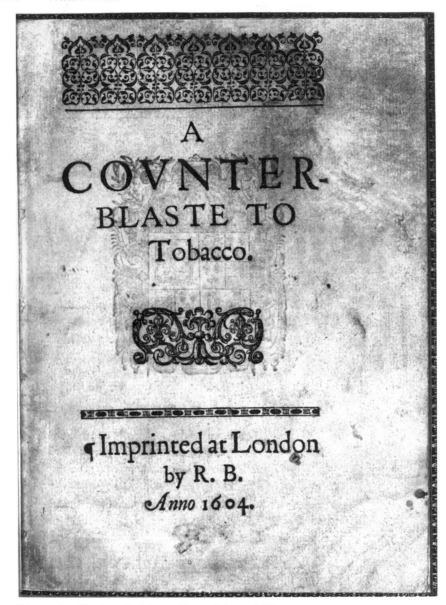

Title page from King James I's *A Counterblaste to Tobacco,* 1604.

Excerpt from James I, King of England A Counterblaste to Tobacco

    . . . The application then of a thing of a contrary nature to any of these parts is to interrupt them of their due function, and by consequence hurtful to the health of the whole body; as if a man, because the liver is as the fountain of blood, and as it were an oven to the stomach, would therefore apply and wear close upon his liver and stomach a cake of lead he might within a very short time (I hope) be sustained very good cheap at an ordinary, besides the clearing of his conscience from that deadly sin of gluttony. And as if because the heart is full of vital spirits, and in perpetual motion, a man would therefore lay a heavy pound stone on his breast for staying and holding down that wanton palpitation, I doubt not but his breast would be more bruised with the weight thereof than the heart would be comforted with such a disagreeable and contrarious cure. And even so is it with the brains, for if a man because the brains are cold and humid should therefore use inwardly by smells, or outwardly by application, things of hot and dry qualities, all the gain that he could make thereof would only be to put himself in great forwardness for running mad by over-watching himself. The coldness and moisture of our brains being the only ordinary means that procure our sleep and rest. Indeed, I do not deny that when it falls out that any of these or any part of our body grows to be distempered, and to tend to an extremity beyond the compass of natures temperature mixture that in that case cures of contrary qualities to the intemperate inclination of that part being wisely prepared and discreetly ministered may be both necessary and helpful for strengthening and assisting nature in the expulsion of her enemies, for this is the true definition of all profitable administration of medicine . . . (London: Robert Barker, 1604 Arents Tobacco Collection)

SOURCES

Andrews, K. R., N. P. Canny, and P. E. H. Hair, eds. *The Westward Enterprise: English Activities in Ireland, the Atlantic, and America 1480–1650.* Liverpool, UK: University Press, 1978.

Burre, Walter, 1612. In Peter Force, *Tracts, and Other Papers, Relating Principally to the Origin, Settlement, and Progress of the Colonies in North America, from the Discovery to the Year 1776.* 4 vols. Washington, D.C.: 1836–46.

Eden, Richard. "The Decades of the Newe Worlde, or West India" (1555). In Hadfield, *Amazons, Savages and Machiavels,* 240–249.

Hadfield, Andrew, ed. *Amazons, Savages and Machiavels: Travel and Colonial Writing in English, 1550–1630, an Anthology.* Oxford: Oxford University Press, 2001.

Hariot, Thomas. "A Briefe and True Report of the New Found Land of Virginia." (1588, reprinted in 1589 and 1590). In Hadfield, *Amazons, Savages and Machiavels,* 266–278.

de Las Casas, Bartolomé. "A Briefe Narration of the Destruction of the Indies by the Spaniards." Trans. M.M.S. (1583) In Hadfield, *Amazons, Savages and Machiavels,* 250–255.

Peckham, Sir George. "A True Report of the Late Discoveries, and Possession Taken in the Right of the Crowne of England of the Newfound Lands, By that

Valiant and Worthy Gentleman, Sir Humfrey Gilbert Knight" (1583). In Hadfield, *Amazons, Savages and Machiavels,* 256–265.

Pocahontas: Her True Story. Biography. A&E Home Video, 1995.

Prothero, G. W., ed. *Select Statutes and Other Constitutional Documents illustrative of the Reigns of Elizabeth and James I.* 4th ed. Oxford: Clarendon Press, 1913.

Raleigh, Sir Walter. "The Discoverie of the Large, Rich and Bewtiful Empyre of Guiana." In Hadfield, *Amazons, Savages and Machiavels,* 279–285.

Rowse, A. L. *The Elizabethans and America.* New York: Harper and Brothers, 1959.

Strachey, William. "For the Colony in Virginea Britannia. Lawes Diuvine, Morall and Martiall." In Hadfield, *Amazons, Savages and Machiavels,* 296–302.

Wright, Louis B., and Elaine W. Foule, eds. *English Colonization of North America.* New York: St. Martin's, 1968.

QUESTIONS

1. Why did Elizabethans and Jacobeans use "magical" imagery to describe America?
2. How successful was the quest for gold in the New England colonies? For silver in South America?
3. Why did the Roanoke Colony fail while the Jamestown Colony survived?
4. Why were South American natives treated cruelly and captured as slaves?

CRITICAL THINKING AND RESEARCH PROJECTS

1. Explore your family tree to find out where your ancestors were in Shakespeare's world of the late sixteenth and early seventeenth centuries.
2. Research the impact of British exploration and colonization on any of the Native American tribes that inhabited the Eastern coastlands during this period of history.
3. Investigate one of the global enterprises undertaken by Elizabethan explorers and describe its outcome.
4. Detail the development of one of the early South American or Caribbean colonies from its founding to the present.

FOR FURTHER READING

Anderson, Benedict. *Imagined Communities: Reflections on the Origin and Spread of Nationalism.* London and New York: Verso, 1991.

Coote, Stephen. *A Play of Passion: The Life of Sir Walter Raleigh.* London: Macmillan, 1993.

Cummins, John. *Francis Drake: The Lives of a Hero.* London: Weidenfeld and Nicholson, 1995.

Greenblatt, Stephen. *Marvelous Possessions: The Wonder of the New World.* Chicago: University of Chicago Press, 1991.

Haskins, Caryl P. *The Amazon: The Life History of a Mighty River.* New York: Doubleday, 1943.

Hebb, David Delison. *Piracy and the English Government 1616–1642.* Aldershot Hants, UK: Scolar, 1994.

Hedgerson, Richard. *Forms of Nationhood: The Elizabethan Writing of England.* Chicago: University of Chicago Press, 1992.

Hulme, Peter. *Colonial Encounters: Europe and the Native Caribbean 1492–1797.* New York: Methuen, 1986.

WEB SITES

http://members.aol.com/mayflo1620/pocahontas.html

http://www.eaglering.com/foundations/virginia.html

http://www.auburn.edu/~lakwean/hist7530/doc1584_hakluyt.html

PHOTO CREDITS

Page 1: Willem Janzoon Blaeu, World Map 1635, with two polar insets in the body of the map and border panels depicting the four elements, the seven known planets, the four seasons, and the seven wonders of the world/The Granger Collection, NY. **page 15:** Black and white print of William Shakespeare/Dorling Kindersley Media Library. **page 18:** The house in Stratford-Upon-Avon in which Shakespeare was born/Shakespeare Birthplace Trust. **page 20:** Sketch of the front elevation of Shakespeare's house, showing the beams used in the construction of the wooden frame. From The Portland Papers, Vol. 438 (291246)/Shakespeare Birthplace Trust. **page 24:** Warwickshire, Temple Grafton Church/Shakespeare Birthplace Trust. **page 25:** Hamnet's burial certificate/Shakespeare Birthplace Trust. **page 26:** An arched niche houses a bust of the English playwright William Shakespeare (1564–1616) in the Folger Shakespeare Library, Washington, DC, January 31, 1982. ©Michael Freeman/CORBIS. **page 31:** Titian, "Lucretia and Tarquinius," ca. 1515 ©Francis G. Mayer/CORBIS. **page 33:** Titian, (Venetian, c. 1485–1576), "Venus and Adonis." National Gallery of Art, Washington, D.C. **page 41:** Title "The Excellent history of the Merchant of Venice"/Courtesy of the Library of Congress. **page 44:** Richard II (1367–1400), King of England from 1377 to 1399 ©Michael Nicholson/CORBIS. **page 44:** Henry V, 1413–1422 Topham/The Image Works. **page 45:** Richard III. The Royal Collection ©2001 Her Majesty Queen Elizabeth II/Royal Collection Enterprises Ltd. **page 53:** Title "The most excellent and lamentable tragedie, of Romeo and Juliet."/Courtesy of the Library of Congress. **page 61:** London in Shakespeare's Day/Library of Congress. **page 72:** The Globe Theatre; From Map Of London/CORBIS. **page 77:** Richard Burbage, English actor and member of Earl of Leicester's company and its successor, The Kings Men. Head and shoulders portrait. From the original portrait in Dulwich College, undated. ©Bettmann/CORBIS. **page 89:** Spanish Armada Advancing Through English Channel/CORBIS. **page 91:** Henry VIII, 16th C., Hans the younger Holbein—c.1497–1543, German. National Gallery of Ancient Art, Rome, Italy/Canali PhotoBank, Milan/SuperStock. **page 92:** Painted portrait of Anne Boleyn (1507?–1536), second wife of King Henry VIII and mother of Queen Elizabeth I. ©Bettmann/CORBIS. **page 96:** Earl of Essex. Marcus Gheerhaerts (1561/62–1636), "Robert Devereux, 2nd Earl of Essex," (1566–1601). Soldier, favorite of Elizabeth I. Copy by Henry Bone, Enamel on copper. Kingston Lacy, Dorset, Great Britain. ©National Trust/Art Resource, NY. **page 101:** King James I. Male personalities; 4 of 56./EMG Education Management Group. **page 108:** Pieter Bruegel, the Elder, (active by 1551–died 1569), "The Harvesters." Oil on wood. H. 46-1/2 in. W. 63-1/4 in. (118 × 160.7 cm). The Metropolitan Museum of Art, Rogers Fund, 1919. (19.164). Photograph ©1998 The Metropolitan Museum of Art. **page 109:** Lucas van Valckenborch (1535–1597), "Winter (February)," 1586. Oil on canvas. Cat. 387. Inv. 1064. Kunsthistorisches Museum, Vienna. ©Erich Lessing/Art Resource, NY. **page 112:** Salomon Koninck (Dutch, 1609–1656), "Old Rabbi Seated by an Altar"/SuperStock, Inc. **page 123:** Michelangelo Merisi da Caravaggio (1573–1610), "The Toothpuller." Galleria Palatina, Palazzo Pitti, Florence, Italy. ©Scala/Art Resource, NY. **page 125:** John Gerarde, "The herball or Generall historie of plantes . . . ," 1597. Pages 508–509. The Huntington Library, Art Collections, and Botanical Gardens. This item is reproduced by permission of The Huntington Library, San Marino, California. **page 130:** Jacopo Tintoretto, "Portrait of a Man in Armor with Gold Decoration," ca. 1555–1560 Barney Burstein ©Burstein Collection/CORBIS. **page 135:** Albrecht Durer, "The Artist's Father" ©Archivo Iconografico, S.A./CORBIS. **page 136:** Elizabeth Regina. Queen Elizabeth I (1533–1603) at prayer. Frontispiece to "Christian Prayers" 1569, color illustration from the Lambeth Palace Library ©Bettmann/CORBIS. **page 139:** Peter Brueghel the Elder, Netherlandish, (c. 1525–69). The Triumph of Death. Museo del Prado, Madrid. Scala. **page 164:** Pieter the Elder Brueghel (b. 1525–1569), "Children's Games", 1560. Oil on oakwood, 118 × 161 cm. Kunsthistorisches Museum, Vienna, Austria. Copyright Erich Lessing/Art Resource, NY. **page 168:** Juan van der Hamen y Leon (1596–1631), Portrait of a dwarf, possibly "Bartolo" or "Bartolillo", a dwarf who was included in the royal progress during the Prince of Wales' visit to El Escorial in 1623. 122 × 87 cm. Location: Museo del Prado, Madrid, Spain ©Erich Lessing/Art Resource, NY. **page 177:** Christopher Plantino, "Theatrum Orbis Terrarum: Map of Europe," 1570 ©Archivo Iconografico, S.A./CORBIS. **page 178:** Quentin Metsys (c. 1466–1530), "The Money-lender (Banker) and His Wife," 1514. Louvre, Paris, France. ©Erich Lessing/Art Resource, NY. **page 200:** The Vitruvian Man by Leonardo DaVinci. ©Bettmann/CORBIS. **page 210:** Anguissola, Sofonisba (1535–1625) Self-portrait, painting the Madonna, 1556. Canvas, 66 × 57 cm. Erich Lessing/Art Resource. **page 212:** London, England: Anatomical drawing of a woman and unborn child in the uterus. A key at the side describes the various parts and their functions. The placenta is also described as the 'cake' as it nourishes the baby. From "The Midwives Book, or the whole ©The British Library/Topham/The Image Works. **page 215:** Rembrandt, Dutch, 1606–1669. The Anatomy Lesson of Dr. Tulp, 1632. Oil on canvas, 169.5 × 216.5 cm. The Hague, Mauritshuis. Stichting Vrienden van Het Mauritshuis. **page 221:** Firdawsi (active 975–1010), "Shah-nameh" (Book of Kings): The Feast of Sadeh. From a manuscript dedicated to Shah Tahmasp (1524–1576). Attributable to Sultan Muhammad. Colors: ink, silver and gold on paper. Painting: Gr.H. 9-1/2 in. (27.4 cm.), Gr. W. 9-1/16 in. (23 cm.). Iranian. Paintings. Tabriz. Safavid Period, ca. 1520–22. The Metropolitan Museum of Art, Gift of Arthur A. Houghton, Jr., 1970. (1970.301.2) Photograph ©1992 The Metropolitan Museum of Art. **page 225:** Giovanni del Vecci (1536–1615), "Map of Africa." From the Sala del Mappsmondo. Fresco, 1574. Palazzo Farnese, Caprarola (Viterbo), Italy. ©Scala/Art Resource, NY. **page 237:** China showing elephant and lake which flooded in 1537 from Theatrum orbis terrarum by Abraham Ortelius, 1592. Picture Desk, Inc./Kobal Collection. **page 239:** Toyotomi Hideyoshi/Library of Congress. **page 247:** Sir Walter Raleigh. From a painting by Nicholas Hillard, National Portrait Gallery, London/Library of Congress. **page 248:** "Horrenda & inaudita tempestas." Illustration from Theodor de Bry (1528–1598), "Americae pars qvarta." Francofvrti ad Moenvm, 1594. (Optional: Urbain Chauveton's translation and notes of Book 1 of Benzoni's "Historia del Mondo Nuovo.") Reproduced with the permission of Rare Books and Manuscripts, Special Collections Library, The Pennsylvania State University Libraries. **page 255:** Sir Francis Drake/Library of Congress. **page 258:** A Native American chief carrying a bow and wearing the warpaint and clothing appropriate for a feast or a hunt. A painting by John White./Getty Images Inc. Hulton Archive Photos. **page 260:** Sir Walter Raleigh, "Discoverie of the Large and Beautiful Empire of Guiana, . . . ," 1596. Title page. The Huntington Library, Art Collections, and Botanical Gardens. This item is reproduced by permission of The Huntington Library, San Marino, California. **page 268:** King James I, "A Counterblaste to Tobacco," 1604. Title page. The Huntington Library, Art Collections, and Botanical Gardens. This item is reproduced by permission of The Huntington Library, San Marino, California. **Insert-1** William Shakespeare, 1610. Artist Unknown, oil on canvas. National Portrait Gallery, London. **I-2** Elizabeth I, Gheeraerts, Marcus the younger—1562–1636, Flemish National Portrait Gallery, London/SuperStock Inc. **I-3** Jan Sanders van Hemessen (ca. 1504–1566), "The Surgeon: the Extraction of the Fool's Stone." Museo del Prado, Madrid, Spain. ©Erich Lessing/Art Resource, NY. **I-4** Michelangelo Merisi da Caravaggio (1573–1610), "The Fortune Teller." Musei Capitolini, Rome, Italy ©Nimatallah/Art Resource, NY. **Insert 2-1** The Sultan Mehmet II attributed to Gentile Bellini ©National Gallery Collection; By kind permission of the Trustees of the National Gallery, London/CORBIS. **I-2-2** World Map from Mercator Atlas Showing Terra Australia, 1595. Royal Geographical Society, London/Bridgeman Art Library, London. ©SuperStock, Inc. **I-2-3** "Air," one of the four paintings showing the four elements ordered in 1607 by Cardinal Federico Borromeo of Milan. Canvas, 46 × 67 cm. Location: Louvre, Paris, France. Art Resource, NY. **I-2-4** Title page of the first edition of the King James Bible, London, 1611. The Granger Collection.

Index